LUMINOUS

LUMINOUS

Ink

WRITERS ON WRITING IN CANADA

Edited by Tessa McWatt
Rabindranath Maharaj
and Dionne Brand

Cormorant Books

The publisher gratefully acknowledges the support of the Canada Council for the Arts
and the Ontario Arts Council for its publishing program. We acknowledge the
financial support of the Government of Canada through the Canada Book Fund (CBF)
for our publishing activities, and the Government of Ontario through
the Ontario Media Development Corporation, an agency of the Ontario Ministry
of Culture, and the Ontario Book Publishing Tax Credit Program.

LIBRARY AND ARCHIVES CANADA CATALOGUING IN PUBLICATION

Luminous ink : writers on writing in Canada / Tessa McWatt, Rabindranath
Maharaj, and Dionne Brand, editors.

Issued in print and electronic formats.
ISBN 978-1-77086-519-8 (SOFTCOVER). — ISBN 978-1-77086-520-4 (HTML)

1. Canadian literature — 21st century — History and criticism.
2. National characteristics, Canadian, in literature. 3. Canada — In literature.
4. Authors, Canadian — 21st century. I. McWatt, Tessa, 1959–, editor
II. Maharaj, Rabindranath, 1955–, editor III. Brand, Dionne, 1953–, editor

PS8077.1.L86 2018   C810.9'006   C2018-900022-8
                                           C2018-900023-6

Cover design: angeljohnguerra.com
Interior text design: Tannice Goddard, bookstopress.com
Printer: Friesens

Printed and bound in Canada.

CORMORANT BOOKS INC.
10 ST. MARY STREET, SUITE 615, TORONTO, ONTARIO, M4Y 1P9
www.cormorantbooks.com

CONTENTS

INTRODUCTION
LUMINOUS INK

Tessa McWatt, Rabindranath Maharaj,
and Dionne Brand

Literature is not only a mirror; it is also a map, a geography of the mind.

MARGARET ATWOOD, *SURVIVAL*

TO BE A WRITER LIVING in, writing from, or about, Canada, now, is to live at a vexed and precarious junction of the past, present, and future. It is to sense and to track what was, what is, and what, perhaps, will be. This junction is a place of many revelations, the coordinates of which are not always clearly defined. Life phenomena are what writers track; and geographies. Geography consists of maps — with borders, depths, gradations, topographies — and people, phenomena, spatial analyses, tides, and the study of change and motion. At the best of times, in the best instances, writers can be the sonar and remote sensors of temporal geography.

At the heart of this anthology are a series of questions about the work of words. What does it mean to be a writer now in this country? What can the literature being written today — the stories, the novels, the poetry, the drama, the creative non-fiction — tell us about Canada's social arrangements, about its political and aesthetic shapes and its preoccupations? In the twenty-first century is a national literature possible, let alone desirable?

In 2015, as faculty members at the Banff Centre Writer's Studio, the editors of this anthology gathered over meals and mountain walks and considered the configuration of what has come to be called "CanLit." In a Japanese restaurant where a sushi train offered, with each turn, some new and tempting dish, we talked over the changes that had taken place in the writing community since Margaret Atwood published *Survival* in 1972 — that seminal work that marked a call for a national literature and ushered in the idea of "CanLit." We talked about place and politics and aesthetics; about our different positions on and location in nation, and to the nation–making projects of Canada's government and cultural institutions. We talked about absences in the official record of CanLit and, in that light, we summoned Wilson Harris and what he called *the unfinished genesis of the imagination* in his essay "Creoleness: The Crossroads of a Civilization?" We talked about universality as Jacqueline Rose proposes it in *States of Fantasy*: "One way to come at the concept of universality" she writes, "might be to note, on each separate occasion, the history which provokes it." We considered the definition of universality that had gathered around the project of CanLit as representative only of and in Euro-Canadian experience. What makes a writer a Canadian writer? What makes the writing Canadian? Is it place? Is it preoccupation with and/or reference to the land; is it modality of voice or of experience? Is it something more elusive, a sensibility that shifts with the tides but yet holds some faint echo of the land; a register that is inconspicuous and hidden — perhaps deliberately — but which works its way into stories, conversations, insights? What are the qualities, ideas, issues, and landscapes one engages when writing from this physical space? Where dispossession of aboriginal land subtends all references, what is landscape? What is land as metaphor? Depending on where the writer is located — in the body, in the land, in history — what literary questions does the writer encounter? In the changing demographic of the population and the growing urgency of writing about race, class, colonialism, sex and gender, and the ways they matter, how are writers responding to these crucial concerns?

In the late 1960s, Atwood, D.G. Jones, Dennis Lee, Graeme Gibson, and other writers were building a literary community that tried to differentiate itself from writers in the U.S. and U.K. There was a flowering of independent presses and the production of works of poetry, fiction, and cultural essays. Indeed, in a few short years, many new presses were established — mostly by writers — and the publication of a new generation of poets and novelists began in earnest. In 1972 Atwood was worried about the survival of Canadian literature and, by extension,

Canada, in the face of U.S. cultural dominance:

> We need such a map desperately, we need to know about here, because here is where we live. For the members of a country or a culture, shared knowledge of their place, their here, is not a luxury but a necessity. Without that knowledge we will not survive.

To borrow from John Berger, *here* is also *where we meet*. And, at the top of Sleeping Buffalo Mountain in Banff, as we watched the hawks above the spruce trees, we considered all that had changed since Atwood's observations and we envisioned a new hermeneutic — new ways of interpreting and making sense of the world. And so we were curious to examine the new forms and aesthetics that might be described, now, if we asked the writers themselves.

Maps are oriented due north.

The literature produced in Canada has changed radically from the moment that Atwood produced *Survival*, positing survival as a foundational problematic for the nation-building project of literature. We wondered, then, if not survival, was there something else around which a body of literature cohered? Was there a common thread stitched through communities and regions so that an observation made on one coast would be understood by someone on the other; a question asked of one community might be answered by another; a description offered in one language seen and felt in another? The forces, on writers, of learned histories, of dislocations, of appropriations and privileges, and of violence suggested that the responses could not be informed by any common understandings or united by any mutual agreements. Certainly we, and the writers in this collection, have differing and wider concerns, wider than national preoccupations. And our aesthetic practices are informed by world literature, pinned yet unpinned from the local. Some straight line of genealogy is impossible — the meridian of writing in Canada passes through every latitude and dislodges any clean or clear expression of a national narrative. There is a real tension between a homogenizing, stultifying, and reductive national narrative — visible, for example, in the political citizen-making machinery — and the vibrant voices of writers writing today. We seem to be living in a political moment that is a reiteration of the first Trudeau era that buoyed the wave of

1960s and 1970s writers who attempted a definition of the space of the nation and the possibilities of naming. The pitfall of the idea of nation is that it creates insiders and outsiders. That moment of liberalism was attended by political upheaval — including the imposition of the War Measures Act. Significantly, another Trudeau is in power as we write today; and this neo-liberal moment is rife with its own upheavals — the unsolved cases of missing and murdered Indigenous women and girls, the unfinished possibilities of the Truth and Reconciliation Commission, to name only a few. This Trudeau shrugged off comments on his commitment to gender equality in his cabinet by saying, "Because it's 2015." In this Trudeau's mapping, the passage of time equals the reason for gender equality. He gestures toward a temporal narrative of progress and alteration, over time, that should be self-evident, but it is undermined by the structural inequalities that remain in place throughout the nation. Then, in the sixties and seventies, as now we understand how easily pluralist ideals can be appropriated, undermined, subverted, or halted altogether.

WE DON'T WANT TO LAND in that narrative of linear progress that excuses the past by saying "we didn't know any better then," thereby imposing a singular experience of that past. We were convinced of the importance of an anthology that would, in a broader sense, illuminate the shape of literature as we see it in Canada today. We have left aside the question of who is Canadian because matters on the ground have exceeded nation and, most definitely, exceeded a configuration of nation where Euro-Canadians dominate that idea. Conversations in the mainstream cultural landscape have arrived at a tacit admission that this is a plural society in which there are many conversations among many communities. Yet that vaunted plurality is still a work-in-progress. What new literary questions emerge in the face of a stumbling, some might say, reluctant, consciousness?

Northrop Frye and later D.G. Jones and Margaret Atwood envisioned Canadian literature in terms of its relationship to the other. This view — and the subsequent unfolding of Frye's garrison model — installed the characteristics of a settler-colonial mindset; the bush and all within were ripe for colonizing, "taming," and "civilizing." This model persists, especially in historical fiction, although it can equally be argued that its frequent focus on outliers and disparities challenges that model and places it closer to books set in more contemporary times. How did writers bridge or maintain this presumed divide between garrison and outside?

We decided to be broad in our provocations and to ask writers for short literary pieces, riffing on what it means to be "here" as a writer in Canada, now, or how a writer abroad experiences the concept of being a Canadian "there." How is Canada in the writing? What new discourses shape literature in Canada? Is a national literature determined — or measured — by a particular, or common, type of engagement, or is this all projection? What is the relationship between literature produced in its own historical time and place and the work of mythologizing that undergirds a national literature? Is writing from or to a place where one is or was, writing national literature? Is it contributing to a nationalist project?

It is the question of a national literature that is at stake. And we are going to let the works assembled here speak, individually and collectively, into the space that follows that question.

The possibilities that arise out of the intersections of cultures, histories, and relationships to place come to light in times of shifting global concerns, communities, and influences. Once public discussion and academic criticism around Canadian literature focused on the two solitudes of the French and English languages, but now the solitudes and languages are legion. Polyglot and silence shaped our own writings paradoxically. Now is an important moment to take stock — in the face of pervasive and invasive technology, of crippling neoliberal forces in publishing and in society in general, and with real momentum in the contest of Canada's legitimacy on unceded land.

As we walked through the town of Banff — evocative of an old-fashioned postcard — and hiked along the trails, watching for that most quintessential of Canadian wildlife, bears, our minds turned to other types of variances. We thought of the current image of the country as benign and inclusive; but notwithstanding healthcare, hockey, and a parliamentary system, we also considered the many things this image obscures. We thought of the hidden dangers of forgetting. In the past, writers who had strayed too far from familiar stories had often been shunted aside and dismissed as adjunct to the known story. We discussed whether CanLit scholarship had kept up with the new or whether it had been strangled by constant backward glances at a presumed golden age — a curious insistence that nothing had changed from an earlier generation of writing and a blindness to the proliferation of newer vibrant and diverse voices.

To address these questions we sought some of the finest writers working today. We included writers who live in the north, in the rural, in the large cities clustered along the border with the U.S., and in the metropolises abroad. We wanted to remain conscious of the depth of voices that living in the country produces in regional, cultural, and linguistic tenor.

In the twenty-six essays gathered here, these writers grapple with our contemporary moment: with lives being lived after and despite Contact; with Canada's history — the colonial past that haunts and still choreographs social relations in the present; with considerations of personal, familial, and communal relations — the havoc they sometimes wreak and the revelations they present. We find in these pages the unsettling, the unresolvable, the unforgivable. Each writer seems to have made a commitment to a rhizomatic seeing; to conscious observation in the presence of rough knowledge; to listening, which is, after all, the great fidelity of writing.

This time in Canada belongs to the "cleaving from" the old narratives of character, identity, and opinion. As writers living the last three decades, we've seen shifts from the homogenous to the heterogeneous and these shifts have neither been seamless nor without discontent. We bear the freight of inconvenient histories, to paraphrase the title of Tom King's brilliant work *The Inconvenient Indian*. These histories include colonization of yet unceded aboriginal land, transatlantic slavery, Japanese internment, South Asian exclusion, the Chinese head tax, and the "none is too many" policy toward Jews seeking refuge from the Nazis. These histories exert tremendous pressure on the words *country* and *nation*. Efforts to produce a common identity through literature are a refusal of the affinities that our present time demands.

Everywhere in the discourses of how and what it means to inhabit this country imaginations are lit with the challenge of speaking many contradictions into being. This challenge was rendered concretely in a stunning exhibition at the Art Gallery of Ontario in 2017. The exhibition is called, *Every. Now. Then: Reframing Nationhood*. It begins at the nexus of these contradictions and asks in one of its installations, "Who's Home on Native Land." The question moves toward several possible answers — as surely this anthology does — the most gorgeous being in the title of one of the installations, *Towards Something New and Beautiful + Future Snowmachines in Kinngait*. In the exhibition there are visual artists who come from the spectrum of communities in Canada, and all are involved, as we are here, with what it means to make a work of art engaged with its time; with how to make something from what we know, what we desire, what hard facts we must take into account. The artists in the exhibition, like the writers in this anthology, avoid national myth-making. Ruth Cuthand's *Don't Breathe, Don't Drink*, a table of containers of water, gestures the Attawapiskat tragedy; Camille Turner in collaboration with Camal Pirbhai stages photographs of contemporary models dressed in apparel worn by and described in ads meant to recapture people fleeing slavery in Quebec, Montreal, Saint John — yes, there was slavery in Canada. In the exhibit, Kim Tomczak and Lisa Steele remind, with a simple inventory, of Canada's participation in Vietnam; and Gu Xiong's wall of photographs of migrant farm labourers who work in proximity to the vaunted Niagara Falls that exposes further the absences beneath the myth. These wonderful works imagine singularly, and collectively, otherwise.

This anthology imagines singularly, and collectively, otherwise, with essays that open up angles of vision and angles of imagination deeply imbricated and luminous.

Literature is a conversation that provokes. Intellectual debate has been fired in the last decades in Canada by controversies of voice, representation, and literary appropriation. These are deep conversations that have, at times, been met with disingenuous proscriptions of literary freedom. The fights have broken out in the pages of newspapers, magazines, and literary conferences like the two *Writing Through Race* conferences and the biennial *Trans-Canada Conference on Canadian Literature*. Social media has also been ablaze with trenchant critique. While we were compiling our list of writers, ongoing concerns about voice appropriation and inherent privileges received national attention and these, too, worked their way into some of the essays. We think this a generative and necessary development.

The provocation of these essays is that the reader is invited, compelled, to reimagine Canada. These essays are full of the glowing conversations that are in progress today. The once prevailing assertion of the statement, "this is Canadian literature" which assumed a singularity of audience and reception, has given way, we contend, to audiences that are more diverse, more discerning, more attuned to multiplicity, to ambivalence, to contradiction.

WE CAN ONLY ATTEMPT HERE, tentatively and partially, to trace points of conversation between and among these writers. In this anthology, Margaret Atwood provides an account of the events that led to the publication of *Survival* and at the same time gives us a glimpse of the Canadian literary scene unfolding through encounter and struggle, through difference and otherness. Rawi Hage places his own writing in the context of Quebec literature and the *Révolution Tranquille* and uncovers a Quebec aesthetic that springs from "the oppressed rebelling against the oppressor, and an appetite for literature that reflects struggle by simple means and against all odds." He speculates that the schism between Quebec and its ethnic minorities springs from the way Quebec views itself.

Many of the essays reflect on the deeply personal: the collusion of events and interactions that reveal the alignments of belonging and clarify the writers' roles. Lawrence Hill traces the ways that his trips to "places of unbelonging" nurtured and sustained his writing journey. Lisa Moore, Heather O'Neill, and George Elliott Clarke focus on the body as a unit of complexity and morality and violation. Clarke writes of the brutal interrogative gaze casually cast on him and his poetic response — "the spillage of ink." Moore locates writing as a way in and out of the body, listening to inner, nascent, irrational hunches as stories come into being, as mystery is uncovered. Metaphor/writing, she asserts, is about making something new, something that never existed before. O'Neill's essay describes some of the early experiences that led her to go against the aesthetic that produces female passivity and violence on the female body as desire. Camilla Gibb's essay, a meditation on travelling and rootedness, describes encounters that might disrupt or alter senses of home. "But isn't that exactly why we write?... Because it is always lonely? Because we are always in want of a home?"

In his essay, Greg Hollingshead asks, "Where is home and how do I get there?" Separating the writer's task from the socioeconomic and political forces of a culture and insisting that "literature focuses attention on what is happening upstream, at the fountainhead, where the problem originates, in the human mind," he suggests that the search for meaning brings us closer to home.

The ecologies of living today, the technological zeitgeist, underline these essays. All of these writers allude that place is not only determined by coordinates or enclosed by latitudinal lines but is a concept into which are folded paradoxes, tussles, bereavements and joys, and a glimmer of understanding — and yet, there are the complications of finding a language to express this understanding. When Sheila Fischman says that in translating she is "searching for the meaning behind words," she could have been speaking for many of the writers in this anthology who suggest that the language to which they come is not simply a parade of glittering words, but an acknowledgement of gaps and echoes and silences; an awareness of the places from which language springs and the spirit sings. Richard Van Camp refers to all the influences — songs, books, movies, essays, stories — circling his mind, the bibliographies of his inspiration. He writes, "Each of these creators have wounded me and I love them for that." David Chariandy brings sharp and tender focus to the particular influence of Austin Clarke, who helped him to "remember a past that wasn't mine and truly was mine, a being that stretched beyond the whitened suburbs."

Judith Thompson describes the effect of trauma on language and affirms that, "A scream has fierce intention, which is what every story, every character in the theatre must have." Michael Helm's boyhood experiences on the prairies in revival meetings, hearing congregants speaking in tongues, and discovering his own gifts, leads him to understand that writing resides in the unsaid, the invisible, the voice made strange.

Linguistic invention is what writers do: they shift the gaze to the lost, the unspoken, the misappropriated, the forgotten. They poke at the shadows and provoke the ghosts. Eden Robinson opens this anthology describing a writing life in a setting that is "deep enough for whales," which she tries to translate for readers even when there are moments that "defy the human tongue." Madeleine Thien writes of the mythologizing power of words and the potential of language as a sloganeering instrument. "But I am free to ... believe that the desire for precision in language is a desire to live in a moral way, not just to live with principle but to understand the nature of principle, how we come by our beliefs, how they shape us and blind us and create us."

What these writers are also telling us is why they write. Witness. Activist. Curator. Interpreter. Rebel. Dreamer. And sometimes there is no option. Lee

Maracle writes of her obligation to preserve, explain, and inspire. "I write because I cannot fall silent into a backwash of Canadiana after having produced fifteen thousand years of story. I write because I want our youth to know that we have value, we have knowledge, and we have a place in this world." Nino Ricci contemplates the manner in which technology has influenced our apprehension of the world and affirms, "In a world of specialists, then, writers remain the last great generalists, madly plugging away at the hopeless task of making sense of everything." Stephen Henighan's essay is really an exploration of the role of the writer. "We need fiction that scrutinizes our society; our fiction requires this challenge to evolve aesthetically."

Nicole Brossard's essay crystallises the notion of writer as someone who immerses herself in the enigma of the present through the pleasure of language. "To introduce into language leaps and bounds and somersaults of joy and astonishment, an abyss of fear and dread, to translate the infinitesimal slowness of the desire scrutinizing the enigma at the very core of this desire."

M G Vassanji outlines some of his frustrations with the tendency to marginalize or pigeonhole writing that is not considered mainstream and admits he has questioned his desire to continue writing. "But now and then an idea comes, the fingers ache, and so it's back to scribbling in the margins and crying out silently." Vassanji continues to write because there are truths to be told, misapprehensions to be shunted aside.

In Leanne Simpson's poem, the voices that encourage her to write her own stories are present and absent simultaneously, are both conspicuous and yet intangible. She says, "Write, but only as labour in bringing opaque to purpose." And Pascale Quiviger sums up a writer's imperative by saying, "For that companionship in unbridgeable space, I write."

Marie Hélène Poitras's fiction is immersed in the world of the *cochers* and *calèches* of Old Montreal, and her celebration and reinvention of the *cochers* culture arises not only out of a desire to reclaim a part of a disappearing history, but out of a writer's place in preserving real communities. This vantage point of the artist — personal, private, and yet irrecovably public — is one which Hiromi Goto and Rita Wong also share. Wong affirms, "Writing saved my life, giving me a place to raise my voice, not to be conscripted into someone else's ideas or stereotypes of what I was supposed to be." Wong and Goto also engage in the discussion on the politics of accounting when one does not belong to white settler nation-making discourses but finds oneself adjacent to those discourses, in some regard, and outside of them in every regard. Goto writes, "My indifference matters. My engagement matters. And there is never neutrality."

And so Michael Ondaatje's essay attends to what is made in flux. In a world of intersecting voices, literary cartography is the space of possibility. "But world literature is full of alternate journeys. And the air currents of literary influences that result in the merging of art forms, subject matter, alternate perspectives, and above all translations, link our world subliminally and more profoundly than we know. We move, drift, climb into, and tunnel from one country to another. It is the central story of our time."

NEAR THE END OF OUR time at the Banff Centre Writers' Studio, the editors took a gondola to the top of what is known as Sulphur Mountain. We took in the panorama — snow-capped peaks, evergreens and scree, and below, in the valley, the snaking emerald *Makhabn* (Bow) River — but we also felt the silence.

At the end of the boardwalk, at the summit of the mountain, is the site of the Cosmic Ray Station, constructed in 1956 by the National Research Council as Canada's contribution to the International Geophysical Year (1957–58) and the study of particle physics. Cosmic rays are subatomic particles that originate outside our solar system and even sometimes the Milky Way. They move through space at close to the speed of light. Observing the rays' movement allows scientists to glimpse the properties of the layers of atmosphere through which they have travelled.

We arrived at the stone hut, one by one, and together stood at its entrance. The station was staged by Parks Canada to portray a moment in the late 1950s when scientists lived there, doing their work. Simple wooden bunk beds, a wash basin, thin grey wool blankets, a bucket of coal, maps on the desk, and even hiking boots at the foot of the bunk bed, demonstrated the exacting and focused lives of the people who would have participated in measuring and data collection. With knowing smiles and nods, the three of us silently acknowledged an ideal writer's cabin.

When cosmic rays interact with the earth's atmosphere they are converted to secondary particles. Magnetic fields deflect and distort the path of the particles, making it nearly impossible to determine their point of origin.

Perhaps a more potent image than that of mapmaker, for a writer in the twenty-first century, is that of an observer of intangibles — one who tracks the personal, social, political, planetary, the painful, and the joyful. After all, a map is a circumstantial account of the state of things. Maps are subject to shifts in perspective and disagreement on coordinates and shapes. Maps are also susceptible to erasure.

To track the minutiae and magnitude of people's lives in the twenty-first century, writers don't need to create maps: literature is so much more. Writing in Canada appears now to be situated everywhere. Rather than provide a map, the writers in this anthology shine exacting and vital light. These essays are porous, liminal, and fragile. Their luminousity reveals what may come into view when all we know is considered.

THE SALMON EATERS
Eden Robinson

*S*ALTWATER GRASSES SHUSHED IN A slough deep enough at high tide that a VW Bug–sized baby humpback swam up, chasing a silver school of tiny herring. The baby bubbled the water like a toddler in a bathtub. His bumpy dark skin glistened like the wetsuit of a scuba diver. His mother called a long, mournful sound in the deeper waters of the Douglas Channel. The baby spouted, the mist shot through with a rainbow and a slightly rotten fish smell. He zipped back to her as I stood in my parents' backyard by their smokehouse. The lowering sun shone molten gold on the calm water so I saw the whales as dark shadows as they swam away, flukes and fins with the occasional geyser of breath.

I walked down to the soccer field located a few minutes away. The Douglas Channel is rimmed with mountains. Evergreens blanket their sides like dark green velvet, shot through with brown seams of logging roads and the new industrial road that leads to Bish Creek. The humpbacks steamed south along the shoreline. Seagulls complained as they hovered over the beach. A bald eagle landed on a giant stump that had washed ashore. He flapped at an entourage of crows that circled him like dark thoughts.

We haven't seen whales like this since the whalers killed off our resident pod back when whale oil was a big thing. The Douglas Channel is ninety kilometres long from the head to the mouth, where the Inside Passage begins. I live near the head, on a reserve that faces the ocean, a small plot of alluvial flatness in a landscape dominated by granite mountains and surging tides. Nearby, eleven kilometres away by a twisting, steeply graded road, is the town of

Kitimat, built by Alcan Aluminum Limited in the sixties to house their workers. Our population on the rez is about six hundred to eight hundred people. Town has about eight thousand, which fluctuates according the rise and fall of commodity prices.

Down the channel, near Coste Island, is a whale rock. Close to shore, yet deep enough for whales, the rock towers up through the water like a spike. Whales scratch themselves against it to scrape off their barnacles and assorted hitchhiking oceanic crud. When they're in a group, they take turns according to their hierarchy. They have clans like us. They fight and make alliances, snub and favour. Some of them are gentle giants and some of them are snarky asshats.

What I love most about humpbacks is how steadfastly they hold a grudge. This is a lost art. In an era of saccharine Hallmark forgiveness, people have forgotten what a real grudge looks like. When you see YouTube videos of humpbacks charging in to save seals or other species of whales from Orca attacks, you know that rivalry runs generations upon generations deep. As a coastal potlatcher, I'm holding grudges as old as Turtle Island. I didn't start them; I won't end them. I stick to my pod. If they fall, I fall. I rise with them or not at all.

EARLY MISSIONARIES TRIED TO TURN the Haisla into civilized farmers. Given that the soil is poor, the growing season is short and the sun is a sporadic visitor in our rainforest, our farming efforts were doomed and we were deemed lazy. We farmed the ocean. We had clam gardens and fishing beds. Our canoes were our horses. We lived and died by the salmon runs, like the bears and the seals and the eagles and the wolves. We revered nature and we ate nature because we were a part of the living landscape, not apart from it, not above it, not dominating it. We ate and were eaten.

We did like potatoes, though. Spuds aren't high-maintenance plants, which was great because we travelled over our territory all summer for our salmon catches. We had potato plots by our fishing camps, rows of potatoes that we fed fish blood. Carbs are not a big part of traditional coastal diets. Our version of rice is the Chocolate Lily root, which we only ate if we were starving. It's icky. It looks like white rice, but it tastes like dead dreams, bitter and cloying. Glik'sam, on the other hand, was our preferred root, soft and yellow buttercup roots, with the texture and flavour of sweet potatoes. Glik'sam loves the mud and you dig for it with the bears, who were our guides. What they ate, we tried. We have similar tastes.

I live in an apartment two blocks from my parents' house. My father is an elder, and when the salmon are running he's gripped by a chronic and incurable condition that my sister calls "Haisla Fish Fever." My father has fished all his life and is frustrated by his lack of energy and strength, which prevent him from keeping a boat and a fishing net. We always relied on salmon. We couldn't afford meat, so I grew up eating salmon for breakfast, lunch and supper. We eat everything right down to the heads and tails — fish-head soup is a delicacy and I remember my mother and my great-aunt fighting over the eyeballs.

The salmon season starts here in May. Winter salmon arrive first. Their flesh is pale like halibut flesh and the meat is oily and dense. They barbecue well, dripping hissing fat into the fire. Spring salmon are also oily, but pink, also perfect for barbecues. They taste more like Atlantic salmon than any of the other B.C. species. They don't can well or smoke well. Sockeye arrive in June and go through July, sometimes into August. They're smaller fish than Springs, easier to lift and tote. When you slice into them, their flesh is ruby red. They fry well. Steamed, baked, barbecued — all good. But they are most perfect as a canning fish. I don't like working with them in the smokehouse because they turn mushy quickly and you need a large crew to work with them. Once they're mushy, the only thing to do is half-smoke the skins and freeze or jar them. You can cold-smoke them after a good brining, but you lose the sockeye flavour in the marinades. I prefer coho for a traditional smoke. They arrive in August and are commercially valued less than sockeye, and aren't as ruby red, but they're easier to slice thin and hold their shape well. We have a word for the virus that forms bubbles on their flesh and liquefies it. It's harmless to humans, but it makes coho inedible. Two years ago, we had a season where eight out of every ten coho taken from the nets was badly diseased and had to be thrown away. This has never happened before. It hasn't happened again, but it was worrisome. Those are the top salmon, the ones we prefer, but we also eat chum and pink. Dog salmon is fantastic for smoking, but the pin bones are tough and need to be picked out if you're going to feed them to children or elders. They can puncture the soft cheek flesh and if they get stuck in your throat, you'll need surgery.

Sometimes, when a run is bad in your territory, you can buy or trade fish with other First Nations, but salmon from different rivers have slightly different flavours. Some fish swim in rivers with more tannin so they have a bitter kick, especially when canned or frozen. Some fish swim farther upriver to get to their spawning ground, so they're older, tougher. When I was writer-in-residence in Whitehorse, I ran into people who fed their fish to their sled dogs. By the time the salmon had swum that far, they were falling apart with age and stress. I can't tell the difference between wines to save my life, but I can tell you which salmon species it is and where they were swimming and how far they had to swim simply by taste.

This is Salmon 101 if you've grown up on the coast. When I whine about preparing more than forty salmon, my dad constantly reminds me that my grandmother put away hundreds of salmon by herself in one smokehouse.

"She didn't have deadlines," I usually grumble.

The coastal First Nations were like the ants in the children's story, working all summer so we could eat all winter. When the snow fell, our sacred season began. We held feasts to pass our culture to the younger generation through dance, song and story. These potlatches went for days and sometimes weeks, a celebration, a reaffirmation of our cultural bonds, a legal case for the chief's and clan's rights. We had dedicated writers, musicians, weavers and carvers who were commissioned to make high-status treasures for the chiefs who hired them. The chiefs gifted their guests with these treasures or threw their treasures in the fire to show their contempt for hoarding wealth. Everyone was fed. If we all worked hard, our life was good.

The First Nations on the coast of British Columbia have built our cultures around salmon. Our sacred season is in the winter and our ceremonies are only possible with the food wealth that salmon bring us. To say that we like salmon is such an understatement, it would be like saying the Arctic can be chilly or Toronto has traffic. When we're protesting things like pipelines or fish farms, what we're protesting is a threat not just to our food security but to our identity. Imagine France without cheese. Greece without olives. Germany without beer.

DAD USED TO SET HIS net near the point. He had a small boat, a fishing net lined with corks at the top and weights at the bottom and an anchor. One end of the net was tied to shore and the rest of the net stretched into the ocean, held up by the corks and a large buoy. Each species of salmon requires a different size netting to catch their gills. Nets can cost up to $1,000. Food fishing means you fish for your family and your extended family. Some families chip in for the fisherman's gas and boat expenses. Others don't.

Traditionally, the chief of a clan would decide when the Haisla could fish. A certain amount of fish had to swim by before he'd allow fishing. We used to set at the mouth of rivers, but a series of laws after Contact meant we had to set in the ocean, which was less effective. Usually, fishermen watch for signs or troll around with fish finders. Once a salmon run starts, people stake out their spots and a certain amount of clearance is given between nets. This isn't as much of an issue, because food fishing is labour-intensive. You need to check your net every three to five hours. Dad would start checking his net at sunrise and finish at sunset. When the fish were running, sometimes it would be hourly. If you have a regular job, you need to take days off or vacation time. You need a boat and gas money. If you set in the wrong place, you have to re-set, or risk getting skunked. There's nothing more discouraging than going through all the work to set a net and then pulling up seaweeds and logs.

When I first moved home, I helped Dad check his net in the mornings. As your boat nears the net, you can usually tell if you've been skunked if all the corks are floating. If they're sunk down, you hope it's not a log, which you have to untangle leaning over the side of the boat. You pull the net up and then pull yourself along the net to the shore. Your arms get very buff. The net is heavy, even without fish. You pick seaweed and jellyfish off as you go. If you have caught fish, you pull them onboard and untangle them. If they're alive, you club them to death first or fight them as they thrash around your speedboat. Sometimes all that's left is salmon heads and tails. Harbour seals cruise along the nets and pick the bellies clean. Their dark heads poke above the water and they watch you with shiny black eyes. You can't really stop them, even if you wait in your boat with a gun.

Dad's not a big fan of seals. He mimes shooting them when he sees them sunning themselves on the log booms in Minette Bay. He cheers when he sees them being run down by Orcas. The seals would follow the spawning salmon when he used to fish in the Kitlope River. The river is wide and shallow, deeper with the high tide, but clear enough that you could see down to the bottom.

Orcas would follow the seals, their dorsal fins cutting the surface as they ripped past Dad's boat. Killer whales are aggressive hunters, and he watched them twist their bodies up the rock and drag the seals into the ocean.

There are different kinds of killer whales. Some orcas are primarily salmon eaters. They have rounder, gentler features. They live on the northwest coast most of the year. Orcas with pointed fins and more angular features are more likely to swat a seal out of the water with their tails, sending the seal tumbling through the air like a badminton birdie. Orcas that live far out in the ocean tend to be rammers. They gather speed and then ram into other species of whales and then rip into them while they're stunned.

The Haisla had the closest relationship with the salmon eaters. When the world was young and we could change our skins, we intermarried. We still consider each other kin. People from the killer whale clan call them ancestors. Orcas visit us, and sometimes they warn us of coming storms by acting strangely, by beaching themselves or hauling themselves up on docks. They can hear things that we can't.

When I write, I'm interpreting a Haisla world through English words. Sometimes the fit is awkward and I can't get the words to match the concepts. Not that my grasp of Xaislakala is phenomenal. But the lens shifts, and the context of culture means that, for instance, when I say "family" in English, what I mean is usually a nuclear family. When I say it in Haisla, you need a good solid grasp of coastal genealogy to make it through the first cousins and their marriages, much less going back into the generations. The concept of time involves my potential great-grandchildren and all the ancestors, down to when we shared our skins with the animals, the other beings who share our planet.

And then there are moments that defy the human tongue, no matter what language you use. I remember sitting in our speedboat, the outboard motor tipped up so it wouldn't tangle in the net. We were close to the buoy, just starting to pull the net up. With the slosh of waves against the boat and my concentration on the net, I didn't notice them until they surfaced around us, bodies longer than the runabout, dorsal fins cutting the surface as they rose, studied us and then moved on. The terrified wonder of a small mammal alarmed by the presence of a hunter met the absolute and unqualified certainty that they wouldn't eat us. They had just popped up to say hi. They were still a part of our world, even if we'd forgotten their names as they spoke them.

SNOW SQUALLS IN MAY
Lisa Moore

*W*HAT IT MEANS TO LIVE in a body. How writing takes me out of my body — how I forget my body. And — *thump* — I'm back. When I write I am not here. Or: I am more here than ever when I write.

But here I am at a protest in the rain outside Her Majesty's Pen with a handful of other people. I only stay for a short while, and the others have been here for hours; in fact, they have been coming for a week just to be present. The woman beside me is wearing a soaked-through windbreaker suctioned to her body, so that the nylon is semi-transparent in patches and I can see the floral pattern of her blouse. She's shivering. There are signs on Bristol Board or pieces of brown cardboard scribbled with Sharpies and wrapped in Saran Wrap to keep them dry. I have a red umbrella, left over from the protest about safety for sex workers two years ago.

The signs say *Free Beatrice* and *#MakeMuskratRight*. I know a couple of these people from the other protests about the Muskrat Falls hydroelectric dam. I introduce myself to a couple I haven't met before. We shake hands; talk about the weather. One of the women tells me Beatrice Hunter has been subjected to strip searches in there.

Hunter was sent to prison because she told a judge she could not promise to stay away from the Muskrat Falls Nalcor site where she is trying to protect the land and water from methylmercury poisoning and further flooding. The prison is an ugly fortress, dull and falling apart, full of rats. My sister, a lawyer, is trying to sue the government in order to shut this prison down because it is not fit for human habitation. It's not fit for animals.

If you tried to give this prison to the SPCA, my sister tells me, they'd say, No thank you.

Beatrice Hunter says, in a tearful CBC interview, that when she was sent from her home in Labrador to the prison in St. John's, she feared she would become one of the missing or murdered Indigenous women.

We just want Beatrice to know we're out here, one of the women beside me says. Five cars pass and hit their horns. One car passes without noticing. Four more cars sound their horns. We wave vigorously at them all. The reason Beatrice Hunter is in prison is because she wants to be a physical presence, to stand outside the gates of the Nalcor site, in order to register her resistance to the project, in order to protect the land and water. She is in prison because her peaceful, physical presence has proven to be a major threat to the project, to the narrative of the dam. People have heard of her presence across the country. Because she refused the authority of the court, because she insisted on standing there, the whole country is awake to the issues around Muskrat Falls.

I only stay at the protest for a half hour. Maybe less, because I have to get to the hospital to visit you.

In the car I am shivering all the way to the Health Sciences. The windshield wiper on the passenger side is broken and the metal rod, stripped of its rubber, screeches so loud and shrill it raises the hairs on my arms. I can feel that sound in my teeth.

The driver's door was damaged in a hit and run and I can't open it. I have to get in the two-door car through the passenger side and climb over the gearshift. Or, on occasions when the passenger side has been buried in snow left from the plough, I climb through the hatchback. Other than that, the car goes pretty well. The brakes, though. The brakes have give. The brakes are soft. You have to press down pretty hard to come to a complete stop.

Yesterday, after a visit with you and before I hurried to my office to prepare for a creative writing class on poetry, I was overwhelmed with hunger.

The nurse had packed a long string, as thick as a shoelace, into your wound. This string of fabric would act like a wick, the nurse tells me, drawing out what they called drainage. The nurses speak of the presence or absence of odour, the different tints and colours of the drainage, and these are the things I want to be able to recognize, because infection might set in very quickly. They are the signs. I want to be vigilant. I have decided I want to attend to the wound. The nurse is laying out his tools. Blue gloves and a sterile bandage he spreads over the bedside table. He cracks the seal on a bottle of clear liquid and squirts the liquid into a plastic tray. Then he rips the lid off a package and topples a pair of sterile scissors and a pair of tweezers onto the sterile bandage. He tears open a package of gauze and lifts the first square out with the tweezers and drops it into the clear liquid and pushes it under with the tweezers until it is soaked through. Then he turns to you. He removes the bandage from your wound. The word *incision* sounds like snipping scissors, it sounds precise and crisp.

But the word *wound* sounds inflicted; it sounds suffered. The word *wound* seems to capture the *ongoingness* of the bloody hole, how it is active, has depth. There are holes in your stomach and a piece of fabric, as wide as shoelace, is sticking up out of each of the holes. The nurse tugs one out with the tweezers. It is very long and crusty with drainage. He tugs and tugs and it keeps coming out. They don't want the wound to heal with seepage trapped inside. They want it to heal from the bottom up. The holes are deep and bright red and fleshy and ragged and the wick wiggles out, a worm from a sick rose.

But I leave, in the middle of the dressing, because I think I might faint. I go to a room down the hall where there is a large flatscreen TV. It's a room for family members who need a bit of quiet.

There are three middle-aged sisters in there with white paper napkins spread on their wide laps and smudges of shiny grease on their lips radiating all over their chins. A giant platter of barbequed chicken legs in front of them. They're licking their fingers and they're very hungry. I realize that I really want a piece of that chicken. Watching over the sick can make one ravenous.

Where did you get that chicken? I ask.

This is takeout, one sister says. She's wearing acid-washed jeans and a white blouse with brass buttons.

It's hard work, I say.

Being here, one sister asks. Is that what you mean?

Being here, I say.

And yes, my dear, that's what it is, another sister says. Her gnawed bone drops down on to a little mountain of bones, an augury, and she picks the napkin off her thighs and wipes her face.

There's a music video on the flatscreen that's hanging over a faux fireplace with plug-in logs. This room had been a gift from a philanthropist who probably spent a lot of time with a loved one in this wing of the hospital. There's a plaque that says the philanthropist's family name. And there's a poster of a pie chart and this same poster can be found in lots of different parts of the hospital.

The biggest wedge of the pie indicates how much of the province's austerity budget goes to health care. It's hard to tell if the poster is a cautionary tale: they are going to cut. Or if they are asking us to be grateful. I've overheard the nurses talk about a shortage of shifts. They can't get enough work.

In the video on the flatscreen TV, a man is singing a pop song: *I love your body.* Just that line, over and over. *I love your body.* A chant. The melody is catchy. I am swathed in the sweet stink of barbecue sauce and charred meat and the image of the wound that I can't blink away, the tattered flesh, and the inside and the wick — the inescapable obdurate truth that we are finite, we are just breath and pumping blood, and it can all fail us. It will stop irrevocably and without argument and of its own accord and we can intervene and beg and be still in the face of it, and sometimes it relents and heals, but, yes, it will stop. It stops. The thought of all of this falling away, disintegrating, being gone, makes me so hungry — for the light on the snow, veils of it shuddering down and shimmering, as if I could put the sudden May snow squall inside me and swallow it. All the ephemeral splinters of light and ice, and the sugary burnt meat and the love of being here. Of being in a body.

What if I could hold it in my fist? All of it? Can I write it down? The pop song was bringing me to the point of tears. I thought: What a good idea, to love someone's body. I love your body.

Being here, I say. I leave the hospital without saying goodbye to you and I go to the university cafeteria. The noise and crowds, the fast food, and someone in the far corner setting up to play some music. There's the static and splats of harsh noise, amps being plugged in.

I sit at the window and the traffic of the parkway drives under the cafeteria and comes out the other side, six lanes and a median. The Health Sciences complex is visible from where I'm sitting, the snow squall chafing at it, rubbing it away. I wonder behind which black window is your hospital bed. From this distance all the windows are no bigger than my pinky fingernail.

I will be teaching about point of view soon in my next fiction-writing class. I will talk about stories that begin with "once upon a time." The phrase lets us know the events in the story happened in the past, and at least one person survived the ordeal (for there will most certainly be an ordeal) in order to tell the story. We also know the story has lasted through time, has been passed down in some way, and so it's worth hanging around to hear it. There will be a golden truth from long ago.

But the urgency of the present isn't there with "once upon a time." That's the trade-off. And my husband is reading about the anthropocene, he tells me, and how nature will act upon us, how nature might have a subjectivity, bite us back. How we might not matter so much, when you take the long view — all this capitalist charging forward and unfolding, the toiling and philosophy, the poetry and pain. A blip.

And you are a long way off, too, the streams of traffic, brick and a tiny window, flashing like mica in the sun, and you and I started this way, with just a wick connecting us in a black tumbling universe.

ANOTHER PROTEST, THIS TIME ABOUT tuition at Memorial. The students gathering at the clock tower. The government had come down hard on the university because of the mounting expense of Muskrat Falls. We will walk to the Confederation Building from the clock tower. But that was once upon a time. That's already happened. The tuition freeze is gone.

I'm explaining in class about Jesus being made into flesh. How he had said: Take this cup. But there was no getting away from it for poor old Jesus. He was flesh all right, nothing he could do about it. Ranted against it in the desert, but nobody listened.

I'm talking about how the character Ray in Miriam Toews' *A Complicated Kindness* is a Christ figure.

How do we know that, I ask the students. What's in their backyard, I ask. Anybody? I say.

Somebody says, A cross.

And then Ray comes across the field to Nomi with coffees and the muffins,

I say, and he's Jesus, but he's dressed in her dad's suit and she's waking up in the field after taking hallucinatory drugs and it's her dad but it's also Christ, remember, I say. That's Christ made of flesh. Take this cup; it's a takeout coffee cup. See? That's Miriam Toews being funny. She's really funny.

YOU TELL ME YOUR PHONE is almost dead.

That's going to die, you say. I was talking to somebody this morning and I lost her.

Where's your charger, I ask.

There's one in the drawer. Have a look in the drawer, will you? The trouble is they have all these things attached to me, these tubes. I can't move. I can't get up.

I'm going to plug it in back here.

And my mouth is dry. These girls, they don't stop. They're going all night.

The vampire is here, says a nurse, announcing herself. You roll your eyes at her, a parody of a complaining patient. But you hold out your arm.

I'm going to take some blood, she says. Another nurse, who is checking your temperature, confirms: She's going to take some blood now.

I'm going into the same vein so it won't hurt as much, the nurse says. And then you won't see me no more. She has a tray of glass tubes.

Got it, she says, as she presses the needle into your arm. The blood glugs into the little vial and you turn your head from it, so as to feel the sensation without the image, the blood spilling out, tumbling all over itself into the glass tube.

The veins are wiggly, the nurse says. But sometimes I get it on the first try. And the other nurse says your temp is up.

Is it up, I ask. How much is it up? The nurse's mouth is in a hard, straight line as she holds up the thermometer to read it against the light.

It's up, she says. Significantly.

Watch out, you say, and you point to me. She writes books. She's likely to put you into a book. That's what she does, and then you're in a book.

The nurse glances my way, assessing. I try to look innocent.

You say: This is going to die. And you hand me your phone.

I AM TRYING TO GET the car out but it's stuck in the ice. The road slants in front of our house and it means the water runs toward the curb and freezes around the tires of my car. I am reversing and going forward with the tires cranked out, the car filled with exhaust and the squeals of the engine. If I go too far back there will be no going forward. Sleet. Rain freezing as it falls.

There's a sharp rap on my window and a woman puts her face too close to the glass, her nose almost touching. Just the window between our faces. Her eyes are ringed with runny black mascara. Teeth cracked and black and missing. Her face so drawn it looks as though her skull is pressing through the translucently white skin, but she is in her early twenties. Her hair is long and wavy and soaking wet. Her little jacket is half unzipped. Sleet slips down the glass between our faces and I scream. It is a scream from my gut, from deep inside, full of terror.

I shout: What? What do you want? But I recover the way you do when you think: not an apparition, but a person. Just a stranger, rapping on the window with her fist.

I'm going to give you a push, she says. All you need is a little push.

Now I have the window rolled down a bit so I can take her in; she's very tall. She's wearing a miniskirt and her bare legs are flaming red with the cold and boots to the knees and heels that are chunky but very high. Maybe three inches? And the whole road is ice and slanting down.

No, I say.

Yes, I am, she says. I'm going to push you out. I'm going to get behind you. She has command and vehemence. She can see the logistics of this. Or algebra or geometry or whatever it is required to get me off the ice and on my way. On my way to poetry class where I am going to talk about metaphors.

But here's what you have to do, she says. You have to straighten your wheels. Straighten them up, she commands.

You have on high heels, you're not pushing me, I say.

I'm pushing you, she says. Now straighten the wheels. Then my husband appears. He's banging on the passenger door for me to unlock it.

Oh good, the woman says. We're going to give her a push, she tells him. We'll get her out of this. The two of us. She just needs to straighten her wheels. Get behind her with me, she orders my husband. I can see now she is maybe twenty-three years old, maybe twenty-four.

I tell her that if I am driving she will get run over and so will my husband. I tell her I will kill them both. That's a certainty. I will mean to go forward, I say, but I'd have the car in reverse by mistake. I am a terrible driver, I say. My husband, I say, he can get this out and he won't need a push. Just watch. We're not going to push, I say.

I have to climb out over the gearshift and the passenger seat and he has to climb in over the passenger seat and the gearshift, and then, because he's very tall, his knees are practically up around his ears. He's in a fetal position, scrunched up, with his head banging on the roof of the car and he reaches under and finds the bar and the seat shoots back. He's ready to drive me out of the fist of ice and sleet and ill will of winter in May. We stand to the side and watch, this young woman and me.

You in them boots, I ask her. How could you have pushed? But she's crossing the street and yelling directions over the revving engine.

Nothing coming, she says. Give it to her, she yells at my husband. I am sliding all over the road trying to get across the street to her.

You're working, I say.

I'd rather not be out in this, she says, and all her charisma briefly dims to a low-watt weariness. She has one of those smiles where the corners of the mouth turn down, despite being a smile. Not grim but determined. Not rueful but complex, not a lie. But a willingness to overlook sadness.

I am on a plane as I write this (well rewrite this, in fact, because I wrote it down on the day it happened). I glance at the open page of a magazine on a woman's lap in the opposite aisle, open to a full-page photograph of Princess Diana. In this picture she is wearing a pearl earring ringed around with gold and a string of pearls on her neck too big to be real (fake pearls on the princess?) and a pink jacket, the collar of the jacket is out of focus. But her eyes, her smile. It's a smile that could be described in the same way, striving hard to not be ironic about the whole shit show, but still vulnerable, not a lie.

But this makes me suspicious of what I've written. Really? Do they have the same smile? Do I read the smile that way because Princess Diana has since died in a car crash? Because I know what happened, once upon a time? Of course they don't have the same smile. Absolutely not. Maybe, maybe their smiles pass one another in the night, maybe the smiles of everyone who is in the prison of a body share something at some point. No, we are not the same. We are the same. We are not the same. We are same.

I was out all night, the girl says. I'm from a little small place, different than this, come into town a few weeks ago. Nobody is friendly here. Nobody talks to you. You say hi on the street and nobody says hi back.

I'm going to give you some money, I say. Just what I have in my pocket.

No, she says.

Yes, I am, I say. She looks at the money.

What are you giving me this for, she says. (I know, because I've been told, that I have given her the price of two blow jobs.)

Because there's sleet in May is why, I say. Because we live in this fucking weather is why. Because you offered to help me.

I'm going home, she says. Big grin. I just live over there. Get a shower. Get some sleep. She points out her house. Then the car roars away from the clutch of the ice, squealing as it breaks free, swaying and swerving and stopping and just idling there in the middle of the road.

If this were a short story I would not write that line because it's too on the nose. *The car breaks free*. And maybe it didn't happen that way. But my husband had been rocking the car, reverse, forward, reverse, forward. The ice gives up its grip. The car shoots out. She says about the shower and stuffs the money in her pocket and I look around for a pimp (they are usually on the island of trees in front of my house and they wear hoodies and pace slowly between the trees but she might be on her own. I didn't see anyone else). Then she is clapping and whooping because the car is out. And me too, I am whooping and clapping. And off she goes down the road with her knobby knees and bare, red legs, not slipping or falling on the ice, hands dug into the pockets of her sopping wet jacket, elbows akimbo.

Several days later my husband will tell me there was a commotion on the street. Down in front of that house. The house where she said she lived. They brought out a body. Who was it, I say. Was it that woman? The woman, the woman? The young woman?

But I can't find out anything on the Internet. Her face scared the shit out of me. Her face appearing in the window of my car when I was so lost in thought, trying to get the car out. The rapping of her fist. I shouted from my gut. Our faces not very far apart, the glass, the water running down the window, her black teeth, the mascara. All the long wet hair. Soaked to the bone.

THE NURSE PUSHING A LONG stick, like a very long Q-tip, into your wound to measure its depth. The public health nurse showing the result to the student nurse. Turning the stick slightly in the light so they can see where the measurements are written and they determine that the wound has closed half a centimetre. And honestly, my stomach is hardening. I am able to stand all sorts of things that I could not before. I marvel at it. This hardening. This pushing back against this revulsion. Because the flesh is torn. Or because there is flesh at all. Because there is mortality. Because it holds the soul or the imagination or the essence. Or it doesn't.

A line from the Alice Munro story I am reading about the mountains as seen through a train window: "What drew her in — enchanted her, actually — was the very indifference, the repetition, the carelessness and contempt for harmony, to be found on the scrambled surface of the Precambrian shield."

Contempt for harmony. I know that Munro is going for the unexpected in this sentence. Doesn't everyone prefer harmony? And earlier, the narrator is thinking about Greek thought. She is a student of Classics. And she has learned that the ancient Greeks have "a considerable attachment to the irrational."

A list of irrational things: Flesh is irrational; desire is ungovernable; love is batshit crazy; Newfoundland is irrational; Muskrat Falls is an obdurate willingness to allow the machinations of bureaucracy to smash human agency. The willingness to carry through with a hydroelectric dam that will poison wildlife and water and land and destroy food security for the people of Labrador is irrational and the destruction of energy security for the whole province is irrational and to go on with the project is irrational; throwing the land protector Beatrice Hunter, an Inuk grandmother, in a high-security male prison where she has been subject to strip searches for peaceably protesting against Nalcor because they are putting the lives of her community at jeopardy is irrational. The sex worker's high heels and her help and the danger they are in and austerity is irrational. The snow in May. Metaphors are irrational and orgasms and loss. This is an incomplete list, obviously. Completion is irrational.

A MAN NAMED ANGUS ANDERSEN from Nain stands outside the Sheraton while Premier Dwight Ball gives a Fortis Energy Exchange speech. Andersen and other land protectors are handing out bottles of water with a label that says the water is from Muskrat Falls and contains ten percent methylmercury. There's a photograph of the Nalcor site on the label.

I've taken a gauze bandage from your bedside table and stuffed it into my pocket. I am stealing it; fuck austerity and the budget pie chart. When I get outside the hospital I grab lungfuls of fresh air and walk the whole length of the hospital parking lot until I get to my car. I tie the bandage around the metal rod on the passenger side, the only thing left of the windshield wiper. The ice freezes it up in a big knot and it leaves a satisfying transparent band through which I can see a narrow strip of road. Of course the wiper on the driver's side still works. Total visibility is overrated.

The filmmaker Almoldovar quotes Munro in an introduction to three of her stories: "The complexity of things — things within things — just seems endless. I mean nothing is easy, nothing is simple." Every time I read that sentence I go straight to the short story I am writing. I don't read any farther than that because it makes me want to write. That line gives me permission.

Permission to write a tangent, to throw out whole paragraphs that move so far away from the centre of the story I am working on that it feels, even as I write, that they are going to have to be cut. But afterwards I see that they are necessary. They have been dictated by some inner, nascent, irrational hunch, and one of two things is occurring. 1) they were always meant to be in the story, and I am simply excavating the necessary pre-existing world of the characters, or 2) the story never existed, is chimerical, shifting as I write, coming into being. Either way a mystery is uncovered. The mystery is coherence. Because there's no such thing.

I'm driving toward the university and I am rehearsing what I will say about metaphor in the poetry class. It's when you take two distinctly different things that have nothing to do with one another (and here I take my hands off the steering wheel and make two fists and hold them up), because I am talking to myself, out loud, trying to figure out what a metaphor is, And they smack together, I say, and I smack my fists together and spread my fingers open.

And make a third thing, I say, a new thing. And they stay apart, those two things, and they come together at the same time, and the paradox is a chemical reaction, the sublime new thing that never existed before. And I put my foot down on the brake as I approach the stop sign at the intersection on Newtown road and there is no brake. The car sails through. There is no stop.

WHERE IS HOME AND
HOW DO I GET THERE?
Greg Hollingshead

*K*INGSLEY AMIS ADVISED HIS SON Martin not to be a writer because he'd end up wandering around the house in his dressing gown trying to think of the right word. A.M. Klein says of the poet, "stark infelicity/... stirs him from his sleep." This is what writers do. We wander the house half-dressed in search of felicity. We don't sleep well. We play around and play around, we wait and we procrastinate, we try this and we try that, until we get it right. The words, the line breaks, the details of character, of plot, the sound, the rhythm, every detail fitting, appropriate, relevant, happy, felicitous, right. And each time something clicks into place — even though we know it will probably need to be cut because we've made other changes and everything is related to everything else — we're home.

So there's that. But I have a friend who some days can't leave the house. It's not the neighbourhood, it's the world. He's a writer who writes out of rage and despair at the dreadfulness of it all. He didn't smile when I told him Pascal said man's misery stems from his not being able to stay in his room. When I mentioned Edmund Wilson's description of a writer — "The victim of a malodorous disease which renders him abhorrent to society and periodically degrades him and makes him helpless is also master of a superhuman art which everybody has to respect and which the normal man finds he needs" — he just laughed.

In Canada, only some readers and reviewers abhor and degrade some of us, sometimes. Society is well-disposed enough, when it notices. But if it doesn't abhor us, we may abhor it or at least what it condones and, like my friend, have trouble leaving the house on some days. How many writers woke up the morning after September 11 to projects that would no longer do? What words could click into place for us now? Nine/eleven didn't happen in Canada, but its effects did. And then there was Harper and, more recently, Trump, 65 million refugees of war, renewed threat of nuclear war, and all the while the mass extinction of life on the planet. One effect of the times has been a politicising of the cultural atmosphere. Another kind of politicising, of literary theory and education, began in Canadian universities in the mid-seventies, though it's been only recently, as those students have grown up in the world they've grown up in, that emulations of Alice Munro have given way to texts radical in more overt and culturally varied ways. But since 9/11, perhaps because by the end of the century there was hope that literature could speak to and not simply mirror entrenched social injustice, there has been despair.

Even Zadie Smith, at Harbourfront in the fall of 2015 — after reading from *Middlemarch* about how knowing and feeling all ordinary human life would be like hearing the grass grow and the beating of the squirrel's heart, it would kill us, and so the "quickest of us walk about well-wadded with stupidity" — said that while people have taken from this the "literary idea" that more empathy would make the world a better place, George Eliot is simply being realistic about our moral limits. Human empathy is fickle, Smith concluded, it comes and goes, and if we want change we must depend not on "human sentiment," but on legislation and the law.

So Zadie Smith would have us look to the life-saving virtue of our stupidity and to our legislators for change. Legislation for *change*, really? In a market-driven society? It's been more than a century since the publication of *In Search of Lost Time* where Marcel Proust describes "that abominable and sensual act called *reading the newspaper*,"

> thanks to which all the misfortunes and cataclysms in the universe over the last twenty-four hours, the battles which cost the lives of fifty thousand men, the murders, the strikes, the bankruptcies, the fires, the poisonings, the suicides, the divorces, the cruel emotions of statesmen and actors, are transformed for us, who don't even care, into a morning treat, blending in

wonderfully, in a particularly exciting and tonic way, with the recommended ingestion of a few sips of *café au lait*.

Who don't even care. That's the intention. We're not meant to. That way *nothing will change.* To judge from the twentieth century and the first two decades of this one, things will only get worse. And meanwhile, what are writers? Buskers in the marketplace, consoling the shoppers, leaving the dreadfulness of it all to the politicians, the lawyers, and the CBC?

I would say that Zadie Smith is directing our attention too far downstream. The barbarism isn't out there, held at bay until brought to heel by government and the law, while artists, safe in here, cultivate our sentiments. It all exists inside each of us, artist or not, at every moment. Literature attends to the reality, the truth, of that. Here's Eliot, again from *Middlemarch*: "Doubtless some ancient Greek has observed that behind the big mask and the speaking-trumpet, there must always be our poor little eyes peeping as usual and our timorous lips more or less under anxious control." Like some ancient Greek, literature is interested in those poor little eyes, those timorous lips more or less under anxious control. Why? Because otherwise the reality of who and what we are is obscured by a speaking-trumpet.

Literature focuses attention on what is happening upstream, at the fountain-head, where the problem originates, in the human mind. Legislation can keep us relatively safe for a while, but without continuing insight into our nature the legislation will erode, becoming ever more selective about who and what it keeps safe, and at some point, even here, as nine years of Harper reminded us, it certainly won't be keeping safe people who don't work for the firm.

The reason, beyond good luck, that I directed the Writing Studio at the Banff Centre for eighteen years was the writers who come there as participants and faculty. These are people, mostly Canadian, most in their late twenties and thirties but also older, into their seventies, who are thinking for themselves about what it means to be in the world. If they're poets they're thinking about what it means to be alive, sensuously, socially, mentally. If they're storytellers they're thinking about what it means to be a person emotionally connected to other people. These are writers, who, like all people who think for themselves, live by their own lights. For some it's all they have, but it's everything.

Most years at Banff I found a way to mention Gregory Bateson on how only a human can relate a theory or name a thing. If your cat meows when she's hungry, she's not theorizing, she's not naming food, she's saying *I depend on you [so feed me]*. Bateson's point is that as humans we think of ourselves as mainly engaged in the first kind of relating, but our dominant concern — befitting the animals we are — is the second. What we're talking about matters little to us compared to our relationship with the person we're talking to. Let's say we think the ratio is 80 to 20 percent, but it's more like 20 to 80 percent. Are we making a good impression? Do they like us?

To this I would add that this fault in the rock face of our worldview, this chronic blindness to the animal primacy for us of our relations with others, is also the site of entry into art. If art is superhuman it's because the animal is bigger for us than the human. In fiction or at the theatre, the audience pays attention to what the character is saying not for what it says about the world but for what it says about what she needs, socially and emotionally, in her relations with other people and the world. And so irony, metaphor, metonymy. Artists use A to signify B. Joseph Conrad said art is indirectness. It's the unsayable by the human alone.

The human mind is conditioned to think of itself as under the control of an agent capable of understanding what's going on and therefore able to protect and extend its power. The self is a strange doubling-down, a way for the mind to commit to what it thinks it is and knows. The artist — something like the skeptical, self-deprecating, bemused Canadian she sometimes is — has been blessed with the intuition that her mind does not know what it thinks it knows and in this it's not alone. This is why she has nothing of instrumental, political use to offer the conditioned mind (not even her own), unless it's *I don't know.* On 30 May 1888, Anton Chekhov put it this way to his friend Souvorin:

> The time has come for writers, especially those who are artists, to admit
> that in this world *one cannot make anything out*, just as Socrates once
> admitted it, just as Voltaire admitted it. The mob think they know and
> understand everything; the more stupid they are, the wider, I think, do
> they conceive their horizon to be. And if an artist in whom the crowd has
> faith decides to declare that he understands nothing of what he sees — this

in itself constitutes a considerable clarity in the realm of thought, and a great step forward.

Chekhov is talking about a clarity-of-mind step forward, not a legislated one. Clarity of mind is why and how the literary writer watches and listens, knowing nothing. A *conscious animal* is not into providing answers of any kind. A *meow* is a wide-open message signifying nothing except relationship. It doesn't mean anything. It's not an answer to anything. D.H. Lawrence says that if you try to nail anything down in the novel, either it kills the novel or the novel gets up and walks away with the nail. Literature will always walk away with the nail. It knows that the nail is only an abstraction, a belief, inimical to the artistic endeavour. Like the personal, art can have a powerful political effect, but that is not to say art is political. Political means the marketplace, where things are supposedly known that are not known. They're hardly noticed. Who's got the time? There's always breaking news! It's the market! Art is about paying attention to what is actually going on for people. It's not about confidence in government and the law, which are fatal to it. This is why, as Chekov admitted in a 4 October 1888 letter to the poet Pleshcheyev, speaking-trumpet expectations of artists frightened Chekhov:

I am afraid of those ... determined to regard me either as a liberal or a conservative. I am not a liberal, not a conservative, not a believer in gradual progress, not a monk, not an indifferentist [believer that all religions are equally valid]. I should like to be a free artist and nothing more...

Consider the animal. Here is J.M. Coetzee, in his novel *Elizabeth Costello*, on a great ape in a cage:

At every turn Sultan is driven to think the less interesting thought. From the purity of speculation (Why do men behave like this?) he is relentlessly propelled towards lower, practical, instrumental reason (How does one use this to get that?) and thus towards acceptance of himself as primarily an organism with an appetite that needs to be satisfied... In his deepest being, Sultan is not interested in the banana problem... The question that truly occupies him, as it occupies the rat and the cat and every other animal trapped in the hell of the laboratory or the zoo is: Where is home and how do I get there?

Where is home and how do I get there? This is the same question asked by the human animal trapped inside a conditioned mind.

Now that the reality of climate change has started to sink in, there has been a shift, visible for a decade or so in concepts like the Anthropocene, toward understanding the human in the context of not only the animal but all life on the planet. This can only be a good thing. But not in the marketplace, where this larger ecological awareness is being framed in the language of rights, which is "human" talk, not about a relationship (we are doing the planet a grievous injustice), but about an object desirable for the injured party to have, or be awarded. So we're conferring rights on rivers and talking about personhood for chimpanzees.

Clearly, this is a matter too unsayable for the politicians and the courts, who will ensure that nothing changes because what is done will be done arbitrarily and piecemeal. Absurdly. Literature has understood for centuries what is at stake here. Witting animal talk, *conscious* animal talk, cognizant of the primary reality of relationship in the life of all animals including the human, is not about *rights* but about *obligations*. Not an abstraction to be pursued and possessed the way we pursue and possess a piece of property but the honouring and maintaining the network of our actual relationships. Like the other animals, we are social creatures. *Rights* talk is government/law/business/media/market talk. It's a way to sell humane behaviour, by turning what should be a galvanizing injustice into marketable emotion, marketable power. It's a way to go on not even caring. How much easier to confer rights on people we're oppressing than to stop discriminating against and incarcerating and otherwise mentally setting them aside. Let the government and the police and the courts deal with it. The last thing the problem can be is that we as individual human beings are plainly failing to fulfill our obligations to other human beings. It shouldn't be surprising that in a *rights* paradigm, other animals and the planet hardly register. To engage in *rights* talk is to create a hierarchy of the oppressed, in which the most clamorous win the most compensation. No wonder impostors. No wonder life in the full death grip of the market, with no voice at all — the life of the animals, of the forests, of the seas — needs advocacy groups and teams of lawyers, or we will destroy it as fast as we can.

Rights are a pragmatic, political tool in a market society. The unsayable isn't sellable. Religions break it down into articles of faith and sell it that way, and then come the rivers of blood. Art isn't an agent for anything, not the Church, not rights, not the Bank of Montreal, not Canadian Tire, not leaders and their sunny ways. The nail is an abstraction, belief disguised as reality. Art comes out of a felt sense of human obligation, of what is going on in the heart, in those poor little eyes peeping, in what that anxious control of those quivering lips looks and feels like. Art is also about the speaking-trumpet, but it's not it. It's about the unsayable. Once my wife Rosa overheard someone on the bus say to the person beside him, "I don't know what that means at all, but I think you're saying something I understand." That person could have been talking to a writer, or to any artist, or to any human being who was even a little bit off script.

As artists, we're not trying to make a picture of how things are. Sometimes our work is felt in the world, provoking the market to accommodate the tremor. What we're focused on is something different. We're conditioned beings who are trying to go home, and that means private digging. Celan says, "There was earth inside them, and they dug." That's us. We're writing drafts, we're performing a succession of replacements, we're digging deeper and deeper as we excavate our own models, our own superficiality, our own commonplaces, banalities, and clichés, burrowing down through the wadding of our stupidity, the language of the conditioned mind that we spend our days inside and that is inside us like a debilitating fog. We dig in order to come at what we haven't ever quite been able to say before, in order to make something that feels fresh and new and right and intelligent to ourselves, and — with enough work and luck — to others. We can sense it glimmering, deep down. The closer we get to it the closer we are to home. This is happiness, the kind that every artist knows.

I don't have trouble leaving the house, first, yes, because this is Canada, legislation is still in place — as a six-foot white male and not, say, a woman of colour, I walk out with a childlike lack of fear of assault, not in this neighbour-hood anyway, though I am getting old, so that day could come — but also because I know I carry it all inside me anyway, and not just the seeds of it, and not just because I'm a writer, and also because I'm not writing to reflect it or to provide solutions, because I have none. To regret this or to pretend I have one would be an error, just as it would be an error to hate myself or give up in despair. This is not a matter of the forces of barbarism being too powerful or art too weak, but of art being not about answers but about the fact of the primacy for human beings of relationship and the implications of that, the obligations that arise from that. I need to go out there, not in order to name but in order to discover appropriate ways of pointing to the world, of elevating aspects of it to attention, to relevance, of saying *meow* and *woof* like a would-be conscious animal addressing a by-and-large, like myself most of the time, unwitting one, who will have no idea what I mean but who I hope, for the sake of us both, and of every plant, animal, and human on the planet, will understand. This is only what art has always done and always will do. It's not useless. These days it might look useless. A marginal activity. Busking in the marketplace. It's not that, it's work at the rock face, it's everything.

A CHAIR AND A BIRD
Madeleine Thien

ASUJIRO OZU, WHOSE BOOKS AND films have always moved me, once said, "Plot uses people, and to use people is to misuse them."

I have been thinking about his words for years. I wrestle with them as I write books and stories and imagine the lives of others. Ozu makes me stop my pen, still my hands, and write nothing.

A novel cut loose from plot is like a child without ancestors; it is hard to imagine such a thing because as soon as we begin to write a thought, the thought changes, expanding from itself in a kind of linearity. Yet I keep returning to Ozu's warning. In imagining the shape of others, their personhood and desires, how is it possible not to use and therefore misuse? I know that art and the word, in trying to represent some part of this reality, have already begun a process of distortion; their hands are tied at the outset.

Between Ozu and physics, there is a beautiful line. In the now-famous story of quantum mechanics, physicists discovered the strange truth that light is both a particle and a wave — two incompatible things — at the same time. Physicists observed that light exists as both wave and particle until the moment when an observer chooses to look. Only then, under observation, does the light choose to exist as one or the other — taking form.

This strangeness is like saying: I am a chair and a bird at the same time. Only when someone looks at me must I cease to be both. Perhaps I choose chair. Not only do I become a chair, I give off the impression of having been a chair from the outset, as if created that way from the very beginning.

Quantum mechanics provides evidence for an idea that seems incredible and mad: simply by observing something, or interacting with it, the observer creates, and thereby alters, reality.

In the process of writing, an idea forms. As we observe it, the idea takes shape. We bend it — use it — to represent an idea of reality.

First one thing, then another. So she built it up, first one thing and then another. Dancing, skipping, round and round the room they went ... "Ah, damn!" she cried (it was a joke of theirs, her swearing), the needle had broken. Hat, child, Brighton, needle. She built it up; first one thing, then another; she built it up, sewing.

— VIRGINIA WOOLF, *MRS. DALLOWAY*

On the surface, plot doesn't ask the existential question of why; plot is built by a manifold string of questions that ask *how*. How will I open the door? How will you address this child? How will the child interpret what was said? How does the belt get unbuckled? How does he crawl through the window and run to the road? How does the drug arrive in her body? How is the rebellion betrayed? How does the day unfold? The process of describing how events occur could be the storyteller's way of answering the question of why.

In order to define plot, the dictionary[1] describes a set of events set into motion. The writer, simply by virtue of paying attention, causes fictional events to occur. By choosing the precise moment at which to observe, the writer forces a decision on his or her imagined reality.

Quantum mechanics suggests that the moment of observation, the *now*, is crucial because it marks the dividing line between what could be (but does not yet exist) and what is. Physicists have floated the idea of retro-causality, a possible though unlikely explanation for the maddening wave-particle behaviours exhibited by light. Otherwise known as backward causation, this is the idea that light and matter somehow have knowledge about the future and can change a previous decision. If the theory of retro-causality were correct, not only does the past shape our present, but the future is shaping it as well: what you do next month may change what you did a decade ago.[2]

But the answer to how light is both a wave and a particle could be far simpler, though not less destabilizing: that time itself is the illusion, and if the human mind could lift the veil of this illusion, we would perceive, writes physicist Carlo Rovelli, "no flowing of time. The universe would be a single block of past, present and future."

Einstein famously wrote, "For we convinced physicists, the distinction between past, present and future is only an illusion, however persistent."

I have a feeling that the novels that I love know this in their marrow; despite the linearity of language itself, they find structures and narrative methods to slip through, double back, and dismantle the flux of time.

TODAY, SITTING AT MY DESK in Berlin, I am thinking of my mother. There is a tree in the courtyard, it is just on the cusp of surpassing the height of the five storey-building. An elevator in a glass box descends, waits, lifts. In thinking about my mother now, I think about how she dreamed of buying a small house on the Sunshine Coast, near to the sea, and how I promised to buy her this home one day. I remember poverty, bankruptcy, and my mother crying because she couldn't afford a pair of shoes for my older brother.

I think of my mother's insomnia and how she never allowed herself to rest. How she never went easy on herself, never felt that what she gave was enough. The racism in her workplace, directed against her, still makes me weep — in powerlessness, in fury, in silence. She died at the age of fifty eight. She taught me to believe that in order to be accepted as equal, I must consistently be better. That I could never work hard enough. A lesson I cannot let go of, even now, even if my heart wishes to.

I HAVE OBSERVED MY MOTHER through the branches of this moment, my own moment, and have forced a choice, a synopsis, on who she was. She would laugh. She would say, You think you know everything.

I look up for the word for plot, 情节, and am inexplicably drawn to the second character, 节. When I look it up (jié — 节 — joint, node, knot) the dictionary gives me only one sample usage: "Your mother was bound by her allotted life span. You must restrain your grief; excessive mourning won't do you any good." The words jié āi are highlighted: to restrain one's grief.

PLOT USES PEOPLE, AND TO use people is to misuse them.

For weeks, I have been meaning to call my father but I'm afraid. I don't want to tell him that I've decided to accept a job outside the country. He will understand, immediately, that the overall time we have together has been shortened. He is getting older and time is neither abstract nor an illusion; time is existence and life. My father's sadness is like a balloon in my chest. I float to the ceiling, unable to breathe. It's not that I think I can save everyone, it's that I don't want to cause pain. When I was young, the thought of causing pain made me want to slip away, to disappear completely. I thought carrying someone's pain was how you expressed love and fidelity. Now I wonder, how did I come to this conclusion? Was I blaming his pain for something that was mine alone? In my own heart, I have not yet accepted the physicists' description of time: that it cannot be shortened or lengthened, and that it is an imagined container. Such a truth would undercut a sense of my entire life, the plot of existence, the movement.

When I finally tell my father the news, via Skype, he says, "Don't worry too much. We will work things out." Before we hang up, he says again, because he knows me through and through, "Don't worry all the time. We will be okay."

We were aware of a marked thickening of the political and social atmosphere, a thickening oppression that was near the point of suffocation.
— DR. YAKOV RAPOPORT, SOVIET PATHOLOGIST, ARRESTED FEBRUARY 3, 1953, DURING STALIN'S "DOCTORS' PLOT"

Those who read have access to words, to history, and to the history of words. They know that language shapes, flatters, conceals, enthrals. He who reads reads language itself; he perceives its duplicity, its cruelty, its betrayal. He knows that a slogan is just a slogan. And he's seen others.
— CAMBODIAN FILMMAKER RITHY PANH, THE ELIMINATION

During China's Cultural Revolution, permissible language became the same as permissible thinking. These were the conditions in which a person had to live: the correct political positions are set by the Communist Party, the government, or the leading political cadres. You must learn a specific political language, because the language will guide your thinking. The slogan is the thought, complete and entire, no longer subject to critique.

Sometimes, if one makes a misstep, it will simply be corrected. But as campaigns intensify, a misstep can cost a person their job or their freedom; later, it can cost their life. Language is the means by which to divide the pure and the impure, the revolutionary and the counter-revolutionary. The political campaigns pit colleague against colleague, students against teachers, artists against artists, but leave the overall power structure intact. No, they do more than that: the campaigns protect and stabilize Mao Zedong's power structure while, at the same time, giving individuals the illusion they are at the vanguard of revolutionary change.

Those who do not appear to believe are denounced in violent meetings that set the crowd against the individual. The targets are humiliated, devastated, tortured, sometimes killed. These denunciation meetings happen every single day. And every day, you must also publicly criticize yourself, confessing any latent idea or thought that is impure; and you must also criticize others. This is an age of denunciation, insincerity, and political expediency. Someone else (a revolutionary committee, the government, your colleagues or friends, your children) becomes the ultimate interpreter of your thoughts. Someone else claims to have access to the true meaning and intent of your words. To be a political person, an upright person, begins to mean becoming one who exposes the corrupted, incorrect, and unacceptable thoughts of others. Retro-causality.

All words become a kind of surface — a public demonstration and evidence of solidarity with, and submission to, the prevailing orthodoxy.

But a world without contradiction, doubt, and paradox is a false world. The denuded world is — of course it must be — an inaccurate representation of the world. Those with certainty believe they know the pattern (the plot) of private lives.

Plot uses people, and to use people is to misuse them.

Hannah Arendt, in her study of totalitarianism, writes that we can introduce a lie into the world and back it up, and in so doing, create a factual reality, thereby turning the lie into fact. She says that totalitarianism's disregard for factuality[3], truth, is driven by the political conviction that, not only is everything possible but, in a totalitarian world, everything is permissible.

Language can turn us against one another: a lie becomes truth; to denounce someone is to be morally pure; to destroy another person is to cleanse society; to wrap ourselves in righteousness is to embrace justice; to burn a book or ban a thought is to safeguard truth.

It is an act of courage to refuse to look at another person with malice, contempt or scorn — no matter how violently we may disagree with their ideas. I have this feeling that, increasingly, what Arendt describes as "judgment without scorn, truth finding without zeal" is becoming a radical and revolutionary act. If we open our mouths to speak and find the words of another, the endless repetitions of slogans, whether of the right or the left, constantly doing our thinking for us, and filling us with righteousness, we have abdicated — what? a moral responsibility to one another? Yes, but something else, too, something that can never be recovered — our brief time here, our very being.

What is it about speaking that fills me with so much dread? And what is it about writing that allows a form of non-speech? This paradox is a refuge. Writing, for me, is a silent act and yet a loud one. No one is forced to read or to listen to anything I say; I am not imposing my will on another. But I am free to make a noise, to think my impure thoughts, to believe that the desire for precision in language is a desire to live in a moral way, not just to live with principle but to understand the nature of principle, how we come by our beliefs, how they shape us and blind us and create us. Plotting a work of fiction is a way of living out the idea that no thought ever ends, ever discovers its permanence, and time, if it exists at all, exists in the spacetime between reader, writer and characters as, to borrow once more the words of the physicist Rovelli, "a single block of past, present and future."

ONCE, WHEN I WAS FIFTEEN, I described something unspeakable to the psychologist assigned to me. I had never spoken of it before. He did not believe me, and asked if I had enjoyed it. I didn't know what to say. I was afraid to go back for another session. The question was like a knife in my heart. This pain follows you, but you learn to stay quiet and give nothing away, to live with what, slowly, inevitably, becomes part of one's nature. Years later, I finally answered the question for myself: No, I did not want it and I did not enjoy it. I also asked myself: Is it possible that something that is received as pain can be enjoyed? I answered yes. What was the difference? I had so many desires, some were shameful and some beautiful and some unknown. I had to look my lovers in the eye, and also, most important, myself. Love is a not a stable, describable form. Beneath that visible layer is the infinite strata below, which is a universe of plots and patterning. We can predict one, or hundreds, but never infinity. Do not misuse someone.

I AM THINKING ABOUT OZU again, who attempted in his films to relinquish the harness of plot. He said he did not want his characters to be sacrificed for the idea of an ending. I think Ozu would enjoy quantum physics, and the idea that all possible states exist, and will continue to exist *until* we observe, at which point one state will become a concrete reality. He would have empathy, I think, for the physicists who are struggling to answer the question: Is it possible to observe a particle without disturbing it?

My mother died before she told us this story: how she watched in horror as a boy stumbled and fell from the roof of her building. I write *before* but maybe she never intended to tell us. To tell it would be to set the ending in motion. If she never told the story, she would not yet arrive at the place where she stood, looking up. The boy's fall from the roof would not begin. Imagine if our understanding of the world was not predicated by the arrow of time, or determined by plot. Maybe she told us about the boy, but at a different moment, an altogether unrecognizable one. It wasn't that she chose to ignore the ending; it was that she refused to be blind to all that came before, to accept that the ending defined the meaning. She would not wish to misuse him.

Strange how science reveals, time and again, that our intuition about the world is often wrong, and that the search for understanding is endless, rich, and remarkable. Space is curved and time is not only relative, it may not exist. Rovelli writes:

Physics opens windows through which we see far into the distance. What we see does not cease to astonish us. We realize that we are full of prejudices and that our intuitive image of the world is partial, parochial, inadequate. The earth is not flat, it is not stationary. The world continues to change before our eyes as we gradually see it more extensively and more clearly… Reality is not as it appears to us. Every time we glimpse another aspect of it, it is a deeply emotional experience, another veil has fallen.

— CARLO ROVELLI, *SEVEN BRIEF LESSONS ON PHYSICS*

Every time I speak the word *mother* I remember seeing her for the last time. I want to remember what it was to see her for the first time, the tenth, the fortieth.

There is no fixed and stable point of knowing. At the moment of having ascertained a very precise piece of information (the position of an atom, for instance) we have foreclosed the possibility of precisely knowing another piece, the speed at which it is moving, moving, eternally moving. Strange and liberating to know that there are 100 billion neurons in the human brain; more than 100 billion stars in our galaxy; and at least 200 billion galaxies in the observable universe. There is no shape to life, no boredom, no end to our questions, and this questioning is, for me, both an art and an experiment, setting me in motion.

MARGINALIA AND NOTES

1. Noun — A plan made in secret by a group of people to do something illegal or harmful: [with infinitive]: *there's a plot to overthrow the government*; the main events of a play, novel, movie, or similar work, devised and presented by the writer as an interrelated sequence; a small piece of ground marked out for a purpose such as building or gardening: a vegetable plot; a graph showing the relation between two variables; chiefly U.S.: a diagram, chart, or map.

2. Note from Charles (first reader): See *Pride and Prejudice* (original title: *First Impressions*) in which Elizabeth cannot marry Darcy because he is against her for being of a lower order and she against him for being proud, but nevertheless she can marry him and thereby transition from the lower social context that was the initial obstacle. Their union shapes the future by improving the family's situation, though it cannot undo the indignity of her younger sister's elopement, even as it explains it.

3. "In a totally fictitious world, failures need not be recorded, admitted, and remembered. Factuality itself depends for its continued existence upon the existence of the non-totalitarian world." — HANNAH ARENDT, *THE ORIGINS OF TOTALITARIANISM*.

IT'S LIKE FEATHERS PASSING
OVER ME

Richard Van Camp

*M*Y DAD TOLD ME ONCE that if you slice a magpie's tongue in two it will speak human to you.

I say this now as I think about my heroes all the time: Taika Waititi, Zoe Leigh Hopkins, Helen Haig-Brown, Amanda Spotted Fawn Strong, Peter Jackson, Carla Ulrich, Tantoo Cardinal, Martin Scorsese, George Lucas, Steven Spielberg, Anita Doron, Christina Piovesan, Alex Lalonde, Michael Mann, Zacharias Kunuk, Kent Williams, Chrystos, Lee Maracle, Robert Kirkman, Menton3, Kelly Kerrigan, Antonio Fuso, Scott Henderson, Ivan Coyote, Sonny Assu, Steven Paul Judd, Gregory Scofield, George Littlechild Nenekawasis, Julie Flett, Eden Robinson, Mike Grell, Ted May, Jesse Moynihan, Sammy Harkham, Sammy Hagar, Nikki Sixx, Hyung Min-woo, Sophie Campbell, James Welch, David Robertson, Craig Lesley. I could go on and on. They're all brilliant and they haunt and inspire me every day because they've all wounded me somehow. Just like the greatest storytellers of our time: Ivy Chelsea, Rose Bishop, Rosa Mantla, Marlene and Earl Evans, my brother Roger, the late Glen Douglas, Terri Naskan, Joel Duthie. Those that swoon me. Those I belong to and those I answer to.

And I think about the great wounding of certain scenes. When you break a bone the body overcompensates in your healing so that the fracture will actually become the strongest part of your body for eternity. That's what I mean when I say "wounding." I think about the parking lot scene in *Wolf in White Van* by John Darnielle where our narrator, Sean Phillips, is slowly being circled by youth as they examine his put-together face. I think about the entire novel of McCarthy's *No Country for Old Men* and how just looking at any page gets me running out of my own skin to get upstairs and write. I think about the claw hammer versus a hundred axe handles fight scene in *Old Boy* set to that gorgeous soundtrack. I think about the nail gun scene in Eden Robinson's *Son of a Trickster*. I think about these scenes all the time now. I want to write something *that* forever.

I couldn't have written *I Count Myself Among Them* without any of the heroes I'm honouring here. Flinch wouldn't have been born to stalk the earth as a giant, to throw a Night Crawler through a wall, to smudge with him afterward as the gang member coughs pink gunk out of his lungs had it not been for the incredible violence of all I've read and watched. This is what I call "the great wounding": all the comics, all the movies, all the passages. I'm drawn to *Imperial Bedrooms* by Bret Easton Ellis. About every two years I need to go back and reread it. It's like a séance for me. I always feel so haunted after. It's a gruesome read. It's like your favourite babysitter because you know what's coming: ghost stories that will haunt you long after she leaves to go to a bush party.

I think of all the writers who are up-and-comers. They are handing me my ass every day with inspiration: I can't wait for you to read their words. They are incredible. Imagine *The Lesser Blessed* on a blackout: Jennifer Storm, Rabecca Lafond, Leslie-Ann Jones, Debbie Doyle, Helen Knott, Catherine Lafferty, Darlene Naponse, Shane Turgeon, Leif Gregersen, Natasha Gauthier, Jessie C. MacKenzie, Tenille Campbell, Joshua Whitehead. It's the hungry writers who are fearless to me. I can't wait to see what they'll create next.

I'm so grateful that I grew up watching HBO, The New TMN, The Movie Channel. I'm so grateful for movies like *Fast Times at Ridgemont High*, *Porky's*, *The Last American Virgin*, *Foxes*, anything with Molly Ringwald, *Conan the Barbarian*, *Krull*, *Back to School*, *Over the Edge*, *Rumble Fish*, *The Outsiders*, *Grosse Pointe Blank*, *Grease 2*, *An Officer and a Gentleman*, *The Color of Money*, all of the Terminators, Predators, Aliens. *Star Wars* changed my life. *Planet Earth* is basically just Planet Star Wars for me now. I'm so grateful for all of the found footage movies: *Rec*, *Exists*, V/H/S. Oh my God, so scary. Want to see something harrowing? Google *The Last Dive* and *Lights Out* on your computer right now. Brilliant.

Sicario came out of nowhere and blew my skull cap off. I want to write stories with a female protagonist like that: curious and strong as she enters The Great Mystery of what's unfolding before her. I hope I have in "The Moon of Letting Go" and in "Night Moves." I hope Celestine, Valentina, and Crow are as compelling as Kate of *Sicario* is or Vasquez or Ripley of *Aliens* are.

I challenge myself now to write stories that I never saw coming. I sometimes imagine myself gone so I can reach into something new from the other side to return it holy and beautiful for you. The best example is *The Lesser Blessed* (my first novel), which came out twenty years ago. It took me five years to write and it was forged from deep inside of me from the centre of my hometown, Fort Smith, NWT. Now I write from the vantage point of floating over a fictional town like Fort Simmer, NWT, to get to the characters and to the marrow of the story. I am no longer bound to anything other than the story when I write. Think Cronenberg; think Lynch. Why didn't more people watch *Twin Peaks: Fire Walk with Me*? Thank God for CBC's *Brave New Waves* when I used to guard prisoners for the RCMP back in Smith when I didn't know what else to do. *Mahsi cho* to *The Power Hour* and *The Wedge* on MuchMusic! Think of all the movies and books you never saw coming. Think of all the music videos that just ripped open so much for me: "Du Hast" by Rammstein, "Are We Still Married?" by His Name Is Alive, "Fight Sounds Part 1" by Circlesquare, "Blinded by the Lights" by The Streets, "Coconut Water" by Milk & Bone, "What's a Girl to Do?" by Bat for Lashes: I could go on and on.

Have you all listened to *Tiny Dynamine: Echoes in a Shallow Bay* by the Cocteau Twins? I think I left so much pain in that album. Do yourself a favour and listen to "High Monkey Monk" right now and try not to leave your body. You know I'm a slave to The Cure, She Wants Revenge, The Sisters of Mercy, Drake, Purity Ring, anything eighties.

I write to music. If you look at the afterwords in my short story collections, you'll notice I thank so many bands. Had it not been for the Pearl Jam concert at Rexall Place in Edmonton, AB, in 2011, with Eddie Vedder singing "Happy Birthday" to his daughter, Olivia, on the phone, I never would have channelled *Little You*, our baby book with Julie Flett and Orca Book Publishers. Thank you, Eddie. I am so grateful for your beautiful spirit.

Twenty books in twenty years working with ten publishers and two agents is a full-time job, but I can go days without remembering that I write books because I love to share stories, too. I can't help myself. Yesterday, while renewing my passport, I told the three women who took my picture about my friend who won a million dollars and how the first thing he did was pay off his parents' house and all of their bills. They smiled. I wished them all a million dollars. They wished it back. I've already won a million, I said. Their eyes raised. My mom beat cancer, I said. They all cheered.

Bloomsbury's 33 1/3 series is a treasure. Every book. Every intention. Brilliance. My favourite is Kate Schatz's honouring of PJ Harvey's album *Rid of Me*. I wanted to write a novella for The Cure's *Disintegration* album but was rejected twice so if you read my short stories "The Contract" and "Blood Rides the Wind" in *Godless but Loyal to Heaven* and *Night Moves*, you'll meet Bear. This was my pitch: a Tlicho Dene teenager named Bear decides to maim the principal who molested his cousin but finds forgiveness along the way as he listens to *Disintegration* and becomes friends with his bully. Because I was rejected, I still decided to go for it. You can read both stories together and play *Disintegration* in the background. I couldn't have written Bear or his trajectory without this album and without being rejected. Twice.

That's how it is for me. I heard "Winter Bones" by Stars and could see everything for "Bornagirl." I see so many bands I still listen to that helped me weave *The Lesser Blessed*.

But think about Steven Jesse Bernstein; think about Wesley Willis; think about beckylane. Think about the pain and love in everything they did.

It's a race now to keep up with all of the ideas I have. I can see them all so clearly. I am blessed to have the discipline to get up at 4:30 or 5:00 a.m. and get to work. It's why I was born. I know it.

Want to read a nasty and gorgeous book? *Vile Men* by Rebecca Jones-Howe. It's raw. They call it "transgressive." Yup. I agree. It's just one big dog bite to your brain with turning you on as it pulls you inside out. I think you should read it. Another great wounder because she'll fracture you with each story.

Want to know one of my all-time favourite novels? It's *Indiscretion* by Charles Dubow. What a book of longing. What a book of a lifetime. Many lifetimes. Except I would have changed the ending. The plane would have gone down with Harry trying to save Johnny. Knowing they would die together.

Knowing he tried. And knowing in the autopsy report that his last act on this earth was trying to save their son. The ultimate love letter to Maddy: *I'm sorry. I tried. I'm sorry. Here it comes. I love you, Maddy. Always have. Always will* …

And I think that's the key: editing while you read. Editing while you listen. It's true what they say: when a writer is reading, that writer is working.

I LOVE TOBY KEITH'S SONG "As Good as I Once Was" but it should be "big biker dude" instead of "big biker man" in the fight scene. And it should be "we'll put a big Texas smile on your face" rather than "I'll put a big Texas smile on your face" because Bobby-Jo and Betty-Lou are sisters, after all. Things like that. I'm always listening. Always filtering.

God, I miss Pat Conroy. God, I miss *Downton Abbey*.

Ernest Cline's *Ready Player One* is perfect. So is Frank Miller's *Elektra: Assassin* with Bill Sienkiewicz. So is *Oink: Heaven's Butcher* by John Mueller and Ariel Schrag's *Potential* and Sarain Stump's *There is my People Sleeping* and N. Scott Momaday's *The Way to Rainy Mountain*. I can still hear that perfect punch with the hat flying in James Welch's *Winter in the Blood*. The question is where are you going to take us where we've never been before: either through plot or character or verse?

Best plot twist: where they are standing with a hostage in *Eileen* by Ottessa Moshfegh.

Best character-driven novel (besides "Clay" in *Imperial Bedrooms*): *Stranger, Father, Beloved* by Taylor Larsen. Michael, I think about you all the time. You're in a room, alone, trying to pet the snowflakes in your head. My wish is Bear, Larry, Torchy, Sfen, Snowbird, Crow, Flinch, Benny the Bank, Juliet Hope, Johnny Beck, Donny Beck, Celestine, Valentina, Grant, Clarence, Brutus: I hope they become your family. I hope they muffaloose or streak by you as you go about your day every once in a while.

Best dialogue-driven novel: *It Ends with Us* by Colleen Hoover. Actually, it's a tie with *No Country for Old Men*.

One of the best post-apocalyptic anythings ever: *The Dog Stars*, the novel by Peter Heller, and the movie *Time of the Wolf*. I hope when you read my stories "Wheetago War," "On the Wings of this Prayer," "I Double Dogrib Dare

You" or "Lying in Bed Together" you are as terrified of the future as I am if we don't turn things around.

Did anyone see *Shortbus*, *Eraserhead*, or *Arrival* coming?

How'd you like to meet deputy Sheriff Lou Ford in Jim Thompson's *The Killer Inside Me*? What a novel. What a villain.

I think that's how my character Torchy was born. Well, he was inspired by two wicked brothers in Fort Smith, but the existence of Lou Ford from *The Killer Inside Me* and Anton Chigurh from *No Country for Old Men* confirms what a galloping monster it is to write from a dangerous point of view. But Torchy, as you see in "Mermaids" and "Godless but Loyal to Heaven," keeps getting pulled into situations where he ends up being a hero. He keeps saving people and, through the flames and bare-knuckle brawls fused with the trust of Snowbird and Stephanie, he keeps saving himself.

My Holy Trinity of Christmas movies is *The Family Stone*, *Elf*, and *Love, Actually*. All three make my soul hum. We need hope. I think that is a major theme of my work: hope, redemption, forgiveness. I was told a long time ago that every writer deals with three themes their entire careers. I think those are my big three. That's a good way to be remembered.

You know which actor I think about all the time? Teddy Kyle Smith, the dad who plays "Egasak" in *On the Ice*, directed by Andrew Okpeaha MacLean. I want to write male characters that strong, that fierce, that smart. I believe I have with Benny the Bank, Jed, Constable Morris, Icabus.

Each of these creators has wounded me and I love them for that. I carry them in my bones now. Some muffaloose me; some streak beside me; some float above me. They're all enchanters.

HAVE YOU READ NICK TOSCHES' *Trinities* yet? It's a hissing grenade spinning under the table you've just sat down to feast upon. Flinch is my hissing grenade. He's the end of humanity. You can see it in "I Count Myself Among Them." He is the beginning of when the world was renewed.

It's up there with *Clean and Sober*, a movie with Michael Keaton who showed me that the human journey through a story never has to be easy. I loved the passion in *Internal Affairs* with Richard Gere and Andy Garcia. Dirty cops. I loved *The Shield*. Loved it. Followed it. Was drawn to it like a bathroom filled with candles and a wish to see "Bloody Mary" in the mirror staring back at me.

Take those with "Snatch" and you'll see how Benny the Bank named himself in Fort Simmer, NWT.

I'm speaking to you in *The Lesser Blessed*'s "Raven Talk" where *"Mkbuh"* means "Okay, bye," "Right arm" means "right on" and going for "a dart" means going for a smoke. I'm also speaking to you in Dypthia: the secret language of twins. I'm sorry we changed the title of two dying brothers in *The Moon of Letting Go*. We should have kept it as "Dypthia" rather than "Idioglossia." "Idioglossia" is too easy and "Dypthia" is the language two twins developed in Victoria, B.C. It's a series of clicks and whispers, nods and sways, a waltz of *sorry*s and *I love you*s. A friend told me about them. Apparently the brothers were beautiful, majestic. Born ancient.

You know who showed me what a perfect galaxy short stories can be? Sherman Alexie, Miranda July's *No One Belongs Here More Than You*, and *Rust and Bone* by Craig Davidson. "K Mart," "A Quite Incredible Dance," and "Waiting for the Call" by W.P. Kinsella are works of perfection for me. I think about "Cathedral" by Raymond Carver all the time: a visit, a collision.

I think about Barry Lopez's last blood line in his essay, "Buffalo": "I awoke in the morning to find my legs broken." I think about Bernie Rose in *Drive*. What a gentleman. Even when he's delegating a crew to break your pelvis for you. He knows where your arteries are. And now you know where mine are.

Mkbuh.

Okay bye.

Mahsi cho.

AS MAN
David Chariandy

*Y*OU TRIED TO TEACH ME how to drink, but I wasn't your best student. Truth told, I often left our sessions both inspired and strung out. Your "lunches" would begin just before noon, but run well over twelve hours, during which three separate meals and countless martinis would be ordered. The Bistro where we sat would transform into a salon wherein the great minds of the city would congregate to discourse grandly upon art, life, the world. I'd mostly just listen, intoxicated equally by the Bombay Sapphire and by the sheer range of topics and references. I'd watch you carefully, always dignified, always styled like it counted. Your linen shirts, your untamed dreds. You often said "As Man" to me, a boast of strength and solidarity in the language of your birthplace, but I seldom felt that I earned this address. After drinking late into the night with you, I would go home and throw up. You would go home and write.

Through the machinations of your friend Rinaldo, we met up many times over the years, although, more than once, when I emailed you proposing a meal and drinks, you feigned outrage. "Who paying?" you wrote back, "You, or this Rinaldo W —? Wha' time the two o' wunnuh dragging-me-way from writing my frictions? Wunnuh is two of the most lawless brutes that my Mother, God rest her soul, warn me to not set horses with, yuh!" Were we truly lawless brutes? Rinaldo, maybe, but quiet Abdi too? Me? Certainly, in the opulence of your Bistro, we were together a scene, Black men cocktailing shamelessly into the morning hours, although Leslie would very often join us, and sometimes Dionne, whom you named, out of her presence, "the genius." When we were six or more, we sometimes struggled for seats, and one time I suggested that we move to the back room of the Bistro, where there was a formal dining space with linen and glassware and polished silverware laid out, with tables big enough to accommodate us all very comfortably, but you insisted on remaining at the bar. And was this the first lesson, Austin, that you offered me as a writer? You entered places that others never expected you to enter, you suggested. You occupied space both alone and with your friends. But in this city, in this country, you never sat at the tables that already had been set for you.

Behind all the opulence, behind your clothes and postures all suave and debonair, I knew there were hard stories. There was the Barbados of your childhood, a struggling single mother that you continued to quote at me, her violent threats to her children countering the deeper violence of history. There were, for you, the difficult emotions and politics of what you phrased "leaving that island place," and then there was your arrival, in 1955, in the imagined "Toronto the good." Like Lamming or Naipaul, you were a scholarship boy sent to an elite school. And if you unapologetically displayed certain class aspirations, your truest sympathies lay elsewhere. You wrote about domestic workers and manual labourers. You spoke out against the prevailing myths of politeness and equal opportunity. When asked, in a CBC interview, about the parallels you drew between a seemingly placid Canada and the racial violence in Birmingham, you explained "In Birmingham ... the Negro knows where he is. He has less of a psychological war within himself." In your first novel about modern Black life in Canada (perhaps *the* first novel about modern Black life in Canada), a woman once optimistic about immigration concludes: "I never knew that this place was so blasted cruel." In your second novel, a man struggles painfully to put into words his everyday experiences of racism. "'*This thing*, man,'" he manages to express before his suicide to a friend, "'This thing does some funny things to a man's mind ... I am talking about the effects, man, the *effects*.'"

I understood in my own way "this thing" and "these effects," but I was not an immigrant like you. I was of the generation after, taught my whole life the official stories of this place. But what you helped me see, Austin, was a bigger narrative, a deeper language. The domestic workers and factory labourers whom you chose to write about were not mere characters in a book, but my very own parents. And you helped me see their dignity, their thoughts and dreams expressed in language of which I'd been taught to feel ashamed. You helped me remember a past that wasn't mine and also, absolutely, was mine, a being that stretched beyond the whitened suburbs, beyond the multicultural amnesia. With the others, you encouraged me to complete my first book, and when it was at first widely rejected by the literary world, you helped me keep faith. Eventually, it found a home; and it surprised me by finding more readers than I imagined possible; and I know I made you proud. Although I also remember you chiding me, more than once, for acting soft "like the young man in your book." The world of writing, you warned, was tough. It was rife with disappointment. You could sacrifice everything for decades for your art. You could write many books, be recognized in many different parts of the world, and the next day be forgotten, lose your publisher, lose your house. You needed to be strong, you explained. "As Man," you always ended your emails. "*As Man.*"

You knew, of course, that we were not only of different generations. We were different people, of different experiences, different aesthetics, different politics. You were to me that living contradiction, a *Black* Red Tory. Yet you scorned what you had once, in the sixties, called "conditioned Negroes," those who seemed content with second-class citizenship. In you I heard, both earnestly and ironically, the heady languages of independence movements, of civil rights, of Black power. I always watched you carefully, and eventually, I realized that you had been watching me too. Soon after my first book was published, you released your own novel about the generation after, about the yearnings of mothers for the futures of their children, and of the cities of today that still permit the destruction of Black youth. Your novel was entitled, so perfectly, *More*. And I knew you hoped it would earn you, once again, the success that you had finally, after decades of insecurity and unrewarded labour, enjoyed with *The Polished Hoe*. But *More* didn't achieve this success, at least not the sort measurable by sales and awards. And afterwards, what you wished for me took on an almost discomforting intensity. My own next novel, you suggested, couldn't simply be one that was personally satisfying. It would have to be what you called a "blockbuster." It would have to win prizes. "You got to lick all them pretenders and play-play novelists," you wrote to me; although you knew, all too well, that I myself often felt like a play-play novelist. You wouldn't hear such things from me, though. You imagined a future "in the hands o' people like you. So, don't let muh down, man. Share some licks. Plax! Plax-plax ... *plax!*"

I understood, of course, that your expressed hopes were not solely for me. By then, you had been working diligently upon your own next book. Your emails would be sent to me at all hours, with little discernable pattern of sleep. Once, at four in the morning, you casually explained to me your "dislike for computers," your "longing to work once more, on my IBM Selectric Typewriter." You explained that "at this grave-yard hour, I here breking my arse writing ... non-friction, as my mother used to call it. But I going make a martini, a dry one, and see what happen." It was in this email that you revealed your new project, a memoir. "On the pages," you wrote, "I don't call um a Memoir. To me it is 'Membering.' Membering sound more sweeter than 'A Memoir.' Wha' you think?" Weeks later, you wrote me again very early in the morning; and when I surprised you with an immediate reply from my home in Vancouver, you seemed to forget all about the time difference. "Horses or duppies riding you, that you can't sleep?" you asked. You went on to explain that you would be "wukking more longer, on 'MEMBERING, the name of the memoirs;" but then you added, wryly, "But I ain' know tummuch ... not one shite, 'bout Memoirs, yuh! I writing what I remember. And sometimes I don't remember one shite."

This wasn't just a joke. Your memory was indeed failing. When we got together at restaurants, I began to notice you hesitating with the menus you had perused many times, squinting at the descriptions of the dishes, maybe at the printed words themselves. I began counting the drinks you ordered, hoping the explanation lay there; but I also began the habit of secretly meeting Rinaldo's eyes. Later, when we were alone, Rinaldo would tell me of health scares you had experienced, perhaps even a stroke, although none of this you ever admitted to me. Only in your emails could you concede to experiencing mild, gentlemanly maladies. You wrote offhand of an appointment "to help curb my gout," but only because you had better news with which to conclude: "I just drive the last spike in the revisions to the Memoirs. As man. Austin." Yet, weeks later, when I wrote to ask if we could meet up, you informed me that your manuscript had been rejected. I wrote back with condolences, but I didn't hear back from you for a very long time. And the next time I wrote to tell you I was coming to town, you wrote back about an appointment regarding "this matter of my

Will." "It is overdue," you explained, "and being men, we are shy of making Wills and Last Testaments." You promised that you would contact me later in the day, after the appointment. But for the first time in our relationship, you didn't.

WHAT WERE WE TO EACH other? I wasn't as close to you as Rinaldo or maybe even Abdi. I didn't know you for as long as Dionne or Leslie. I've heard you called by some the father of Black Canadian literature. But we both knew your reluctance, to put it kindly, about most things concerning fatherhood. We were different writers, different minds, different bodies moving through the world. You would always sign your emails to me "As Man," but, in all honesty, I rarely saw myself in the men you invoked. But all the same, I recognized in your writings those characters who understood themselves to be fugitives from conventional masculinity, unwilling or else unable to live up to prescribed ideals and roles. The title of one of your collections of stories was borrowed from those devastatingly ironic lines by Derek Walcott: "There are no more elders/Is only old people." But there are always elders; and you, Austin, were one of them. And in the moments I now best remember, it wasn't just strength you affirmed between us, but also vulnerability. In your very last email to me, you acknowledged that we both, too often, could feel very frighteningly down and alone. "Depressions are a serious part of being a writer," you put it. But I remember that in your second-last email to me, your prescribed solution came from a woman: "As my Mother wouldda say, to me, if she was still living, 'Take my foolish advice, and follow what I say.' Drink a rum … one! … straight. And say yuh prayers." This message ended with your predictable "As man!" But then you added three more words: "Love," you wrote, "Your Brother."

On my last walk to your home, my last time visiting you alive, Rinaldo tried to warn me. He explained that you had changed. He said that I needed to come prepared for what I would see now. But for the rest of the walk, I could only think of times past. I remembered a night, years before, when I had been hanging out with a mongrel bunch of young writers at The Grand, and I called you up and you appeared, like a legend, among us. You were in yet another moment of poor financial shape, but you splurged insanely upon food and drinks for all of us. Afterwards, you invited us all back to your place for more drinks, and I remember the looks on people's faces when we entered. Your home was amazing, walled completely with books. There was your lifetime of collected art, that photo of Malcolm X, and also that photo of you meeting Queen Elizabeth. King Coltrane ruled the air. I remembered another bright time of music and language, when Dionne pulled from one of your shelves a book by Derek Walcott, and read for us in that voice of hers, arriving eventually at those lines: "I had no nation now but the imagination." Your home, as I had known it, was the living and sublimely complex archive of Black genius in the Americas. It was a home that you had kept neat and opened generously to others. But now, arriving finally at your doorstep for this last visit, I suddenly felt afraid of entering. There was a digital lock box outside; and Rinaldo punched in the code 1934, the year of your birth. And then he held the door for me to step in.

Your place was much the same, still neat, your many books still shelved high up and all around us, but you had changed. You were thin and couldn't stand. You could not do many of the things that a man takes pride in doing for himself. You were not always lucid. For some reason, you held on your lap 'Membering, which had happily been published, but you didn't seem to know what to do with it. At times, you opened it to the first pages, as if attempting to read. You fumbled with a pen, gestured towards a page as if contemplating edits. You tried to autograph it but failed. After long minutes of silence sitting there beside you, I excused myself and walked away to the kitchen. I stood alone until Rinaldo hugged me and very gently urged me try once more. And then you saw me again. You asked about my writing, about the novel that, months after your death, I would dedicate to you. I said that it was going all right. I was, you know, still working on it. And then, very reluctantly, I asked about you, about your own writing. You sharpened. You recovered every atom of your old dignity. You lifted 'Membering, saying "I suspect this shall be my last."

Sometime, in those last moments together, I asked you, one more time, if you ever found it difficult to complete a book. If you ever doubted. You said that, yes, you had doubted, every writer doubted, but that you had always pushed yourself to finish. "Because I felt it was important." Shortly afterwards, you were helped to bed by the caregivers, immigrants of colour both like and unlike the ones you had represented so many years past. It was time to go. But, before leaving, I looked once more up at your shelves. Books by Baldwin and Wright, by Morrison and Walcott. Books by Giovanni and Brand and Brathwaite. All of the luminaries, all of that desperate brilliance. I saw among the spines your own books, Austin. For when you had the strength, you'd placed them where they belonged.

WRITING IN MONTREAL

Marie Hélène Poitras

Translated by Susanne de Lotbinière-Harwood

I AM A MONTREAL WRITER BORN in Ottawa, where my father taught
French to immigrants in a COFI (Centre d'orientation et de francisation
des immigrants) and my mother worked as a nurse. My childhood was spent in
the Outaouais region, in a small, open-minded and bilingual town called Aylmer,
until the age of eleven. Then we moved to Saint-Jean-sur-Richelieu because my
father had been hired to teach at the local military base. I worked there a few
years ago, as well.

Located forty-five minutes from Montreal, Saint-Jean-sur-Richelieu is an
attractive, comfortable suburb by the Richelieu River. My mother and sister
still live there, in that town which offers the best Belgian-style *gaufres* in a café
close to the canal. Saint-Jean is a quiet place. It exudes order and a certain sense
of normality. My teen years and early identity were shaped by that suburb and
community where I felt I had no room to breathe. When I reached sixteen,
Montreal became a magnet. I followed my best friend's older brother to concerts
and independent record stores. Those were the days when we listened to cas-
settes, the early years of Weezer, the Doughboys, and Me Mom and Morgentaler.
The indie rock scene was exploding with bands like Sonic Youth, Lush,
Mudhoney, and, of course, Nirvana, which I was lucky enough to see live at the
Verdun Auditorium. Music and my journalism studies brought me to Montreal
at the age of nineteen.

Despite all the excitement of this new adventure, setting up in my little apartment in the Hochelaga neighbourhood came with a big sacrifice: I had to move away from horses.

One passion gave way to another: once in the big city, my love for words and literature exploded. After a year in journalism, I reoriented myself to the study of literature. Back then I might be found asleep with books under my pillow: Anne Hébert's *Le tombeau des rois* (1953) and *Regards et jeux dans l'espace* (1937) by her cousin, the poet Hector de Saint-Denys Garneau. Reading gave me a fever. I still loved music, but literature took up more and more of my time and — one thing leading to another, allow me a huge leap in time here — I completed my M.A. in literary studies with a "profile" in creative writing at l'Université du Québec à Montréal. Like many lit students newly let loose into the working world, I took on a small job in a bookstore and hoped to be hired to teach at the college level.

In the spring of 2003, a friend came by one day with a clipping from a local paper. It read *"cochers recherchés."* (*calèche* drivers wanted). Suddenly the prospect of spending the summer outdoors with horses instead of indoors with air-conditioning felt exciting. I registered for the three-month training period given by the Institut du tourisme et de l'hôtellerie du Québec in order to learn how to introduce tourists to Montreal while driving a horse-drawn vehicle.

The adventure allowed me to discover two areas that I knew little about: Old Montreal and, not far from there, in the *sud-ouest*, what looked to me like a stage set, behind-the-scenes, hidden from tourists, a neighbourhood which for years I had confused with Pointe-Saint-Charles before realizing that it was called Griffintown. I immediately liked the word; it sounded like the name of a town in a western.

I SPENT TWO SUMMERS WORKING as a *calèche* driver. In 2003, my hands were full learning how to do this physically demanding and dangerous job among colleagues who often proved less than diplomatic. During that first summer, I put all my new know-how into practice while doing my best to avoid accidents. Not everybody is cut out to drive a *calèche*. What made it possible for me were my years of horseback riding and my knowledge of horses.

It was during my second summer that the idea of writing about the Griffintown drivers, horses and stables came to me. By then I had mastered the tasks required and could spend more time observing what was going on around me. From atop my driver's seat, I was the all-knowing and -seeing narrator; a fascinating play was unfolding before me, with its larger-than-life characters — urban cowboys! — who somehow seemed to be just waiting for a novelist to pick up on them! On days when rain forced us back into the stable to wait for the inclement weather to pass, they would tell all kinds of unlikely tales. They were anything but boring. I was part of this community of horsemen and horsewomen. I understood their codes and learned to master their vocabulary, a colourful idiom rich with expressions often drawn from a Western-inspired landscape, such as *"voler le gun"* (stealing the gun), which meant taking the best spot in the queue without respect for the order of *calèches*; old-fashioned and often beautiful words to describe parts of the horse's harnessing and of its anatomy, including breeching strap, noseband, nose; or linguistic inventions in order to discuss money among themselves, quite impossible for a novice to decipher: *une cloche* (a bell) equalled $100. To underscore their self-made legends, the drivers even had names for their characters: *Grand Galop* (Full Gallop), Walley, *La Couette* (the duvet), Alice (for Alice Cooper), etc. Some drivers even had secret nicknames, like Psycho. As for me, several had started calling me *La P'tite* (Little Lady). Horses, too, have their personalities and affinities. Some salute one another with a courteous whinny, others can't stand each other, and former racehorses sometimes have racers' egos and compete with other vehicles, such as the Amphibus, which can cause the *calèche* driver to sweat bullets. It is an atypical environment, a highly inspiring one, so at some point I sensed I wanted to portray the drivers and horses now part of my life.

Sketches and short stories flowed from my pen. I felt energized by these men and women, by their territory and cowboy aura. It seemed to me I'd never read anything about them in literature.

In 2005 I published a collection of short stories inspired by the stories of Raymond Carver, *La mort de Mignonne et autres histoires* which contained a few texts set in the *calèche* drivers' world.

One day during the 2009 Salon du livre de Montréal, I sat at the same round table as Monique Proulx, a Montreal writer for whom I have huge respect. She was familiar with my writing and helped me to realize that the world of horses and drivers somehow belonged to me, and that this was something precious.

Her remarks prompted an awareness of the fact that this world, which faces extinction, had not been put into story form in Quebec. I was engaging with a declining world whose entire history was threatened with oblivion. Monique Proulx's advice ripened inside me and for the first time, I felt responsible, as a writer, for preserving the past of this *cochère* culture, for recreating it in language. Here lay a vast territory and many places to name; I felt like an explorer and all of this excited me greatly: I was thrilled.

A major question came up immediately: how to write about Griffintown?

As well as many sub-questions:

How to turn Montreal stables into fiction?

How to enter that world through my writing without betraying them?

How to render these characters — almost too large to be credible?

How to stitch together a good story using the truth of what matters to life in Griffintown while avoiding the documentary aspect?

It took me several years to figure out the answer. In fact, seven years separated my short-story collection and my novel *Griffintown*. During that period, I even had the time to publish a thirteen-volume youth series inspired by the Montreal music scene.

I found the core of an answer in Cormac McCarthy's Border Trilogy,[2] especially its first book: *All the Pretty Horses*. This former horsewoman, experienced in classic equestrian style, became interested in the landscape imagery of the Far West. I watched the classics of the genre again, Sergio Leone's movies, and understood that I, too, would employ the tropes of spaghetti westerns by avoiding the white Stetson/black Stetson mindset and the glorification of America inherent in traditional Westerns. I wanted anti-heroes, their excesses, their urges and misadventures. Of course, Leone's movies had Ennio Morricone's fabulous soundtracks, which added a layer of lyricism to their desert-like settings. McCarthy taught me that writing rich with a poetic style can elicit the effect of a melancholy trumpet line or of a haunting melody. My editor Antoine Tanguay found the correct description: "the flowery brutal style."

Thus, the Western genre became a kind of blank canvas on which to unfold my characters and their story. I learned to deal with the clichés typical of Westerns and discovered that, basically, a cliché is such an accurate and powerful image that it speaks to the collective unconscious of a group of people. But in order for Western clichés to fulfill all their meanings, I had to recharge them with a new and different energy. For example: in Western movies, duel scenes are often preceded by a tumbleweed shown rolling along the ground. This wind-swept ball is made of various kinds of dried leaves and roots. Obviously, there are no such plant masses blowing through the streets of Montreal, so here is what I put in *my* tumbleweed:

"Clumps of old yellow grass; dried flower buds and forked horsehair; pow-dered horn; even a little marrow tangled in the grey sand with dandelion rootlets; veins of leaves from autumns past; seeds of sainfoin; bits of string and rough cord; pollen and crumbling iron; sparrow's fluff."

I thoroughly enjoyed writing *Griffintown*. I'll never forget what fun I had working on it. And, more generally, my identity as an *author* found its definition in the process of writing this novel: I write in French, in North America, from Montreal.

Over the years I have often spoken out publicly about horses and *calèches*, a living heritage frequently criticized in Quebec. In the spring of 2016, Montreal mayor Denis Coderre imposed a moratorium on *calèches*. There was opposition to his decision and *calèches* were allowed to return to Old Montreal. In the last ten years, Griffintown has changed dramatically. Condo towers have sprung up like mushrooms, the area is a vast construction site, making it increasingly hazardous for horses and drivers to circulate in its constantly shifting environ ment. This formerly unloved area is now a hip quarter, due to its proximity to downtown. This spring, one of the oldest stables still in operation in North America, the Horse Palace, on Murray Street, was torn down. It was built in the middle of the nineteenth century. People who know very little about horses regularly take a stand on the matter. *Le Devoir* published an open letter I wrote to Mayor Coderre in which I made a few recommendations:

(…) there is the large stable, the one I call the "tin castle" in my novel *Griffintown*[3], because that's what it is. I worked there for two summers (2003–2004). The place is inadequate for housing horses that work as hard as the Belgians, the Percherons, and the Canadians employed in the *calèche* business. The building is dilapidated, but worse is the fact that these great titans are kept in standing stalls instead of in proper loose boxes. A standing stall is a narrow space contained between two low half walls. The horse is tied to a chain. Not all horses lie down, but those who want to should be able to do so by lying down to the full length of their bodies. This is possible in a box stall but not in a standing stall.

They also need a sufficient quantity of hay or sawdust to allow their severely tested hooves and joints to rest upon comfortable ground, but this is not always the case. Also, these animals should be able to freely move about in an enclosure from time to time without being harnessed to a *calèche*. Let's imagine there is a big tree providing them with shade and, why not, grass for them to quietly graze on during their days off. It seems a lot to ask, yet these things are provided for the horses of the SPVM's mounted police.[4] I know because I visited their stables. Why don't *calèche* horses enjoy the same conditions? They too are in the service of the city. Photographs of them hang on the walls of Pierre Elliott Trudeau airport, to be seen immediately upon landing in Montreal.[5]

Horses have their place in the city, and if the sound of their hooves on the asphalt disappears, part of Griffintown's soul will go with it. The idea of preserving a living legacy matters to me. Last year marked the 350th anniversary of the arrival of horses in Nouvelle-France. I feel we should also spotlight the Canadian horse, a beautiful race bred here, an animal that merges elegance and resistance, an excellent companion for coachmen. In fact, the Canadian is called "the little iron horse." That is yet another aspect of this horse culture which, in my opinion, should be recognized and celebrated to a much greater degree.

WHILE CANADA CELEBRATES THE 150TH anniversary of Confederation, Montreal is celebrating the 375th anniversary of its foundation. The city is currently topsy-turvy with construction sites and orange cones everywhere; parking is a pain, mightily exasperating suburban commuters. The city is changing, businesses close, sometimes our landmarks disappear. Then life picks up again, neighbourhoods transform and reinvent themselves. Montreal does not have the dizzying energy of New York, Paris, or Mexico City; it is a mid-sized city where people know and greet their neighbours. My city has imprinted on me its memories and whenever I move about it, a sensory mapping comes alive, places and areas are emotionally charged.

One is never done discovering this city where people write, sing, dance, create, and demonstrate. Despite all its flaws, its residents have two major qualities: tolerance and openness to others. That's why I feel good here. But you have to be able to keep up with its pace and welcome change. As for me, I embrace its chaos.

With *Griffintown*, my literary preoccupations intersected with my citizen's fibre. When asked what it means to me to write in Canada or even in Quebec, a somewhat deflecting reply comes to me, but it's the correct one: I write in French in Montreal, in North America. This is my anchoring and my perspective. I see the world from this point of view. I absorb it and reinvent it through every word I write.

NOTES

1. Marie Hélène Poitras, *La mort de Mignonne et autres histoires* (Montréal: Éditions Alto, 2017)
2. Cormac McCarthy, The Border Trilogy, *All the Pretty Horses* (New York: Knopf, 1992).
3. Marie Hélène Poitras, *Griffintown* (Montréal: Éditions Alto, 2012, p. 111; Toronto: Cormorant Books, 2016, p. 81. Translated by Sheila Fischman).
4. SPVM: Service de police de la Ville de Montréal.
5. Marie Hélène Poitras, "Le cheval, fière incarnation de notre patrimoine vivant. Lettre à Denis Coderre, maire de Montréal," *Le Devoir*, Montréal, May 26, 2016.

WHY?
Sheila Fischman

*A*FTER AN INTRODUCTION TO A hero long retired, I was asked for the first time in my life about my chosen, no, my accidental, career. He was Maurice "Rocket" Richard, hero and star of *The Hockey Sweater*, a now-classic children's story by Roch Carrier. Roch had introduced us, saying that *"Sheila traduit tous mes livres en anglais."* Asked the Rocket, *"Pourquoi?"*

Why indeed.

I don't remember ever being asked How? How do I take a story by Carrier or one by Christiane Frenette, a novel by Jacques Poulin or one by Larry Tremblay — how do I take these texts written in French and turn them not only into English, but into a kind of English that will make the reader feel that she or he is reading something written in French, written in French but with English words?

I don't have a general theory of translation, an explanation of how I come to choose certain words and not others, how I decide that a long French sentence can be broken up with a judicious application of semi-colons and em dashes or that some short ones can be combined. Always, it is a matter not only of meaning but equally important, of rhythm, of the musicality of a sentence or a paragraph. How do I know when I've been successful? *It sounds right.* Certain authors have made me very happy by telling me that they had found the same *petite musique* in my translation as they had laboured over in the original. Because of course that's what I aim to do, to keep that little music. A good translation is never just a matter of writing words that mean the same as the words in the original. We've all read that kind, where the translator has been skating over a text word for word. Reading them is not a pleasure.

Let me tell you a couple or three translation stories. They all relate to me because I was the translator. They're very different, as different as the authors and their books. As is the process and experience of translation in each case, which I will try in a while to relate.

In the beginning, my attempt to translate something written in Quebec in French was strictly an exercise, a way to force myself to look up unfamiliar words in a dictionary, enlarge my vocabulary and, I hoped, be able eventually to speak French with people whose first language it was. It took a while to find something that seemed possible, but one day I met a young writer who had just published a first novel that I was told had been written in "simple French" and he encouraged me to try putting it into English. The young writer was Roch Carrier, the novel *La Guerre, Yes Sir*, a book that would change my life. Amid events both grotesque and infuriating, it tells a story of how a small francophone Quebec village is touched by the Second World War: a man chops off his hand with an axe and avoids conscription. A village boy who answers the call is not so lucky and is killed in battle. His body is brought home in traditional fashion by a group of soldiers, all unilingual Anglophones. And we are told, as we have been and will be, time and again, about how these events and relationships will play out over years and generations to come.

This first translation was readable and, I thought, possibly important and so I sought a publisher. In Toronto the House of Anansi had just been founded by Dennis Lee and Dave Godfrey and it became their tenth fiction title, AF 10, as you will see on the book's spine. The publication date, 1970, coincided with a period of great political unrest in Quebec, culminating in bombs in mailboxes, kidnappings, the invocation of the War Measures Act, and the murder of a Quebec cabinet minister, one of the kidnap victims. Outsiders asked, puzzled, "What exactly is it that Quebec wants?" One small novel featuring French-English hostility could not answer such a question, but it could set the scene in a way that might locate one source of that hostility.

Sitting at a small pine table with a stack of yellow paper, a portable typewriter and a dictionary, I plunged. How long it took, how many drafts, I could not tell you. I only know that after some weeks the language suddenly seemed familiar, in places almost translating itself. I was understanding the book even in places where I didn't know the words. Still, there were huge gaps in my understanding. I remember a sentence: *Calice d'hostie de tabernacle*! What? Why?

To me these religious terms were utterly incongruous, coming as they did in the midst of an angry tirade. There would be more, often combined in very creative, hilarious ways. Now it's a truism to observe that in Quebec the vessels of the altar are used where Anglos would use terms related to the body, especially ones pertaining to elimination or sex. I decided that such terms, the emotional equivalents of the French curses, would be out of place and unfaithful to the speakers, that the best translation would be no translation at all. As I wrote in my introduction at the time, "Literal translation would have been at best perplexing, more often simply absurd. A *chalice of a host of a tabernacle* just doesn't yield the effect of *calice d'hostie de tabernacle* — pronounced *calisse* and *tabarnaque*."

It seemed to have worked because the novel became a bestseller in English and some of those curses and oaths would later be found in the speech of francophone characters in English-language novels.

The success of *La Guerre, Yes Sir*, encouraged me to tackle more translations, of Carrier first, then of some other writers of his generation — Jacques Benoit, Jacques Poulin, André Major, Marie Claire Blais — and eventually work by a younger generation.

Gaétan Soucy's puzzling and brilliant novel *La petite fille qui aimait trop les allumettes* was untranslatable, of that I was certain. It presented countless challenges and a central dilemma that defied translation. The narrator of *La petite fille* uses self-referential masculine pronouns and, as French is a gendered language, the character's own, presumably male, sexuality is clearly established at the outset. Or so it seems. To indicate the meaning of the pronouns I was sometimes able to use nouns such as *brother* or *son*, not so economical — or as shocking — as *il* or *le,* but it made the point. Confusion sets in, though, when we read remarks such as "father's balls were bigger than mine when I still had them," and later, references to the regular bleeding that results from their having been cut off. Eventually the truth will out and the reasons for some most inappropriate words made clear. The narrator will finally admit to being female and the troublesome pronouns will be made to fit.

But it's not only grammatical gender that the author, the great Gaétan Soucy, played with, but also the sounds of words that play off one another. The book's language, a reflection of the narrator's restricted reading experience, is archaic, and her command of it is uncertain, resulting in approximations that are in fact plays on words extremely difficult to reproduce in another tongue.

At one point she refers to a *cornemuse* (bagpipe). But it is clear from the context that she is referring to an *arquebuse* (an ancient weapon). How, in English, to salvage both the sense and the wordplay? Well, there's an old weapon called a *musket* — which suggested to the brilliant punster who dreamed it up and gave it to me — utterly unrelated in meaning but perfect in its sound, *muskrat*. Nothing to do with bagpipes, of course, but everything to do with the play on words in the French.

Another example: the narrator seems to be obsessed with body parts, not unexpected in a teen. There are references to swellings on the torso, *enflements*, in the French, but that word is too conventional for this most unconventional personage. They became *inflations*.

Anne Hébert's great novel, *Les Fous de Bassan*, is told in three voices, a test for the translator's ear. They are relatively easy to distinguish, and reproducing them was a demanding but enjoyable exercise, but first I had to take on an enormous challenge: how to translate the very first phrase in the book.

La barre étale de la mer.

Six words.

Once I had English words for that very evocative image, the rest, I thought, would follow.

It took me a good three weeks.

Short words, simple words, a poet's words. For Anne Hébert was of course first and foremost a poet.

La barre. Étale. A powerful image, a suggestion of rhyme, assonance. A *barre* can be a bar of various kinds, including a *sand bar. Étale.* A technical term, describing the sea, whose technical equivalent in English is … *slack.* Correct meaning aside, it suggests loose, sloppy, lazy, limp, sagging, all of them a logical impossibility when associated with *barre.* And compared to *étale*, an ugly word. I drew up lists of all sorts of alternatives, none reasonable or appropriate.

I was lucky enough to have a French friend who used language like a musical instrument, achieving perfect pitch with every word he spoke. Better yet, he didn't know a word of English. What I needed was a visual image that would suggest a verbal image, whose words would be chosen by me. And so Alain simply described the sea, as observed from land. No tidal motion. No waves. No wind. A stretch of water. Narrow. And still.

This was helpful. First with *barre*, which now suggested to me a strip of sand. A sandbar. A strand? That refers to a strip of land bordering the sea but I decided to use it in reference to the sea itself. A strand of sea. But I still had that limp-sounding technical term *slack*, for *étale*. Here, I was lucky, but I have no idea how the phrase came to me, or from where. Or why. All I know is that "poised between tides" suggested the sea, motionless, but capable of moving at any moment. And so, "A strand of sea poised between tides" became the first phrase of a translated novel that would be entitled *In the Shadow of the Wind*.

The three examples I have just recounted are my attempt to answer *how* I translate. The *why* is not so easy to pin down. All I can say is that I like words, I like the potential of the music of words, of moving from one instrument to another to produce something that is familiar, recognizable, yet new.

Why do I translate? I translate, first of all, to share enthusiasms. Anyone who knows me is aware that it's rare for me to get up from my dining table without a book, or at least a title, about which I am enthusiastic, that I want others to share. It's simple. Urging someone to take a book home for a week is quicker and simpler than sending a version of it out into the world, theoretically available to thousands of readers. For me, making that version is one of the great reading pleasures. As the late translator Philip Stratford used to say, translating a book is by far the most detailed and profound and intimate way of reading it. I translate for that reason and for the pleasure of going deeply into a text, a sentence, a paragraph, a chapter … a book. Searching for what lies behind what lies behind the words.

FIRST LANDGUAGE
Hiromi Goto

$\mathcal{I}$ THINK ABOUT STORY A lot. I think about how it moves through the world, a particular arrangement of words, a narrative of ideas, ideologies. I think about how the nation relies as much upon its story as it does upon its constitution. How the story of our self frames and guides us our entire life. Story tells us how Turtle Island came to be, one of the many origin tales from all over the world. Story is how we understand our existence. It is a remarkable thing. If we are made of atoms in a vast universe, maybe it is story that binds people and their world together.

One of the key aspects of stories is that they render representations. In Canadian literary fiction, much of the representations are of people; characters who interact with each other in a variety of relationships, within a social context, in a geographical setting, in a particular time. I've been writing on the edges of this genre (because literary fiction is a genre, just as much as detective fiction, and speculative fiction) since my early twenties — I'm now fifty years old.

Having immigrated to Canada as a young child, I grew up seeing misrepresentations, particularly around Asian characters, in film, television, and books. Small flare-ups of racism, in word and deed, experienced in school; I moved through different periods of denial and loathing. Both against those who would cast me as other, and for myself.

When I first began learning my craft I wrote in ways that I thought were "literary," not fully understanding that I was writing whiteness into my fiction, as if it were a *style*, rather than an *ideology*. Fred Wah, who was my first creative-writing instructor, was nudging me toward developing a greater culturally critical awareness of what was I performing on the page, but I wasn't yet fully ready to hear what he was saying.

Some time between my first and second year of writing workshop, I slowly began to include Japanese Canadian characters into my stories. One of my classmates, an older white man, offered feedback on the young female Japanese Canadian character I had written. He asked me if the depiction of the young Japanese woman as shy and quiet wasn't a cliché.

My blood burned, splashed across my face, crackled in my eyes. "No," I snapped. "That's *your* cliché!"

That moment marked a pivotal point for me as a writer and cultural worker. I began to understand that these creative sites were in no way neutral, and that ways of writing and ways of reading were loaded engagements. This learning was supported by conversations with people of colour collectives, antiracist and queer activists, feminist teachers like Aritha van Herk, and my cohorts who were exploring, questioning, learning, and doing alongside me. I began to consciously approach my creative practice as a place to refuse and resist white hegemony even as I worked to disentangle myself from internalized racism. Alongside this learning/unlearning I was also disentangling myself from intern-alized sexism, homophobia, transphobia, and other forms of oppression… This is ongoing work. It is never "done."

My writing has mostly been centred on depicting the lives of Asian Canadian women. Writing fiction has allowed me to speak back to erasures and (mis) representations of Asian characters as imagined and inscribed by white writers. The capacity to frame diverse Asian Canadian experiences on the page was creatively exhilarating and politically empowering. There is a vast difference between being written about versus being the one who writes. This is the differ-ence between object and subject.

But is the colonial subject ever free?

My earlier books focused on identity, representations (particularly in a Canadian context), feminism, and queer lives coupled with aspects of folklore, the magical or the monstrous. These still remain areas of strong interest and relevance for me. I am also feeling the necessity of a mindful shift in my creative/

political practice. My writing life and my work have been guided by ideas of social justice, framed by my particular subject positioning. I demonstrated resistance to systemic racism, sexism, homophobia in my stories by critiquing and exposing the systems that affected my life and the lives of other Asian Canadians the most.

I've been a long-time reader of Stó:lō writer Lee Maracle's powerful books. One of the most meaningful workshops I've ever participated in was facilitated by her in the mid-1990s in Calgary, and I look toward her as a respected teacher.

In April of 2016, Lee Maracle shared her wisdom at the Earth Day: Voice of the Elders event in Vancouver. Lee spoke of many issues, but, as it often is with me, one lesson shone bright. Lee told the audience of how she often hears people talking about their rights. *You don't have rights*, Lee said. *You have responsibilities.* Her words echoed inside my mind/heart. And they are echoing still… It's important to note that she wasn't suggesting that we didn't have inherent human rights — her focus, as I understand it, was on the misguided foregrounding of an individualist sense of entitlement prioritized before collective/community/historical responsibilities.

Later, in May of the same year, I was asked to participate on a panel at the Congress of the Humanities and Social Sciences, "Decolonial Solidarities and the Work of Sharron Proulx-Turner: An Aboriginal Roundtable." Sharron, a groundbreaking Métis writer, had terminal cancer, and we were honouring her vision, activism, and creative and intellectual work. Tlicho writer, Richard Van Camp, was one of the hosts. He asked all who were there — poets, scholars, students, activists, grandmothers, children, settlers, unsettlers, to learn fifty words of the First Nations language of the place where we lived, as one way to engage with Reconciliation.

That same summer, Aboriginal Storyteller in Residence at the Vancouver Public Library, Cree and Salteaux multi-disciplinary artist Renae Morriseau, and Mi'kmaq artist/poet Michelle Sylliboy, brought together a group of writers and artists so that we could share what Reconciliation meant to us. In order to prepare for this gathering I read *Honouring the Truth, Reconciling for the Future: the Summary of the Final Report of the Truth and Reconciliation Commission of Canada.* The reading of the Summary and hearing the stories, poems, songs, film, and personal histories presented during the event affected me deeply.

The confluence of these events and a subsequent year of reading, considering, learning, has finally seen me arrive at a place where I must rethink everything.

I am a slow thinker, and a slow learner. *Jimi*, my mother has called my writing path. Not as in Hendrix (although that would be righteous), but the Japanese word for "plain" or "simple." There is a need for theory and scholarship, a need for activism and public dissent, a need for both reshaping policy and for tipping over police vans. And there is a need for plain brown female Mallard ducks who are a vibrant part of the wetlands just at the edge of the city...

I understand that the work of the Truth and Reconciliation Commission was not without issues, missteps, and elisions. I doubt that anything of that scale could be free of such troubles — how can one commission undo all the wrongs, heal all the traumas, and end the violence embedded in the colonial apparatus? I also mistrust the state, and question its true intentions. Apologies and recommendations are not the return of land and sovereignty.

I can also perceive that the Truth and Reconciliation Commission is a significant national moment that asks all Canadians to begin the work of decolonizing their understanding of this nation's history, to listen to stories that were brutally and purposefully silenced by the state and the church, and to rethink our relations with the Indigenous, Métis, and Inuk peoples of Canada, in the present and into the future.

This is a massive shift in how we imagine Canada, our citizenship, our identity. It affects how I think, and my relationship to writing. The act of writing (toward publication) brings with it a complex array of philosophical questions for me, especially now, after having considered the implications of reconciliatory engagement.

No matter how my personal identity (as shaped with/in resistance to a colonial nation) was understood by me and affected how I lived and what I wrote, I was living and continue to live on occupied First Nations territory. Even though my writing and art practice has been guided by a strong commitment to social justice, it seems to me that I've been trying to make my voice heard, to be recognized as a "legitimate" colonial subject, rather than speaking back to the original theft and commodification (i.e., resource extraction imperative) of Turtle Island. I wonder now, if what I'd written about these past decades has been for my "fair share" of colonial pie...

I think my weakness (and a sometimes strength) as a thinker and writer is that I have a tendency to approach complex things with an eye toward understanding them in their simplest form. I think this is a learned trait, because of my early childhood shock of English as a second language. The world collapsed into incomprehension when I found myself in kindergarten with absolutely no clue as to what was happening around me. It was a dissolution that created in me a sense of panic as I realized Things Were Expected Of Me, but I had no way of understanding what they were. This made me hyper-vigilant: observe, decode based on the behaviour of others, don't draw attention. Most of all, figure out what was being said, what I had to do.

How do I write, now? How can I write? Does my writing engage with Land and the First Peoples, here, in a way that acknowledges and shapes respectful relations? Does the writing invisibilize, look away, or, at the very worst, reinscribe colonial violence? These questions are a matter of ethical urgency, and, more and more, it's becoming increasingly clear to me, that the long-term collective well-being of all People, human and non-human, depends upon fundamental shifts in thinking about these relations.

Engaging with these questions is also self-serving because I've reached a conundrum: I want to write about Land and the People of this land, but I can feel the colonial apparatus affecting my ways of perceiving and writing. I find myself unable to do the thing that I love to do, for fear of reinscribing what I deplore. Because, don't kid yourself, one's imagination is not exempt from being turned into a colonized nation...

The embeddedness of the colonial imperative is made clear in the English (or French) language we use as Canadian subjects/objects. Early this spring I was in Victoria, B.C. — traditional lands of the Straits and Coast Salish peoples, including the Lekwungen, WSANEC, and the Wyomilth. There, for the first time, I was introduced to a remarkable tree, the "Garry oak."

That is not your true name, I thought, even as I admired the sturdy tough limbs, the rough thickness of their grey bark. *That is the colonizer's name for you.* I walked in the "Garry oak" meadow, among the beautiful camas, searching for the name of the tree as spoken by the original peoples of the land, and could not find it among the information plaques placed throughout the park. Later, when I returned home, I did some online research. The oak tree, I read, had been named after Nicholas Garry, deputy governor of the Hudson's Bay Company. In short order I found kwetlal (camas) and its important place in Lekwungen food and land systems, but my searches for the First Peoples' name of the tree led me nowhere.

A tree's name might seem a small thing against the scale of the struggles before us in a human-troubled world, but, in fact, it is much like a synecdoche … it points to a larger and deeper core issue. "Garry oak" tells us about the colonizer's attitudes toward place and people (both human and nonhuman), it tells us about imperialism, it tells us about taking without asking. It also tells us that the relations and long history (that moves perpetually into the unfixed future) between the tree, the land, and the First Peoples, who still live there is insignificant.

I've long been a reader of speculative fiction, and it is also one of the kinds of writing I do. In tales of magic, folk legend, and traditional lore, the knowing of "the true name" of some one or some thing is a powerful knowledge. The importance of names and naming is found throughout the world, across histories and cultures, religions and philosophies. If I were to write of "Garry oak" [sic], I would want to write of them with their true name. Because if I began to signal the [sic]ness embedded in the English language as we write about Turtle Island, there would be too much [sic]ness for it to be legible, coherent, or interesting (although I think poetry could perform this aberration in powerful ways …).

The impossibility of writing about "Garry oak" is, in a nutshell, a colonial imperialist tale.

I want a different story. I want a different language. But more than that — what is urgently needed in this time of extreme climate change, and the growing spectre of mass migration due to unrest and war as a result of rising temperatures and drought conditions[1] is for those of us in the "developed" nations, who live in positions of privilege, to begin to perceive that our mindset has a direct impact upon our relationship to the lands and waters. What is urgently needed is a critical mass of people to theirembark upon a fundamental shift in their philosophical worldview.

This may sound grandiose or preposterous, and maybe it is. But our collective long-term future depends upon it. Because somehow the idea of "democracy" has become embedded with capitalism. We are not living in a sustainable way when a nation's "wealth" is measured by the gross domestic product. A nation built on unsustainable, ever-increasing "resource extraction" is a story with only one possible ending — death.

Whether a tree is felled by a windstorm, is burnt in a fire, or is beset upon by insects who eat all its leaves so it cannot survive the especially harsh winter, in its dying the tree returns to the earth. The cells break down, aided by other arthropods, mold and fungi, into elements that are moved throughout the ecosystem to nourish other creatures, near and far.

When I have been at my most despondent, it has always been a source of comfort to know that even out of the ashes of our species, should we affect the environment of the Earth so much that we make it uninhabitable for our species (and uncountable others alongside us), Life will arise from death, as Life always does.

Less than a month after I was introduced to "Garry oak" I arrived in Treaty 1 land, Winnipeg, and checked into the Fort Garry Hotel. I tilted my head as I gazed on the name. *Garry with two r's*, I thought. *Just like the tree. Could it be?* I looked it up online and, yes, as I suspected. The tree and this hotel, named after the fort, were honouring the same Hudson's Bay Company man...

All over Turtle Island this appropriation is enacted and reenacted every time we speak the false names of places and of all the different Animal People (except for a few words like moose and wapiti...). They are not "just words." Language is culture, identity, power, and relations. The Canadian state knew this very well — it was one of their reasons to create the Indigenous children's prison system otherwise known as "residential school." Their attempts to kill Indigenous languages was an act of long-term and systemic violence, a state policy bent on destroying the First Peoples' distinct cultures and identities. Language matters profoundly. It is how we speak the world alive.

And whose world do you live in, now? How have you arrived here?

I was staying at the Fort Garry Hotel to take part in the Pierre Elliott Trudeau Summer Institute. One of the Trudeau Fellows in attendance, I learned, was Dr. Nancy Turner, an ethnobotanist who has spent her life working with Indigenous communities of northwestern Turtle Island, to document, retain, and promote traditional knowledge of plants (the uses for foods and medicines), land management, as well as language and names! After lunch I saw that she was sitting alone for a moment so I self-consciously set myself down beside her. We exchanged introductions and our areas of interest and then I placed before her my desire to know the oak tree's true name. I know the name, she said, her eyes lighting up. I can email it to you later.

In the Upriver Halkomelem dialect the tree is called *p'xʷəlp*. The Straits Salish (Saanich) call the tree *chəng'-élch*. I cannot pronounce these true names. I have much learning ahead of me. But it is the seed of a start.

In Robin Wall Kimmerer's beautiful book on ecology and reciprocal relationship with the living world, she states: *To be native to a place we must learn to speak its language.*[2] Yes, my mind and spirit sang. This is the language I wish to learn, to bring alive into my vocabulary. Because everything is connected and I cannot speak of the Land, here (where I live, love, resist, fight, and dream...), without first perceiving and accepting with an open spirit my responsibilities as an uninvited person to Indigenous territories. I love this Land and all the many Peoples here; not just human, but also the People of fur and feather, hoof and claw. Those who fly through the air, who swim and flutter in the oceans, lakes, and rivers. The People who croak and burrow. The People who live hundreds of years, every spring, rising with sap and brilliant leaves. Rivers, lakes, and mountains. These are relations that have existed for millenia upon millenia. These are relations to which many of us who live in urban centers have lost. These are the relations to which we must return. Renew. And speak alive.

Reknowned Okanagan writer Jeanette Armstrong had this to say about N'silxchn in her essay, "Land Speaking"[3]:

All my elders say that it is land that holds all knowledge of life and death and is a constant teacher. It is said in Okanagan that the land constantly speaks. It is constantly communicating. Not to learn its language is to die. We survived and thrived by listening intently to its teachings — to its language — and then inventing human words to retell its stories to our succeeding generations. It is the land that speaks N'silxchn through the generations of our ancestors to us.

This is where I find myself — rethinking the way I language my writing, shifting away from what had been a focus on representation. Instead, I want to develop a deeper understanding of what it means to build relationship or kinship in story through a framework that honours and is respectful of Indigenous knowledge systems, philosophy, and spirituality. To see if it's possible for me to bring my story closer to a landguage that has always been in and of Turtle Island. It is my response to the call for reconciliatory actions.

If representation can be claimed as a key component of story, then even more significant is *relationship*. For if stories have in them peoples and places and situations, it is the relations between these things that creates the world of story. A story without relations is merely a kind of list. Representation, of course, still remains an important part of reclaiming identity (especially those of us whose faces, experiences, voices, and lives have been erased by systemic racism, homophobia, transphobia, ableism, misogyny, et al). We all arrive into our voices and art, our being at different moments of our lives. It is still necessary and important for us to represent ourselves with passion, compassion and love.

LEE MARACLE'S WORDS RING OUT, again and again. *You have responsibilities.* I can finally hear this call, not as a burden of obligation, but as an invitation to be a part of community, and, in fact, to understand that I matter. My indifference matters. My engagement matters. And there is never neutrality. In Maracle's call I hear an invitation: engage in a relationship that you have not accepted as your own; a responsibility to the First Nations of this Land, to the vast Lands of Turtle Island. Learn how to live this knowledge. I embark upon a path that has me moving toward understanding the true meaning of "all my relations."

AUTHOR'S NOTE
I would like to mention that Prince George poet Ken Belford has a book of poems entitled *lan(d)guage*. The title of my essay is not a direct reference to his collection, but I like to think that the land makes all these connections for us. Much gratitude to Rita Wong, who sent me a copy of Jeanette Armstrong's beautiful essay and

provided editorial feedback, and to my partner, Dana Putnam, for being my first reader and so supportive, always.

NOTES

1. "Climate change will stir 'unimaginable' refugee crisis, says military," *The Guardian*, December 1, 2016. *https://www.theguardian.com/environment/2016/dec/01/climate-change-trigger-unimaginable-refugee-crisis-senior-military*.

2. Robin Wall Kimmerer, *Braiding Sweetgrass* (Minneapolis: Milkweed Editions, 2013), 48.

3. "Land Speaking" in *Speaking for the Generations: Native Writers on Writing*, ed. Simon J. Ortiz (Tucson: University of Arizona Press, 1998).

AN AMBIGUOUS VOICE

Stephen Henighan

ONE SATURDAY WE WENT TO two parties on the same day. The first party was in a house with high ceilings and varnished hardwood floors. The hosts were a young couple with PhDs; the parents of each partner, well-known academics, presided over the festivities. While our toddler played with other children in English, I talked to my fellow upper-middle-class white southern Ontarians: left-wing people from think tanks, right-wing people from banks. Conversation was strained; my every comment elicited granite-faced politeness. After an hour I went to find my partner. "Can we get out of here?" I asked. She nodded. She was having a good time but saw that I was miserable.

We crossed town to a rental property on a side street. The house was cold because the tenants couldn't afford to turn up the heat. The hostesses, from Colombia and El Salvador respectively, had invited Colombians, Brazilians and Central Americans. Manual labourers mingled with doctoral students, united by the languages they shared. Conversation went back and forth between Spanish and Portuguese. While our toddler played with other children in Spanish, I sat in the stained cushions of an old chair. I talked about politics and told stories of my travels. I was happy and relaxed when my partner reminded me that it was past our toddler's bedtime.

In the morning she said: "It's strange you were so tense with those WASPy people, and you relaxed with the Latinos."

I stumbled to find an explanation. What I should have said was: "That's why I write."

I COULD SAY THAT I write because I grew up in houses full of books, a few of which had been written by the occupants. My father published more than twenty books of fiction, poetry and criticism; my stepfather published four scholarly books; one of my sisters is an academic; I have an aunt who published poetry. Some of those who haven't published, write in private. Even my immigrant grandfather, a man with little formal education, took a turn as a newspaper sports columnist after his athletic career ended. It was inevitable that I would write; it was not predictable that I would persist in writing for decades. I write out of psychic necessity, bolstered by the conviction that the next book will earn me the unimaginable: the attentions of a literary agent, publication with a major press, invitations to festivals that have turned me down again and again. The next book comes out, gets a few reviews and fades away. I barely notice because I'm already submitting the *next* book, which, I'm convinced, will be the successful one.

Like all writers, I am tussling with my personal "demons," as Mario Vargas Llosa calls them; at a more conspicuous level, I am wrestling with the English language, and with Canada. My English is a battlefield. Once, when a polite Canadian writer told me that a column I'd written had shocked her — "I mean everybody knows it's true, but you can't *say it* ..." — I responded that it was my culture to state matters as I saw them. If she respected other immigrant Canadians' cultures, why didn't she respect mine? "My mother is an upper-class Londoner and my father is a working-class New Yorker. The only thing those two cultures have in common is that they both let you know exactly what they think of you. That's my inheritance." A Jewish intellectual, overhearing this exchange, said: "How did those two ever meet?" To which I had a simple answer: "On a beach in Yemen."

This part is true, though I may exaggerate the class difference between my parents. By the time my mother was born, during the London Blitz, her family was a decade removed from mansions, gold chains and titles. After the Second World War, my grandparents maintained certain upper-class presumptions in the absence of an upper-class stock portfolio. My father, by contrast, may have grown up the eldest of five children of immigrant parents who were often unemployed, sleeping on the sofa in cramped apartments, but he got a good education in rigorous Catholic schools and won a scholarship to university.

The discrepancies between my mother's British English and my father's New York English were my initiation into language. According to my maternal grandmother, my parents, who were in their early twenties when I was a toddler, would point to objects and say, "What does Mummy call it? What does Daddy call it?" Pivoting from "drawing pin" to "thumbtack," or "lorry" to "truck," or "Alsatian" to "German shepherd," or "tom*ah*to" to "tom*ay*to" as I was learning to speak, introduced me to English as a zone of conflict.

From Yemen, my parents moved to Hamburg, Germany, where I was born. German-ness pursues me: the accident of birth is only an accident, yet it can also be an unsought destiny. I've returned to Germany more than a dozen times. Not long ago, as I was getting off a ferry in Helsinki, the Finnish customs official, seeing my birthplace in my Canadian passport, switched from English to German. After I had answered a couple of questions in this language, she asked me to move from the "Other Passports" to the "European Union" gate.

I learned to speak in rural northeastern England, a heritage that has left me with an ambiguous voice. Some Canadian friends tease me about my "English" accent. On the U.S. east coast, where I studied as an undergraduate, I was told that I talked "like one of those hockey players on TV." In England, where I lived for most of the 1990s, I was instantly identified, even after years in the country, as an "American." An *Anglais* in Quebec, my home for much of the 1980s, a Brit in Ontario, a Canuck in the States, a Yank in the UK, I am at home nowhere in my own language. In the nine years that my parents were married, we lived in seven houses in four countries. Movement became my stability: as long as we were packing the hope endured that we would find that elusive place where we could live in harmony. Each time we settled down, my parents' fighting resumed, the clash of American English and British English making every syllable I might utter an inadvertent repudiation of one parent or an unplanned declaration of loyalty to the other. I took refuge in other languages, armouring myself with verb conjugations. As my partner observed, I feel sheltered in the cultures whose languages I've learned. I relax, and even experience a kind of ebullience, as I never do in English. From my late teens onward, I read voluminously in Spanish and French, as well as English; in my thirties I began reading in Portuguese, German and Romanian. I travelled, cheaply and in solitude, in Latin America, Central and Eastern Europe, and later Africa.

As my contemporaries became infatuated with women or men, I fell in love with countries. I explored all of their regions in endless bus and train trips; I learned their histories and read their literatures. Peru, Nicaragua, Hungary, Romania, Guatemala, Angola, Mozambique succeeded each other as my obsessions. Yet, unlike Joseph Conrad or Samuel Beckett, I could not become a writer in another language. I was stuck with my turbulent English. I needed a country to which I could attach this language. Only Canada would allow me to take this liberty.

AFTER MY PARENTS DIVORCED, MY mother bought a rundown farm in the Ottawa Valley. We had arrived in Canada three years earlier, and lived near two villages closer to Ottawa; yet these houses had been mere stopoffs in my parents' wanderings. The end of their marriage brought our meandering to a halt. The prospect of stasis awed me: it offered the possibility of integration. The world to which we had moved was an organic society, where everyone was each other's cousins, surnames repeated, and acceptance required mastery of the local language, a pungent Ottawa Valley dialect, spoken out of the corner of the mouth, which combined derisive rhymes ("number nine binder twine") and quaint exclamations ("Holy Jumpin'!" and "Jesus Murphy!") with a puckish formality ("If a person was wanting to do this, would a person …"). I half-adopted this language: like any child of immigrants, I wanted to be Canadian. At first I was beaten up at school for having longer hair than the crewcut farmboys; later, I was half accepted. On farm evenings, I read and read and read, and began to write. At fifteen, enthralled by *War and Peace*, I observed how Tolstoy opened the essays that began after the novel's action ended with the statement: "The subject of history is the life of nations, and of mankind." The collected novels of Sir Walter Scott, with which my stepfather lined the walls of our living room, also spoke of an emerging nation. From beyond our enclosed community — some of my classmates' parents had never been to Ottawa, less than an hour away — came echoes of the modernizing Canada of Pierre Trudeau. The Ottawa Valley, by contrast, was Red Tory country. Radio stations played Stringband's "Dief Will be the Chief Again." Our teachers urged us to respect people who signed U.E.L. after their names to attest to their descent from United Empire Loyalists; "Yankees" were widely despised. On the wall of my grade six classroom hung a vivid poster of the heroic Nova Scotians burning Washington, D.C., during the War of 1812.

My early attempts at writing mingled pseudo-Victorian diction with blasts of Ottawa Valley dialect. In my mid teens I seized on George Eliot's *Adam Bede* as a revelation that taught me it was possible to write an intellectual novel about the countryside. Yet my attempts to match my creative material to my personality and language remained stuck until my late teens when I discovered Mario Vargas Llosa's *The Green House*, the only novel I have read six or seven times. The interlocking planes of Vargas Llosa's narration, in which vast realms of time and geography intersect, and a character who appears in one location under one name turns out to be the same person as someone who lives in another place under another name, provided me — fatally, perhaps — with a literary model. *The Green House* was set in rural areas and used avant-garde techniques to evoke a huge, marginalized nation. I burned to write a similar novel about Canada.

My Canada was the Ottawa Valley. Among the more than eighteen hundred students in my high school, I remember only four or five non-Indigenous students of colour. In addition to English, the sounds of both French and Anishinaabe occasionally resonated in the halls. The farmer from whom my mother had bought our farm had an Irish surname and sharp, burnished features that local people described as "Algonquin." The English, Scots, Irish and Indigenous people had mixed here; crucially, so had French-speaking Canadians. The Ottawa Valley was *la vallée de l'Outaouais*, where my divided English was subdivided by English-French dualism. French was spoken in villages half an hour's drive away; bilingualism was the key to a job in Ottawa. By my late teens I was imbibing the dark visions of Marie-Claire Blais and Hubert Aquin, which I saw not as guerrilla actions against the Canadian state, but, unproblematically, as elements of the bilingual national culture I must imbibe to become Canadian.

When I arrived in suburban Philadelphia to start university I made a beeline for courses on Latin American literature. Studying in the United States taught me that the aesthetic ancestor of Vargas Llosa and Gabriel García Márquez was William Faulkner. I realized, in retrospect, that I had grown up in a Faulknerian landscape: a rural place rich in myths and repeated surnames, a region whose conservative nationalism pitted itself against modernizing cultures stemming from the U.S. east coast, whose economy had subordinated the rest of the continent. Marginalized regions became my theme. After studying and travelling in South America, I was ready to weld this vision into a novel.

MY FIRST NOVEL, *OTHER AMERICAS* (1990), melded the Ottawa Valley with Bogotá, Colombia, to evoke a vision of shared marginalization. Employing a structure derivative of *The Green House*, I was writing Canada into the Americas in order to write myself into Canada. By the time *Other Americas* was published, I was living in Montreal. The 1988 election had ushered in the Canada-U.S. Free Trade Agreement. My dismay at this sapping of national sovereignty was offset by pride that all but two ridings in eastern Ontario, traditional Progressive Conservative territory, had voted Liberal to try to stop the deal. As the Cold War ended, trade agreements replaced ideological blocs and communications were digitalized. I skirted the challenge accelerated globalization posed to my aesthetic and ideological vision by discovering urban diversity. I vowed to reinscribe the nation in a contemporary form by writing an urban, multicultural novel. To make the stakes clear, I set my novel in Montreal during the 1988 election. I produced a manuscript of over eight hundred pages, whose narrative delved into the feelings of characters of different languages, cultures and gender identifications. I wrestled to give this behemoth shape. A section broke off and became a short novel about a woman from Ecuador who immigrates to Montreal, *The Places Where Names Vanish* (1998). Fifteen years after I had started my urban novel it was published as *The Streets of Winter* (2004). By the time it appeared, I felt as though it belonged to the past. How to write about Canada after the 1988 election, and after NAFTA, was a dilemma that nearly stymied me. I had always defined myself as a novelist, yet as time passed I published more and more short stories. The child of perpetual motion, now living in an era of national fragmentation, I contemplated the possibility that the Canadian nation might no longer be a sufficiently coherent entity to support a novel. As my life was episodic and peripatetic, so, too, was my fiction. My collections of international stories, *North of Tourism* (1999) and *A Grave in the Air* (2007), influenced by Mavis Gallant, Graham Greene and Henry James, received encouraging critical receptions. A new collection of international stories, *Blue River and Red Earth*, will be published soon. Yet I refuse to give up on the novel.

Now living in southwestern Ontario, a region with whose history I feel no emotional or cultural connection, I am trying to reconstruct my engagement with Canada. *The Path of the Jaguar* (2016), which is about a Mayan woman in Guatemala, was my first novel without substantial Canadian content. I'm hoping, though, that this won't become a habit. I'm aware that my strategies for novelizing Canada cannot be those of the past. In *Mr. Singh Among the Fugitives* (2017), as in some of my recent short stories, I make Canadian realities present by satirizing them. The longer novel I'm finishing assumes an interdependence between changes in Europe in the 1990s and changes in Canada. Rather than accepting globalization as amorphous and all-consuming, I am trying to dramatize how this fabric is sewn together. It's essential that we do this. Novel and nation remain inseparable, even though the nation has been rendered diaphanous by globalization, and the novel may be an unnatural art form for generations whose literary attention span is geared to a WhatsApp message. Canada may not — yet? — have succumbed to the far-right rejection of cosmopolitanism, under the guise of opposition to globalization, that has plagued other countries in the Global North; yet Canadian complacence about economic globalization — celebrating it as "multiculturalism" to ignore the inequality it instills — has wounded our fiction.

We need fiction that scrutinizes our society; our fiction requires this challenge to evolve aesthetically. As a reader, I am frustrated that Canadians rarely novelize Toronto or Vancouver with the confidence with which Zadie Smith novelizes northwest London, or tackle middle Canada with the all-encompassing gaze that Jonathan Franzen brings to the U.S. Midwest. The glare of the globalized lights has given us stage fright. We retreat into the simple moral calculus of the historical novel, or, having been inspired by events in Quebec, set our novel in New England to avoid troubling the global publishing market with Canadian names and places. Our assumption that Smith or Franzen have the right to name their realities, and we don't have the right to name ours, betrays our colonization. There is no easy solution to this dilemma. The fact that many Canadian writers are, like me, immigrants who have uncertain relationships with Canadian history and tense up around southern Ontario WASPs, compounds the problem. Yet, since no individual can relate to the entire planet, the nation remains the indispensable filter between local and global connections; between the constituent threads of our lives that are personal and those that are societal. Nearly thirty years after the end of the Cold War, we recognize that accelerated globalization, which has sapped the nation of its authority, has not eliminated it as an imagined community. Only once we accept the paradox that by novelizing national idiosyncracies we participate in a global culture more vigorously than we do when we retreat from this challenge, or when we try to pass ourselves off as someone else, can we harmonize the ambiguities of our individual and collective voices.

PORTRAIT OF THE ARTIST AS A YOUNG CORPSE

Heather O'Neill

*E*DGAR ALLEN POE WROTE THAT "the death of a beautiful woman is unquestionably the most poetical topic in the world." Dead women have always been popular in art. For example, Sir John Everett Millais's esteemed painting of Ophelia: spurned by Hamlet, she is depicted as a corpse floating on the top of the water, her delicate body adorned with wild flowers. Images of Ophelia are everywhere in fashion spreads in women's magazines. Their white stockings and dresses are bloated like stingrays. Their hair curls around their heads, in tangled, fairy-like knots. Their dead eyes are closed sweetly, as though they are eternally prepared for a kiss.

The fake dead spread is hugely popular in fashion editorials. On a 2014 episode of *America's Next Top Model*, the contestants were asked to pose as though they had just been murdered. While I was working on my novel *The Lonely Hearts Hotel*, I began to be acutely aware of the image of dead girls in fashion spreads.

Female passivity has always been highly prized in art and fashion as an ideal of beauty. But the models in some fashion magazines weren't only despairing, depressed girls like Shakespeare's perturbed lass. These girls appeared in images that suggested gang rape, murder, and extreme physical abuse. Jimmy Choo had an ad that featured a murdered woman lying in the trunk of a car, while a man rested against it with a shovel. CK ran an ad where Lara Stone appeared to be in the midst of being gang-raped. Marc Jacobs had Miley Cyrus seated next to a dead girl. *W* magazine ran an editorial featuring a half-dressed woman, lying unconscious in the woods. To give you but a few examples.

WHILE WRITING MY LAST NOVEL, I decided to investigate this idea of the brutally murdered woman as art. I presented a series of images of murdered girls as still-life paintings: as though they were flowers that were plucked, at the height of their bloom, and arranged by men in a manner in which their beauty could be fully appreciated. There were girls with bullet holes in their heads. They were standing at the bottom of the river, their hair blowing magically and effortlessly around them, as they opened their mouths in perfect O's of surprise.

This was perhaps the most violent depiction I had ever created of girls in my novels, and I have, at many times, subjected them to all manner of degradation. Why, you might ask, do I find myself writing stories from the broken bodies of young women?

My own body was subjected to repeated physical abuse as a child. I was abused so badly that once I was rushed to the emergency room for stitches. I was wearing grey tights. I remember the leg of one slowly turning red. Physical abuse creates a break in consciousness, a divide between the physical and spiritual self. Which leads me to my interest in writing from the perspective of an alienated female body. I was drawn to this, because I existed in one.

AS A GIRL, THE WORLD began to scrutinize me in a perverse way when I hit puberty. The neighbours looked out their windows and gave me dirty looks because I was walking the dog in jean shorts. Or just sitting blowing bubble gum on a bench, or twirling a baton while talking to the garbage man. Suddenly the world became obscene and I hadn't done anything. Everyone was just projecting these thoughts on me.

I WAS SURROUNDED BY PERVERTS as any girl was. I was attacked twice in public: once on a bus at rush hour. Once I was sitting on a public bus at rush hour and the man next to me took my hand and put it on his penis. I was buying milk at the corner store when a man opened up his trench coat to reveal that he had nothing on underneath. I looked up at the convex mirror at the end of the aisle. There was nothing that the mirror could do. In any case, the owner of the corner store could rest assured this man wasn't stealing anything. I was walking my toy poodle once and a gold Coupe de Ville drove up next to me. The man inside inquired whether I would like to star in pornographic films. I answered the telephone and the man at the other end asked me if I would like to sit on his face. Like telemarketers, they always called at dinnertime.

I was a blank screen with the pornographic male gaze being projected onto it.

IT WAS OBVIOUS TO ANY onlooker that I was not only a girl, but I was a poor one. I wore tiny dresses with holes that I got second-hand. I had a blue leather jacket I'd pulled out of the garbage. Because I was poor, men particularly thought they had a right to say whatever they wanted to me. And I often felt myself separated from the herd, like a gazelle with a broken leg.

BECAUSE OF ABUSE, I USED to run away from home. Montreal in the late eighties was in a state of disrepair and it seemed as if so many buildings were falling into a state of ruin. There were abandoned apartments and warehouses and churches you could crawl into to sleep. There were many abandoned nunneries, their doors and windows boarded up, that were turned into squats.

I crashed in a nunnery once. There was an Edwardian couch with blue felt pillows. I slept on it curled up in a ball with my ski jacket as a blanket.

I thought I would wander around having a few good times and laughs, and then be murdered. That's what happened to girls who ran away from home. Underneath the ground are girls in basements. Maybe they are alive, maybe they are dead. They are like bulbs that bloom into all our treacherous and beautiful ideas.

I HAD NO INTEREST IN boys, not really. I wasn't mad about them the way that I was about other girls. I looked for fascinating girls on the street, the ones who had the strangest thoughts.

There was a girl with bangs to her nose who was always reading Shakespeare's *Antony and Cleopatra*. There was a girl who made miniature furniture out of bits of clay and kept them in a tin lunch pail. There was a skinny girl who had a voice like Grace Slick. There was a girl who had a scrapbook filled with images she cut out of pornographic magazines. One girl played a toy accordion she wore on her back like a school bag. There was a girl whose fingertips were always covered in black ink from drawing in her notebook. She drew tattoos all over my arm with a ballpoint pen. I was like Sleeping Beauty protected by a huge rose bush.

I met a girl wearing a rainbow-striped dress that went down to the ground. She had a pink beret over her thick, black hair. I adored her look. Girls dress for each other, not for boys. She was so mad it was lovely. She spoke about the moon and sadness so eloquently, I would be almost jealous. Once she stole me a can of cranberries from the supermarket. I wasn't sure what I was supposed to do with it. Once she was committed in the psychiatric wing of the hospital. I could never see her. I would write her letters and leave them at the desk.

Everyone says that girls are crazy. But really it's because we are geniuses. Nobody pays any attention when we are unhappy or outraged. The reason these states are delusional are because they assumed we are taking ourselves seriously. And that is the madness. To assume we have any value. Everything that girls did was considered trivial.

There are people who hate a free-spirited girl. You are supposed to choose a role and perform it. There are only a handful of roles you are supposed to play. Men all have Pygmalion complexes. They wanted to use your body to transform you into the girl of their dreams. They never understood that girls weren't put on this earth to please them.

There is a moment when you are a teenage girl where you don't belong to anybody. You aren't really a daughter. You aren't anyone's partner. You aren't related to anyone at all.

I fell madly in love with everything. Everything made me excited. Drinking coffee out of a cracked cup with a yellow rose on it. The covers of paperbacks in bookstore windows. The smell of skunk as I walked along the train track. A row of plastic horses on a windowsill. The gold songbirds on the wallpaper in a motel room. The stack of television monitors in the store window, each playing a different television show. A trumpet player in the subway.

You see the world in such a strange and intense and creative way in that brief time when you truly believe you don't belong to anyone. When you are most likely to be murdered. When abuse cannot touch your personhood. The way I saw the world then was what I wanted to capture in art.

PEOPLE HAVE ACCUSED ME OF writing weak characters, or disempowered females. That's because everything about women is an attribute for being weak and shallow and vulnerable. If an intelligent and serious person is judged by their similarities to a middle-aged white male, then yes, I fail, and my characters fail at that.

But girls contain multitudes. We are made up of so many odd parts. The reason that the monster in *Frankenstein* is so memorable is that after a being is fashioned out of cheap, castaway body parts in a spectacular feat of biomechanical engineering, when it opens its mouth, out of it comes the voice of an alienated teenage girl. Brought back from the dead.

LOREM IPSUM

Nicole Brossard
Translated by Susanne de Lotbinière-Harwood

*P*OETRY IS THE FORMAL AND semantic intuition our desires put forward even though unaware of their own laws.

POETRY IS THE HIGHEST PROBABILITY of desire and thought together in synchronized time.

> *"Political language is destined to make lies sound truthful and murder respectable, and to give an appearance of solidity to pure wind."*
> — GEORGE ORWELL, *POLITICS AND THE ENGLISH LANGUAGE*, 1946

SOMETHINGHAPPENEDTHATTRANSFORMEDOURSAPIENCEOURREVELRYOU
RDREAMSWEOFTENFINDOURSELVESONTHEFOLLOWINGDAYSHAPEDBYTHE
ARTICLESWEREADTHEPREVIOUSDAYWHICHCOMEBACKATUSWITHTHESME
LLOFCOFFEEANDFRESHNEWSPAPERSTHESENTENCESWEREMOREANDMORE
SIMPLEASSIMPLEASEACHONEOFTHECAMERASSPYINGONOURLIVESINPUBLI
CPLACESANDSOMETIMESININTIMATEONESTHESENTENCESBECAMEMOREA
NDMORESIMPLEWITHACORECALLEDSAPIENCESAPIENCE

Whether we like it or not, the writer is a symbol of humanism regardless if he or she is rebellious, transgressive, or immoral. Eventually, because of the freedom available in democracy, the writer is expected to fulfill her/his obligation to remember (*devoir de mémoire*), and ethical and linguistic obligations as well as the dual solidarities, identity-based and universal. Theoretically, the writer is a symbol of humanity because, from the inside and from the remotest locus of the species, he/she seeks the laws that govern emotion, beauty, evil — a meaning to everything exploding before our eyes, inside our chests. To seek from the inside, to listen to the resonant flow of conscience. To introduce into language leaps and bounds and somersaults of joy and astonishment, an abyss of fear and dread, to translate the infinitesimal slowness of the desire scrutinizing the enigma at the very core of this desire.

A writer is always of his time, wrote Gertrude Stein. How could it be otherwise? As for me, I have always wanted to be of my time, meaning that very early on I assigned myself the task of understanding the world I live in. What are the values, the standards, the social and literary currents that have transited through me? How have they contributed to my existential stance, the one hiding within the body and its many folds of meaning, in the gestures, sentences and thought processes that make one gloomy or happy? And how did this stance generate my behaviour, attitude, and narrative logic regarding writing, language, and literature?

Only over time does it become possible to grasp the facts and recurring evidence of our existential postures and attitudes, of our formal behaviour in language, and of the aesthetic and ethical consequences rendered toward writing itself as well as toward language and others.

Some writers write with the raw material of their childhood, of their singularity, others with their thoughts and questions. Others accuse or marvel, while others write their inner life; that is to say, with a narrative and emotion that keeps them circulating from inside to outside and vice versa, so their thinking becomes perpetual movement, a vertiginous vividness immersed in the subterranean vastness of language. This being said, one must not confuse a private life with an inner life.

The present, I must discuss the present. I have long said: I am a woman of the present, meaning by this that the present makes me happy and/or stimulates my clarity of vision. The present as a source of well-being that brings the joy of extreme presence. And now, so very suddenly, after just a few decades into digital civilization, the present is deleting all prior eras to become, all on its own, a bottomless pit of the ephemeral, of consumerism, an invasive means of distraction. And yet the present is not ephemeral once it vibrates in language.

Now that the idea of present has set in. I can no longer dislodge it. I am the ambience of the text and of my own existence. Impossible to separate them. This atmosphere serves a single purpose: the vibrant spirited well-being of the present. Some welcome it without words, others require words that raise body temperature.

Yes, one must, beyond reality, risk one's own insertion into the vastness. You say it, you do it.

So, then, does consciousness really need our bodies? It no doubt circulates the same way as do cosmic waves, which now are easily captured. Therefore, how is it that the so highly knowledgeable consciousness of Europe has transformed into the chaos of war, of dull noises, and the ceaseless stridency of violence. In the night.

Can knowledge temporarily delay the repeated evacuation of our singularities by the ephemeral and thus save us from total amnesia, from that state of ethical and philosophical weightlessness that seems to be looming over us? Knowledge as an infinite resource, bruising and renewing the imaginary landscape and our abiding melancholy.

Yesterday, amid the cypress trees, beside a joyful little turquoise fountain, in the tranquility of the terrace at Casa de Velázquez in Madrid, I wrote. Writing fills me with a well-being I had almost forgotten. Or does living in the freedom of floating, astonishing, ingenious and sensory thoughts also give life meaning? Between yesterday's writing of desire and today's controlled writing (whose processes of performance and consequently of marketing[1] are well known) lies a semantic and time-space zone that effectively throws me into a paradoxical criss-cross of ambivalent logics, ethical certainties, and fierceness which, although real, sensual, rebellious, and innovative, seem less and less viable semantically, whereas in times past, the heart and emotions, Eros and Thanatos, origins and memory, displayed our vulnerability as a species.

In the hallways of Casa de Velázquez that week there was an exhibition titled *Las maletas de Walter Benjamin.* The suitcase is us, inside-outside, content which is fragile or not, a heavy weight to carry; manuscripts, a survival instinct, or an urge to be elsewhere or for travel with dawns fragrant of lilies and lilac. Since the twentieth century, the sound of trains has resonated through our conscious minds, the noise of convoys in the suitcase, but also a surrender of the self, reaching the world's ends, a figure of speech that intersects with matter, metaphor, and virtuality, as if we were no longer going to die from having done it so often before. The suitcases made me think that women often must choose between the suitcase and the child.

Beginning in 2000, I often said that the world had changed. The leitmotif was still mysterious; it elicited questions, a veritable jolt of concern and of an excitement bearing lyricism. Then the world kept on changing, but with the difference that it started to seep into me, to fragment my use of time, to disjoint and unravel my gestures, my projects, to change me into a drone soaring above knowledge, history, my feelings and emotions. Little by little the relationship to time, to space, but also to others, to the idea of humanity, was transforming as if we were soon going to have to choose between our old humanism (grow its secret gardens of emotions, beliefs, compassion, solidarities with the species) and the concept of post-humanity (grow its algorithms without shifting moods, intelligence nonetheless remaining attentive to the *last call* for freedom, justice, and democracy); intelligence casually recycling fire bombs of lies and *fake news*.

In every century, women, be they docile or not, have been massacred simply for being women. This was rarely mentioned in a twentieth century plugged into death, nihilism, and destruction. In any case, for men and women entering life in 1943 and who would begin to discover literature, the values of rebellion, transgression, and deconstruction prevailed, from Tristan Tzara to Alfred Jarry to Emil Cioran to Samuel Beckett to Jean-Paul Sartre, then differently with Gaston Miron, Léopold Sédar Senghor, James Baldwin, Aimé Césaire, then differently again with Virginia Woolf, Monique Wittig, Mary Daly, Adrienne Rich, and Louky Bersianik.

Two world wars and a holocaust, ongoing misogyny and sexism at the heart of Western civilization have made humanity repellent and humanism deceptive. Technology and the anthropological knowledge we have of our species have done the rest. From now on we can get an aerial view of our species in most of its behaviours. Just like a good designer transforms the "table" principle, or the "chair" principle, into an aesthetic object, we will soon be in a position to *design* the basic materials of our inner self far beyond the idea of fiction. What I mean is that, conceptually speaking, we will be able to, and desire to, not so much express ourselves in order to discover our self, but more so that our self will be sufficiently aroused by the idea of an "I" that it will create itself as a work of art.

In the second half of the twentieth century, many of us in Quebec cultivated and retained a form of hopefulness linked to a search for identity, renewal, and an ownership of speech, thus giving the impression that we took root at the same time as tenderness at the heart of the North American landscape, of the French language and of modernity. But just as suddenly came the disenchantment of the Western world absorbing memory's slow-moving time at a speed never before known. Today quantic, biogenetic, and cybernetic mysteries juggle with the shadows and smiles of our species which, nonetheless, continues to love salt, apples, turmeric, the sea, caresses. A species which, in any language capable of philosophy and theology, crosses out, deletes, still does not love women. And yet I am a woman.

I am constantly redesigning my life, I mean the life of others, giving me the impression of inventing mine. A non-invented life does not exist, cannot belong to our species. Our happiness comes from knowing how to invent, to move here and there or someplace else where freedom flows into the pleasure of solving enigmas. Each one of us is free to pretend we live in the space reserved for us without complaining or in a different manner. The idea is to maintain our status as a free person for as long as possible.

Every writer inserts her/his presence, an imprint, on the world. Be it insignificant or significant. How do we insert our significant presence in the world now; how do we allow our gaze to convey the excitement of extinction that dwells in our eyes?

Desiring, imagining for some time to create sentences, narratives, enthusiasms that temporarily unburden the human condition. How, with our angel wings, do we thread our way through the wounds, circulate between the stories, the deaths, and our skillful sentences? How to express that we are breathing and that this is something simple?

How to hide pain behind a story, how to use it to imagine, to walk around, in a living body, in smart cities, to play at "sowing a vital spark" some small seed of happiness throughout the existential labyrinth. Must we hide pain to avoid thinking about it? Certainly we can conceal it in a tree trunk, in the sand, under a pebble, at the edge of a cliff, under our tongue or inside our chest. This is more complicated in literature, where it must be downplayed in order to retain only the viable part, for our humanity will agree to rejoice only once a certain pain threshold is reached. Below that point, it will just ruminate.

THE VIABLE PART OF OUR humanity hides somewhere in the cosmos and in our genes, in some village along the St. Lawrence River, in a tiny microphone pinned to the wool sweater of a woman who is recording a poem in front of the little Koksoak River. In the brief description of an artificial palm tree behind a hotel on Okanagan Lake, on the dark, vibrant surface of the fourteen paintings in the Rothko Chapel, in the drawer of a bedside table in a Tadoussac hospital, in a reply from a Chekhov play, in the belly of a woman, in the grand staircase of the Palazzo Grassi, in the abusive use of the word absolute, between my lips about to kiss you, in the ongoing poem.

Will there come a day when algorithms are able to act as meaning and emotion, to design sentences so perfect that all of art will simultaneously take the shape of desire and enchantment? Maybe, but then why all these serene scars in our thoughts: *dawn's rosy fingers, the rapture of deep middays, the cinco de la tarde, night and its glimmerings of syntax.*[2]

Oriane Ossilk tends to worry about her lack of sensitivity. She envies Hilda Sogol's ability to live with disturbing images which she seems to naturally cultivate like the one of her son laid out, chest offered up on an operation table, awaiting the scalpel and the oblivion that will shift him to an elsewhere with a thousand names, surfaces and myriad planets. For Hilda, death is at work everywhere, she sees it or she doesn't, but forever seeks to understand how the darkness, how it inserts itself into light so far as to aspirate its every manifestation,

infinite comings, infinite goings, which the invisible and the visible map inside her without her awareness.

Therefore writing, therefore I should say "Why" and "How I do it." I have done it, I can do it again, I can even summarize: extreme present, pleasure of language, and progressive immersion into complexity, the enigma of presence. That pleasure will admit certain constraints but will not tolerate any coercion. It is because we go to the far reaches of ourselves that we are able to throw ourselves into the void.

My notes, your thoughts: LIPSING.

Basically I know nothing about my ties to others. I have never investigated their solidity or their fragility. I know or don't. One thing is certain, I confuse my relationship to others with prose and narrative. I never really talk about other people, only about what can arise from the simple fact of being together. I do not seek out encounters with others, and so there is little left for me to describe, understand, interpret, regarding their presence. Nonetheless, I know that every gesture, word or silence counts as do the landscapes where we come together, the time of day, the light, the noise, have meaning and occasionally this gratifies me. Wounds, pain, misfortunes, and little joys make sense only once organized in language, otherwise I die.

I don't want to be me in a text. I want only the essential of what can make me say "I"; and to live from this by combining grammar, punctuation, breathing words, and a point of view on the world. Dust, resplendence, etymology, verb. Then redesign the sentences with the emphasis that writing is the most refined of the technologies that concern our species, a form of *jouissance*, body and soul. Grant me one more minute in the body's logic. Grant me one more moment in the logic of happiness.[3]

Something happened that transformed our sapience, our revelry, our dreams. We often find ourselves on the following day shaped by the articles we read the previous day, which come back at us with the smell of coffee and fresh newspapers. The sentences became more and more simple, *so sorry I forgot to talk about my self,* **as simple as each one of the cameras spying on our lives in public places and at times in intimate ones. The sentences became more and more simple, with a core called sapiencesapience.**

NOTES

1. The vocabulary and referents concerning literary writing have been incorporated into neoliberalism: storytelling, fiction, morphing of the self, emotion, shifting of meaning for specific political or commercial goals.

2. Homer, Anna de Noailles, Federico García Lorca. Translations by SLH.

3. Thinking of this quote from Albert Camus: "Happiness is generous. It does not feed on destruction." *Caligula*. Translation by SLH.

NIGHT THOUGHTS: SOME NOTES FROM THE MARGINS

M G Vassanji

*I*N SOME WAYS, BASED ON my experiences over the past three and a half decades, this is the best time to be a writer in Canada with origins such as mine, in another place, another time. Not long ago — the story may be apocryphal, but it's more probably true — a representative of then, no longer now, *the* Canadian publisher said that their typical reader was a housewife in Mississauga; meaning, white and suburban. Today a woman — housewife or professional — in Mississauga might well be wearing a hijab or a salwar-kameez, and, if we go by statistics, she is more educated on the average. Her knowledge about the world is greater and her life experiences are more diverse. She reads books that reflect a greater variety of human experiences. The publishers have caught on, though to what extent is debatable.

Times change, and Canada is one country that has embraced change readily, some might say enthusiastically and proudly. I am comfortable in most places in Canada (except Quebec) and feel as Canadian as anyone else, speak of "our" country without a sense that I'm being a hypocrite. This feeling has arrived after a long gestation, because it had to be genuine and not an expression of gratitude or a craven, flag-waving gesture. I know that there are people who think differently — whose historical relationship with Canada is different (I recommend an article by Nigel Thomas on the works of Cecil Foster[1] and the works of Marlene NourbeSe Philip and Dionne Brand), and that my brown skin and education put me in a typical in-between position; and I have wondered, am I a sellout? I believe not. Where on this earth is perfect? I would be a "minority" anywhere I went, including the places I love, and face some discrimination accordingly.

Canada today is vastly different from the racist country I first came to, somewhat nervously. When I completed my first novel in the late 1980s, so discouraging was the literary scene in Canada — you could tell from the bookstore holdings and the literary and cultural discussions in the media — that I felt no qualms in sending the manuscript straight to London to a well-known, respected publisher of African literature. My novel was set in East Africa, with a scene in Toronto, and another in Gujarat, India. The African Writers Series had published the most prominent African writers and its first series editor was Chinua Achebe (who had visited my high school in Dar es Salaam). Being published by them mattered to me. But I still thought that the novel should be published in Canada. And so with the ammunition that Heinemann was publishing the novel in U.K. (albeit under a special imprint), I approached the big Canadian publishers. That's how I came into contact with Ellen Seligman of McClelland & Stewart. We had many phone conversations, she sounding sympathetic and, it seemed, quite agonized (I was persistent, and there was already a clamour for greater representation in publishing), saying always, Not decided yet, and finally coming out with a definite, No, but what about the next one? My next novel, fortunately for everyone concerned, was set in Toronto. Ellen Seligman said, Yes. We became lifelong friends.

Perhaps a modicum of success, say local acceptance, raises more concerns. And you ask — vainly perhaps, though one does get philosophically desperate with age — surely it's not enough just to get published? Where do you *belong* — let's say, in a literary and cultural sense, for now — in this wonderful world of ours? There's a dynamic, global culture out there, effervescing in New York and Los Angeles and London, from where it spreads. Where are you, where is your place when they speak about the exciting developments and new frontiers in art, in literature? The colonial feeling that everything is happening out "there" persists in Canada. I've come from a minority (I dislike the term, and I don't consider myself a minority anywhere, but the term has its uses and the world doesn't always care how I see myself) in a small and marginal country to become a minority in another small country; and I cannot help but see myself as belonging and writing in the margins of the margins. Indian but not quite; African, but not quite; Canadian, but. Telling stories, describing lives of small people. Essentially irrelevant to a politically turbulent and technologically hyperactive world. What does it matter what I write? I've had enthusiastic receptions by different Canadian communities, and I am grateful for that; and yet more and more I cannot help feeling, what does it matter what I write? Whose life does it really touch? Would it be different if I were white or black, American or English? To paraphrase Rilke slightly, who would hear me among the angelic orders?

WE OFTEN HEAR THAT ART is universal; great art has the power to touch anyone, anywhere. But this statement is disingenuous, if not outright dishonest. The universalists who proclaim it are often white and privileged. They come from limited knowledge but claim to speak for all of us. Leaving matters of language aside, how would a college student in Dodoma, Tanzania, relate to a work by a Canadian writer set in small-town Ontario — evoking the angst, let us say, of a middle class, middle-aged white divorcee? The only argument left the universalist is that that poor soul in the dry middle of Tanzania is not cultured, sensitive, or civilized enough. Whither universality, then?

Recently I found an apt statement about how one understands a work of literature; it's by Herbert Grierson· A writer is connected to his audience, he says, "by a body of common knowledge and feeling to which he may make direct or indirect allusion, confident that he will be understood ... He knows roughly what his audience knows, and what are their prejudices."[2] Colonialism and imperialism have given many of us a "body of common knowledge," therefore what's produced in Britain and the United States often (but not always) sounds universal in the English-speaking world. The most manipulative television guff comes to us in North America from England (as well as some brilliant stuff) and is happily consumed because people recognize the tropes: the quaint English village, the friendly helpful bobby, the intrepid Englishman, the upstairs-downstairs *Downton Abbey* world that is obsolete and false yet so charming and sweet. Say Regent Street or Park Avenue, Harvard or Oxford, and a Canadian nods with understanding. A terrorist attack takes place in London, and we see a map of the London tube on the front page of our national newspaper. Say "Nairobi" and for most people it could be on Mars.

THE WRITER AS SALESPERSON; SOMETIMES huckster; and sometimes engineer. Publishers' "author portals" advise us how to pitch our works and personalities on social media in order to sell more books. Sales figures appear at the touch of the fingertips. Publishers and agents can watch and judge us from afar like gods. Amazon ranks our popularity. The first lecture a novice writer attends at a workshop is about the art of hustling — the tantalizing first sentence, the seductive first paragraph to draw in some — surely inexperienced or incompetent? — editor. You would think that writing schools should combine with MBA programs. A joint MFA-MBA. Recently, a doctor, after asking me that singular question he's asked me twice a year for more than twenty years — "Are you still writing?" — sometimes adding, "Writers don't make much, do they?" — told me out of his goodwill the story of a friend who's become a novelist. This author-friend researches his market carefully — what's "trending" out there — before beginning a novel. He has adopted a pseudonym — something like Jon Grinn (let's say), so his books will always get shelved close to those of John Grisham. And he sells. The rest of us have to perform in order to sell. It's the way the market is, I realize that. How many times have I been told — by friends — "Write like so-and-so!" "Write something like *Game of Thrones!*"

I've thought sometimes of simply giving up. I do have a body of writing behind me, so all has not been in vain. How long can you, and until what age do you parade yourself, a literary snake-oil salesman or a stand-up comic — putting on smiles, meeting eyes, being charming, answering the same questions that you've answered for a quarter of a century, just to keep those numbers up? Some of us are not charmers or beautiful persons. We don't have the eyelashes or the ready jokes. We forgot to train ourselves as actors.

When I brought up my thought about quitting with a few people who know my work, expecting shock and vainly hoping for encouragement (M G, you can't mean that! Your work is important!), I was met with only, "So what will you do now?"! Nevertheless, now and then an idea comes, the fingers ache, and so it's back to scribbling in the margins and crying out silently, But who cares?

THE COLONIAL CULTURE. SITTING HERE in Canada, a small country, we might argue — we *should* argue — that it is possible and desirable to promote and burgeon our own, Canadian culture — literary and otherwise. A culture that speaks to us in all our diversity, aware of our multiple origins and cultures and histories and languages, that makes us what we truly are. There *are* flashes of uniqueness in this country, politically. And being Canadian in its truest sense, I believe, is not just saying "Eh" (half the world says it) or celebrating hockey (some of us, blasphemously, prefer soccer or cricket), or sticking a maple leaf on the luggage; it is a state of mind, an attitude towards life and the world, sharing certain concerns. But we are a small nation. We are, culturally, Western, which some of us call universal. And we are also largely colonial. While we are diverse and proudly thump our chests as we celebrate our multiculturalism, and like Little Jack Horner pick out a Canadian plum and say how good and better we are, we are essentially Western in the culture we celebrate. The so-called international literary festivals in our cities are international only in the sense that the World Series is a world series. It's mostly Europe and America on display. Not the lands that the rest of us come from. Look at the school English syllabuses and despair; look at the library collections, the bookstore displays. Multicultural? Yes and no.

Recently I was at an awards ceremony for Punjabi fiction. A handsome prize of $25,000, modelled on the Giller Prize and called the Dhahan Prize, has been established in Vancouver to be awarded annually to an author of Punjabi fiction from any part of the world, written in either of the two scripts, the Hindi-related Gurmukhi or the Persian-related Shahmukhi. A fine ceremony took place at the University of British Columbia's beautiful Museum of Anthropology (we can skip the irony). Money was spent. There was a special promotion: staff and media were invited. Not one specimen showed up. You would think the local CBC if not the national (and why not the national?) would take pride in highlighting this outstanding and unique literary enterprise, originating in Vancouver, reaching out across the globe.

Speaking of local and universal, and of prizes, why should our most prestigious literary prize, one of our most exciting cultural initiatives, feel the need to have foreigners on its juries? I mean British and American. Can you imagine the Australians allowing that? Or have I got the Australians wrong? If we want foreign literary notables to add impartiality to our juries, why not a Ghanaian, a Zimbabwean, a Malaysian, a Pakistani? Perhaps that's coming; change does happen in this country, which was the premise I started with.

It's not that we — people like me — are not Western. We live here, were brought up and cultured in the colonies, we have studied and we admire Western cultural and scientific achievements. More and more I have come to realize how Western, or Canadian, I am in certain attitudes, especially those that have to do with the presence or absence or irrelevance of religious faith and with the acceptance of differences and disabilities (or different abilities). I can accept, partially, my cultural heritage going back into the roots of Europe, even back up to the Bible (the "Great Code"). But I am also something else. I am culturally, and historically, Indian (or South Asian) and African. I admire the stories of Tagore, the poems of Faiz, the vocal performances of the two Misra brothers, Rajan and Sajan. I am currently reading ten volumes of the *Mahabharata* (each of more than four hundred pages) and hope to finish them before my sun sets. I have recently read the Persian epic the *Shahnameh*. And I enjoy reading novels translated from Arabic and Hindi. I've recently read authors as diverse as Naguib Mahfouz, Doris Lessing, and Christopher Logue. For one of my novels I discovered and studied Swahili historical poetry, especially that dealing with the Maji Maji War against German colonialism. Where do I fit in? Does this so-called multiculturalism, anxious about London and New York, have room for me?

I SPENT MY FIRST EIGHT years in North America as a student in the United States. It was a thrilling period in my life, in which I think of myself as having been reborn, and I'll be eternally grateful to the generosity of the American university that made it possible. One morning in 1975, while walking along a street in Washington, D.C., I happened to glance at a display window of a bookstore and saw something called *The New York Review of Books*. An entire magazine devoted only to a discussion of books! This young man from Africa was impressed. Not long after, I saw the magazine in someone's hands at a laundromat in Philadelphia. I began subscribing to it. Over the years I learned much from it; the writing was brilliant, the letters columns learned and combative and often as exciting as boxing matches, not to mention the intriguing personal ads and trying to figure out the initials. But three years ago, with a bit of regret, I stopped my subscription. A drastic act. But it had seemed more and more over the years that a select group of people wrote for it, predictably, and about the same subjects — European and American history, music, literature, and even science. If the rest of the world was occasionally touched, it was from the same peculiar Western-American viewpoint. More and more I had come to admit to myself that the world they wrote about did not include me; it felt like being at a party with excellent wine (and Scotch), sparkling conversation, yet no one speaks to you or understands you. There's no point complaining — who asked you to walk in, anyway? It's their party. You can only drink the wine (or Scotch) and walk out, leaving the hum behind you. You are not missed, were barely noticed.

(TO ANSWER A QUESTION THAT should arise in the reader, Yes I have read Canadian literature, mostly the new and diverse but sometimes even mainstream: the works of a few dozen writers as a mentor and several hundred books as a juror; in addition, six thousand pages of a literary magazine that I edited and produced for twenty years, and more than two hundred books of poetry and fiction, which I also helped to produce and promote as founder and editor of a small press, set in or inspired by Ethiopia, Smyrna, India, Pakistan, Sri Lanka, Bangladesh, Trinidad, Guyana, Zimbabwe, Ghana, South Africa, et cetera, that are very Canadian but have had to struggle for the light to fall on them.)

IT'S NOT ENOUGH TO BLAME the so-called establishment. We are even losing our own next generation. At readings sometimes young people come and thank me for writing what I do. They might make reference to our common origins, cultural or geographic. It's flattering to be so appreciated; the heart glows — so maybe it's all been worth it, what's the despair about? "Oh yeah?" I say as I sign the book proffered to me. "Yes, I'm buying this for my father. He would love it." Well. And what about you? *Game of Thrones*?

In the 1980s and '90s there was some provocative literary commentary from academics of South Asian origin explicating the new Canadian writing and confronting the "mainstream." Universalism was attacked, post-colonialism was confronted, icons were brought down like the Bamiyan Buddhas. Unfortunately those scholars have retired, or discovered subjects and literatures in their countries of origin to interest them. This is unfortunate. The younger ones are not interested — there are Derrida, Foucault, Bhabha, and Spivak to preoccupy and titillate them. Do we, Canadian poets and novelists who share their origins, frighten them? Are we not exciting or relevant enough? Are we sellouts? Or is this phenomenon an illustration of the Indian proverb, *the chicken cooked at home tastes like daal*? Or are they simply under pressure to read mainstream? We cannot have a literature without a thriving body of commentary that understands it and promotes it.

In universities now, more and more fiction and poetry are taught for their special interest: Black, minority, feminist, LGBTQ, etc. While it is desirable to highlight special literatures, if only to counter the historical biases and ongoing thrust of the mainstream and the Western, or to study certain cultures, traditions, geographies, and histories of our world for their own interest, surely "minority" status or "native informer" is not what a novelist or poet aspires to; surely it's the beauty of the language, the originality of thought, the depth and novelty of perception, and the excitement of composition ("art") that has called him or her to the vocation or compulsion or madness of writing? That sounds old-fashioned and clichéd. It would appear that, in the modern classroom at least, if you don't belong to a stream, a special interest or identity, you don't belong anywhere.

Referring to recent developments in music in the United States, Nitsuh Abebe, a *New York Times* editor wrote recently:

This is what we talk about now, the music-makers and the music-listeners both. Not the fine details of genre and style — everyone, allegedly, listens to everything now — but the networks of identity that float within them. Maybe decades ago you could aim your songs at a mass market, but music does not really have one of those anymore. Artists have to figure out whom they're speaking to and where they're speaking from. The rest of us do the same. For better or worse, it's all identity now.

Is this where Canadian literature has also arrived? And is that good or bad?

NOTES

1. H. Nigel Thomas, "Marlene Norbese Philips's Poetic Response to Western Hegemonic Discourse," in *Confluences 1*, ed. Nurjehan Aziz (Toronto: Mawenzi

House Publishers, 2016), p 17; "Cecil Foster's Sleep on, Beloved: Reflections on Afro-Caribbean Immigrant Existence in Toronto," in *Confluences* 2, ed. Nuriehan Aziz (Toronto: Mawenzi House Publishers, 2017), p 46.

2. Herbert Grierson, quoted by Cairns Craig, *Times Literary Supplement*, Jan 15, 2010.

THE RETURN

Judith Thompson

I THINK MY EPILEPSY IS back.

I was sharing Japanese food with a friend who was recovering from surgery on both of her feet. I had had two glasses of wine, and hadn't eaten for about six hours. I was deeply tired from weeks of very challenging rehearsal and I was ravenous. I somehow found myself with a huge gob of wasabi in my mouth and as it began to burn I ran to the sink to spit it out and drink some water. The next thing I knew I woke up on the floor with my friend pounding my back, as she assumed I was choking.

Even though she assured me that I had fainted, and that there was no convulsing whatsoever, there was a terrible, familiar feeling. A sinister feeling I cannot put into words yet. When I cannot find the words, but I must find the words, the only way to find the words is to start writing. The burning need to put into words these seemingly indescribable moments is, I believe, why I write.

Maybe by the end of this essay I will have found the words to conjure that sinister, familiar feeling I had when coming to consciousness. At first I was greatly relieved and highly amused when I discovered that there is a bizarre phenomenon called "wasabi syncopy" — fainting as a result of a mouthful of wasabi. But then it happened again. Without the wasabi.

And again.

I AM SHOCKED AND YET not surprised; after all, I am a sixty-two-year-old woman. My body has betrayed me in the past, and it will again. I hadn't had a seizure for thirty-two years. I had taken myself off anti-seizure medication before getting pregnant with my fourth child, who is now twenty-two. Why has it come back?

I was very proud of not having had any medication whatsoever except the occasional Advil for twenty-two years. I am a healthy, strapping woman who rides my bike everywhere and swims fifty-six laps at least four times a week. I have two dogs I walk at least twice a day.

Is something brewing inside of me?

It is ironic that my best hope is that the epilepsy has returned. I'm not naive, though. Shit happens when you are in your sixties.

The neurologist has no idea why it might have come back. I have a few thoughts: three people I was very close to died last year, including my mother. The experience of trauma stays in the body and it will be expressed through the body. As a playwright and theatre creator, my body is my instrument. I have learned not to repress the physical expression of my emotions. This is the basis of all the theatre I create. The neurological forest fire that is a seizure was possibly my brain releasing the trauma.

Here is another explanation: in the play *Wildfire* (RARE Theatre with Soulpepper, May 2017), which I wrote for performers who all have Down syndrome, we explore the horror of the many institutions in this country that warehoused and abused people with differences or delays, people with epilepsy, and anyone else the doctors deemed would be better off in a hospital. Huronia (in Orillia) was called the "Hospital for idiots and imbeciles." Peter Park, the founder of a survivor's organization called People First, was admitted because his seizures were not being controlled. They assured him they would control them. Once he was in, he was a prisoner. He had no rights at all. His seizures continued. When he was finally released, twenty years later, and put on the appropriate medication, he became seizure-free.

So as I wrote and researched this play with the cast, I began to feel a bit guilty for my privilege. I had never been in a place like that. I hadn't had a seizure in over thirty years, though when I was younger and had tonic-clonic seizures (used to be called "grand mal") if my parents had been submissive, I might have been sent to a place like that. Was my epilepsy back as a gesture of solidarity and extreme empathy? The most basic element of all theatre practice is empathy.

The playwright and actor especially must deeply empathize with the characters in order to inhabit them, to feel what they feel, speak what they speak, and move the way they might move. For theatre to succeed, there must be empathy almost without control, something a social worker or therapist or doctor would never let happen. They need to be objective. We need to climb inside, and objectivity only happens when we need to structure, or give the stage manager their cue for the next lighting shift; but those refinements only come after the surrender to empathy.

As I spoke with our sound designer about my adventures with epilepsy, I learned that he also has epilepsy. Our lighting designer, who has M.S., was having a flare-up. I wonder if the power of the play, of the performers bringing the dead and forgotten back to life, right there on the stage, day after day after day, entered us all.

MY MOST DANGEROUS SEIZURE HAPPENED when I was fifteen. I was at the local Catholic high school in Kingston, Ontario: Regiopolis-Notre Dame. It was the worst year of my life. I had horrendous acne. I was an outsider. I spoke up in religion class and I questioned everything. I was weird. There was a gang of boys who targeted me viciously. They spat at me. They threw pennies at me (as in "whore"); they made throwing-up noises when I walked by them. I looked straight ahead. I never answered them. I cried at home, of course. I poured my mother's Valium pills into my hand and I considered suicide, but I could not go through with it.

One hot June day, at the end of the lunch hour, I was smoking a Kool menthol cigarette with my friend Micheline. We were on the back steps of the school, facing a lawn full of bright yellow dandelions. Suddenly I knew I would die. I had no doubt whatsoever. I kneeled on the ground, as if waiting for a gunshot through my temple. The next thing I knew I was speed-tumbling down to the centre of the earth, upside down. And then I was there. And it was a long, long way up to the surface. I knew absolutely that I would die there in the dark if I did not scream my way out. So I did. I took a great big breath and I screamed my way up from the centre of the dark earth and to the bright summer surface. If I hadn't taken that breath, I would have died, in my green plaid kilt and my rumpled white shirt, on the back steps of Regiopolis-Notre Dame, in

Kingston, Ontario. I know I would have died because, according to Micheline, my face was dark, like an eggplant, which means I was hypoxic.

That scream, I now understand, became writing for me. In order to save myself from falling, falling down, down to the middle of the earth, I must write. I must create theatre, with others. To write, I need to breathe in the world, as it is, as it was, and as it possibly will be and the screaming is my outrage, what I want and need the world to see. A scream has fierce intention, which is what every story, every character, in the theatre must have.

When the scream is listened to, it becomes voice, and voice utters words. I have always written for the theatre because I revel in the music of the human voice, either alone, or in dialogue with other voices. Every voice is music, part of the symphony the playwright creates with characters' voices. We remember the words that were said when we were rejected, accepted, condemned or praised, hired or fired. We remember the lies we told and that were told to us. We remember our mother's words, our father's words, our friends' and our lovers' words: they are carved into our very being. I write to honour the poetry of the spoken word at this place, in this time in the history of the world.

I try to find the scream in my character's monologues; for it is only in monologue that a character can truly become/reveal who they are; their essence through words, through a free associative stream of words that nevertheless has that fierce intention; the unique intention of that character.

SOMETIMES I AM ASKED IF my voice as a playwright is a Canadian voice. Is the scream a Canadian scream? I do not know the answer to that question. I do know that when I began writing, it did not occur to me to set my plays in the U.S. or the U.K. in hopes of production. I did emerge as an artist in the exciting and naive roar of cultural nationalism. After being exposed only to American and British plays, almost all from male writers, we (generally privileged white Canadians) were finally asserting ourselves. We had a voice that was all our own, unhindered by commercialism. The support of the arts meant we could live on small grants, and it was acceptable if 150 people saw our plays. No place names changed, or regional idioms. Even Canadian chocolate bars like Smarties and Crispy Crunch were featured. The sensibility was often one of social justice. These were the plays spawned by the Pierre Trudeau era policy of support for the arts, the era of Passe-Muraille and Gwendolyn MacEwen and Linda Griffiths, Lillian Allen, Leonard Cohen, Margaret Atwood, and Tomson Highway. The very beginning of our real awakening, which I believe is only actually happening now. I am not a Canadian playwright. I am a playwright. As we have learned from the Indigenous Peoples, borders are constructs. I am a global citizen, yes, influenced by spending my formative years in Canada in the sixties and seventies, just as I was influenced by my indoctrination in the Catholic Church, something I threw off like a heavy cloak as soon as I was capable. It is all part of the mosaic of Judith, but what is me is what I do with it. I have rejected almost everything I was taught growing up. What remains is the image of Lake Ontario on a stormy day, the time the "tough" girls on the Wolfe Island ferry stole my purse and dumped it in the garbage can, the red cardinals at my mother's bird feeder, my grade seven teacher with the thick blue eyeshadow forcing me to get up and speak my speech in front of the class, the yellow-and-green garter snakes on Garden Island, and those extraordinary, seemingly indescribable moments that I will someday put into theatrical form.

I look back on that moment of pride in Canada, the joyful singing of the silly song created for Centennial year: "one little two little three Canadians … weeeee love thee. Now we are twenty million!" with sadness. I remember my pride in winning gold in swimming at our local YMCA, a place that smelled deliciously of chlorine and french fries. I look back at all of it with shame at our ignorance. How can there be any pride in being a citizen of a country founded on the genocide of the Indigenous peoples? How can we have any pride in a country that celebrates murderers such as Edward Cornwallis, the so-called founder of Halifax, who ordered the scalping of Mi'kmaq men, women, and children (he is quoted as saying "nits turn into lice") and John A. Macdonald, who ordered those building the CNTTTT railroad to "starve the Indians out"? They are celebrated with statues and the naming of hundreds of schools and boulevards.

SO, I HAVE REACHED THE end of this essay and I still have not found the words to express that sinister, familiar feeling I had after fainting. I suppose the closest I can come to it is the idea of running into them. The boys who spat, coughed, and barrel-bombed me daily with every vile name they could think of. The boys who almost killed me, because I have no doubt that my big seizure was triggered by the stress of unrelenting persecution.

I have not ever run into them, but every time I would visit Kingston, when my mother still lived there, I would feel dread when we were downtown, or in the mall.

If I were writing an essay about resilience for *Canadian Living* magazine I would say that if I ever do run into those boys, they would be men, with their own serious problems. They may not all be alive. They very likely would have forgotten about their persecution of me, and if they remembered it, they might feel very bad about it. I would forgive them, and get past it. After all, many people have suffered much worse. And so with my epilepsy: yes, it might be back, but it can be controlled with medication. The boys had no real power, and the epilepsy doesn't, either. Neither the bullies nor the epilepsy will hinder me. In fact, they have made me stronger. All this is true, and at the same time, none of it is true.

It is easy to see the link between the return of that sinister feeling, the possibility of running into my tormentors, and the cycle of history: the alarming swing to the far right, the recent unleashing of bigotry and hate crimes in unexpected places. People who have lived through the Holocaust have been telling us that what happened to them can happen here. It can happen here. It did happen here. And it could, once again.

Those boys did have power. What I could sense, even at fifteen, is that those boys were the same boys that, given an opportunity, a uniform and a weapon, could easily massacre women and children; their eyes had no life: zero compassion. My other threat, epilepsy, doesn't care if I am on a bike or in the bath. When it comes, it is unstoppable. And it could kill me.

I have never written that play. As I write this I realize that I must.

It will be a play about how we respond to the sinister, the familiar, what has been dreaded for a lifetime and now appears again.

So I have another play I must write thanks to this essay.

But ...

How much is me writing the play and how much is a kind of collective unconscious flowing through me? The most powerful art runs through us and all we can do is help it along with our faith, our craft, and our need to scream. All we can do is take a deep, deep breath and scream the play up and out and into the waiting world.

WRITING IN QUEBEC
Rawi Hage

*Y*EARS AGO, AT THE VANCOUVER International Writers Festival, Noah
Richler moderated a conversation between two established Quebec
novelists, Yves Beauchemin and the late Gaétan Soucy.

I was in the audience watching the debate unfold. What I remember of
the conversation is a brief segment, an argument between the two writers on the
topic of *la necessité de la naïveté dans un roman*. Naïveté, Beauchemin argued,
is essential for a novel. Depth, or profundity, should not be self conscious, and
the quality of *Moi, je sais*, of Look, I know!, is pretentious. Depth, Beauchemin
seemed to be arguing, would be determined by the reader or critic, the passage
of time, and maybe even a posthumous historical context.

I remember how Soucy's entire body language was one of contained protest.
For Soucy, this demand for a kind of latency, suppressing the urge to emphasize
thought, appeared to be the most anti-intellectual thing he had ever heard
within the subject of literature — or so I speculate. Perhaps for Soucy, a teacher
of philosophy, the author's invisibility, and the delegating out of thought and
critique, was a false humility, even an assault on the discourse that a novel can
and should provide.

To my great pleasure, the two giants of Quebec literature appeared oblivious
to their Anglophone audience eager to shout, "But what about Canada?" The
conversation between Soucy and Beauchemin was a distinct conversation. In
my memory, they were entirely taken up with *naïveté et invisibilité* versus *une
pensée claire et visible*.

NAÏVETÉ ET INVISIBILITÉ IS NOT the idea of the writer as a simpleton, or aspiring to belong to *l'art naïf*. I suspect that Beauchemin meant accessibility, and the necessity for an egalitarian literature. I perceived that the argument was about inclusion and class. And further, what I heard in this debate was a conversation not confined to literature, but opening on to a specific history, Quebec's history. Here, literature reflects on, and has *une appartenance*, a sense of belonging to, the local history of working-class Quebecers. Written stories are heir to the oral history of an oppressed nation that has managed, despite hardship and through, for the most part, non-violent resistance, to rebel against a religious and imperialist hegemony.

But then, I found myself wondering, who should be credited with the 1960s *Révolution Tranquille*, the secularization of Quebec and abolishment of the Church's power? Should credit go to the intellectual efforts of Quebec artists and writers who, as the story goes, were influenced by the French Enlightenment? Or should credit go to the oppressed working-class Quebecers who rose up against centuries of authoritarianism of the Catholic Church? In short, who will take credit for Quebec's revolution: Rousseau or the Paris Commune?

In my reading of Soucy's novel, *La petite fille qui aimait trop les allumettes*, Soucy suggests the answer to this question is Rousseau, and that Quebec's encounters with the elsewhere provoked its transformations. The novel tells the story of a family who live, in complete seclusion, on a farm. The children are kept in captivity by an authoritarian father who practises a sado-masochism reminiscent of religious rituals, periodically flogging himself. The sole link the children have to the outside world are the books on Japan that their father collects, pushing the little girl to seek contact and learning beyond the farm's boundaries. The novel provides an analogy of Quebec society before *la Révolution Tranquille*, when a nation kept by the Church was liberated through literary knowledge that had its roots elsewhere.

On the other hand, I suspect Beauchemin's response to the question I posed would be the Paris Commune, believing that Quebec's roots lie in local grassroots uprisings. Revolution is a response to harsh and unjust conditions, he might argue, and it is the lack of essentials that cause the little girl to rebel. The argument that literary and/or intellectual thought triggered *la Révolution Tranquille* ignores *les causes simple* that cause the oppressed to rise.

One of the aspects of Quebec most misunderstood by the rest of Canada is that Quebec's current unresolved state is a condition not only of the history of British hegemony, but the dialectic argument that it has with France. Quebec has all the symptoms of a colonized past: a British empire that reduced them to second-class citizens, and a Church that stripped them of agency and power, forcing them to accept a single religious narrative. Soucy might argue that one turns to the elsewhere, to something in the distance or the past (even France), to replace that religious narrative. Beauchemin, I suspect, might reply that this turn to intellectual histories of elsewhere is not authentic to the experience of French Quebecers. Rather, Quebec has been built from an essential experience: the experience of suffering gave rise to the naïf — natural or innocent — message which in turn led to the simple and powerful act of rebellion.

During my activism years in Montreal, I worked closely with Quebec activists — some of whom belonged to the Separatist movement — on various solidarity issues. Separatist Quebecers at the time saw themselves as in complete alignment with other international struggles. Quebec literature has many of the qualities of anti-colonial literature: incorporation of the absurd, humour in defeat, political engagement, and certainly attention to questions of language. In Michel Tremblay's plays, for example, the working class and the particularity of their language are asserted and celebrated with distinction and pride.

But still and for some reason, the post-colonial literature produced by writers of colour in Quebec appears to operate apart. Where do Rodney Saint-Éloi, Roland Menuau, H. Nigel Thomas, Maguy Métellus intersect with the literature of Michel Tremblay? Saint-Eloi's book of poetry, *Jacques Roche, je t'écris cette lettre*, is a superb *deuille* on the death of a friend, and implicitly the assassination of his place of birth; an eloquent lamentation that is sublime in its rhythms, expressing a profound sorrow. Thomas's *No Safeguards*, the first in a planned trilogy, portrays, among other experiences, the impact of fundamentalist Christianity and its colonial ideology exported onto a small Caribbean nation. Thomas's novel, like Soucy's, exposes and refuses the devastation of religious oppressions.

But to return, momentarily, to my earlier question, I am no closer to answering the curious question of who created *la Révolution Tranquille*. Was it a handful of Montreal artists, writers, and intellectuals with their famous 1948 anti-establishment manifesto, *Le Refus global*, or Total Refusal? I say no, and here I might agree with my imagining of Beauchemin's stance. Artists and intellectuals are often opportunistic. They are masters at sensing deep resentments within the populace and acting upon them by giving them poetic expression. Quebecers were ready to free themselves from an oppressive church; the lack of essentials were the backbone of the uprisings. It is injustice, what power belittles as the lack of biscuits or cake, that compels people to march, denounce, and behead society's perfumed, powdered aristocracy.

And where do writers of colour fit into this equation? Which writers of colour are celebrated in Quebec and which writers cause a certain uneasiness? Dany Laferrière is one of the great literary giants of *La Belle Province*. His media engagements have a certain popular approach, and his journalistic engagements are notable for their accessible humour, injecting a kind of intellectual and witty naïveté into a heated argument. The poetic and powerful novel *Ru* by Kim Thúy is an unprecedented success in Quebec. When Thúy appeared on the popular Quebec talk show, *Tout le monde on parle*, her accessibility, her life as a survivor of war, her admiration of Quebec as a welcoming society, her unpretentious, joyful personality, her celebration of sex, were all embraced. Jack Layton's appearances here — his ability to speak joual, as well as his physical similarity to an everyday uncle from every small town — won his political party the election in Quebec.

Let me be clear: Quebec is not in any way anti-intellectual. The raising of its population from poverty, and the transformation of its society into a highly educated liberal democracy are grand achievements. The art scene of Montreal is on par with any other global city. Quebec's embrace of a seeming-naïveté and the celebration of *simplicité* could be seen as a desire to acknowledge the defiance and triumph of its own Commune, the oppressed rebelling against the oppressor, and an appetite for literature that reflects struggle by simple means and against all odds.

Quebec sees itself as *la commune en marche*. And those who celebrate the ever-existing spirit of *la commune*, be it in courage, simplicity, frank discussions of sexuality, farcical and absurd humour, and accessibility are acknowledging everything that Quebecers were once deprived of. *La commune* continues a spirit of perpetual protest. Rabelais's Gargantua and Pantagruel are ever alive in the province: only by embracing our attainment of open expression, buffoonery, and even scatological humour, can you acknowledge and understand our pain. What Quebec disdains most is austerity, a state of being which represents past religiosities and royal orders.

IS IT ANY WONDER THAT Quebec has produced the best circuses in the world, some of the grandest street festivals, and a vibrant comedy industry?

Fundamentally, the schism between Quebec and its ethnic minorities is about the way in which Quebec sees itself. Quebec history took a different turn, changing almost overnight from an important post for colonial French power, to an oppressed and isolated *nation* controlled from outside by a victorious imperial power, and from within by theocratic practices. Quebec sees itself as a colonial subject to this day. Guided by this feeling of existential threat, it allows itself the most flagrantly discriminatory employment practices. The current employment statistics in Quebec's crown corporations are startling. A mere thirty-eight out of six thousand employees in the *Société d'Alcool du Québec* are from visible minorities. Of the more than twenty thousand employees at Hydro-Québec, 312 are visible minorities. That's 1.56 percent in a province where at least 11 percent identify as a visible minority.

Quebec's implicit argument is that its refusal to integrate others is based on a perpetual emergency and sense of besiegement, which entitles it to operate in a mode of *survie, évasion et résistance*.

Moreover, Quebec feels absurdly rejected by the unwillingness of the exile, the refugee, the survivor of war, as well as the non-white Quebecer, whose roots go back generations or centuries, to recognize Quebec's long struggles as a colonial subject. But how could a survivor of residential schools, or a recent refugee from the war in Syria, or a Congolese who has just arrived from on-going war and extreme hardship, ever take Quebec's sufferings as a serious issue, including past injustices against French Quebecers who currently live in a prosperous, relatively privileged and safe society?

IN MY NOVEL COCKROACH, I wrote of a newly arrived refugee in a dire situation that leads him to suffer from mental illness. And to my ignorance, or perhaps pain, I disregarded the suffering of Quebecers. As a matter of fact, the only non-immigrant character is a psychologist in a position of power. Looking back at the contents of the novel, I realize what heresy I've committed towards my city, my province, and my home.

To make matters worse, there is, in addition my aloofness, my reluctance to compensate for my sins by appearing on various media outlets, as well as the fact that I am a francophone who chooses to write in the English language. But all that could have been rectified had I possessed the skill of appearing on screen as a joyful, chatty personage, or could tap dance.

In my own defence, my invitations to appear in Quebec media are primarily requests to act as a spokesperson for the Middle East. Naturally, I refuse. (When journalists ask an Arab to discuss the Middle East, what they really mean is Islam, and it's "problematic" existence, and since I am not a Muslim, I think my credibility on the subject of the Middle East has, with time, faded away.) Once I was invited to speak on the topic of: Can literature stop terrorism? I refused to even consider it, for the obvious reasons.

But a deeper reason for not taking part is that I am afraid. I have too much in common with Quebec politics, though not necessarily its *joie*, or what Russian literary theorist Mikhail Bakhtin calls the "alternate succession of enthusiasm and irony." And frankly, my political positions on religion, my admiration of *la laïcité*, secularism, in combination with having lived through ten years of the civil war in Lebanon, might make me sound like a kiss-ass for France and an enemy of Islam. But my *laïcité* does not, in any way, have its roots in French secularism, but in the various Arab heathens I read as a child, among them the great eleventh century Syrian poet Abul 'Ala Al-Ma 'arri, who concluded, *One, man intelligent without religion/The second, religious without intellect*, or Taha Hussein, a twentieth-century Egyptian writer and intellectual who spear-headed a renaissance and modernist movement, or the skeptical mu'tazila movement of the eighth to tenth centuries. I cherish Quebec for many other reasons beyond its quest for *l'apparence d'une naïveté*. I am for a complete separation of church and state, I cherish Quebec's overt offensiveness, and its *simplicité et joie* when it comes to sexuality. I also marvel at some of its socialist laws of rent control and affordable daycare, its long tradition of unions, its eagerness to protest in a large and strong voice (Montreal had one of the largest protests in the world against the invasion of Iraq). I live here in three languages.

As the political climate around us grows more oppressive, Montreal has become even more of a refuge.

During my years of driving taxi in Montreal, I hosted in my car a man who proclaimed that Montreal is the last bohemia. We all know that this place will eventually change, but nevertheless we enjoy our precious strolls in its godless, libertine gardens. And in spite of the current age's demand for writers to shine, to dance, and act like villagers marching with La Commune towards the barricades, many writers choose to stay in Quebec, to live in solitude and practise Soucy's form of solidarity.

SURVIVAL: THE ORIGIN STORY

Margaret Atwood

*T*RAVEL WITH ME BACK, BACK in time, to an age before there was Canlit.

It is 1961. The Cold War with the USSR is at its height. Segregation is still in effect in the United States, although the Civil Rights Movement is well underway. John F. Kennedy is president. The unsuccessful Bay of Pigs invasion of Cuba takes place in this year. America is tripling its troop involvements in the Vietnam War, although major protests against that war have not yet begun. Rachel Carson is about to fire an effective warning shot against DDT, but climate change and the poisoning of the ocean have not yet entered the public dialogue. The Residential School System that snatched young children from First Nations families is still in full swing, though the average Canadian knows nothing about it. In the Canadian Arctic, James Houston has already helped to develop a market for Inuit carvings, though Inuit printmaking was introduced by him a mere three years earlier.

Coal heating is being converted to oil, adding one more item to the list of Things Men Used To Do: stoking the furnace. Catholic kids and Protestant kids throw frozen snowballs at one another. These have replaced the frozen horse buns they used to throw: the end of horse-drawn milk wagons has put an end to that venerable practice.

There are no personal computers or cellphones; there is no Internet. Hate mail, with phrases such as "parasite," "Communist," and "running dog capitalist" underlined in red and blue pencil, is sent in envelopes, with stamps on them.

Newspapers, radio, and television are the major social megaphones. Talk radio and cable TV are in the future.

A young person's worst fear is death by nuclear explosion; if female, getting pregnant comes a close second. Abortions are not legally available. The Pill exists, but is off-limits to the unmarried. Pantyhose has not been devised: two stockings attached to some kind of apparatus such as a garter belt or rubberized girdle are the norm. Female hair is backcombed, beehived, and strictly glued: there are no windblown locks.

Male hair — except sometimes that of beatniks — is not long, not ponytailed, not dreadlocked: it is short-cut and firmly stuck down with hair cream. Female eye makeup is blue, the lids heavily lined. Gay people are in the shadows: sex between men is still illegal, and is usually punished under the designation of "gross indecency." Lesbians are not much discussed.

There are no hippies, although there are beatniks, who are serious if not morose in demeanour, and existentialists, who are even more serious. Cool jazz is cool. Folk-singing is rampant, and is likely to take place in coffee houses, where poetry readings also occur. Prose readings, author interviews onstage, and literary festivals are all as of yet unknown, as are creative writing programs — all except the one in Iowa — and big grants for authors, and major literary prizes. There is one prize cluster — the Governor General's Awards — but most people have never heard of it.

In the folkie coffee houses you might actually meet a black person, who will likely be a singer up from the States. In universities, black students are predominantly from the Caribbean or from Africa. Although Canada was the desired goal in the days of the Underground Railroad, Canadian black history is almost a blank. Anti-Semitism is receding from its high-water mark of the 1930s, but is still very much a living force. There are quotas for Jews at — for instance — various medical schools. The Canadian Civil Liberties Association will not be formed until 1964, though the Association for Civil Liberties exists in 1961. It is preoccupied with landlords who deny accommodation on the basis of race or religion. There are still service providers such as barbers who refuse such things as haircuts to non-whites.

"Feminism" is something archaic, if spoken of at all. It has to do with suffragists and women getting the vote, long ago, back when ladies wore big hats; but now women have the vote, so why worry further? True, there are a lot of things you need to know as a young woman. "Candy's dandy but liquor's quicker" is a phrase often repeated, meaning lads who want sex should get girls drunk. If you are raped by a boy you know, don't tell or you will be spoken of as someone who "got herself raped." (If you are murdered as well as raped, it will be "got herself murdered.") Don't go into law or medical school, as you will be assumed by your professors to be inferior, and marked accordingly. Many departments at many universities refuse to hire women, because they have standards.

Toronto is a pipsqueak of a city in a small, recently ex-colonial country that is being rapidly branch-planted, with the head offices of many businesses located in the States. It is a Protestant-controlled enclave, known for its blue laws — these decree who can drink what alcoholic beverage, when, and where — and is a joke to the citizens of the larger, more cosmopolitan, more exciting, and more bibulous city of Montreal.

Fifteen years earlier, Canada was emerging from World War II with a proud record, having played an important role in the conflict. It entered the war in 1939, and punched above its population weight on the battlefield, as it did in World War I. Its port city of Halifax was a major staging point for shipments of essential goods overseas. But now, in 1961, that time seems very remote to the young people who were teens in the 1950s and who are now wondering who they are and where they live. What is this "Canada" supposed to mean and be?

There isn't much help on that front in the education system. In public school children learn explorers; in high school, mining and wheat. The interesting history is Ancient Egyptian, with its ever-popular mummies, or Roman, with assassinations and oratory, or European, with colourful robes and crowns and decapitations, or American, with the Revolution and the Civil War and — lately — the atomic bomb. Canadian history has, instead, many dead beavers, which were sent to England and made into hats. When younger I thought these hats were like Davey Crockett raccoon hats, which would at least have been eccentric, especially with the tails left on. But now that I am twenty-one I have discovered the mundane truth about them.

It is standard to think, as poet Earle Birney did, that Canada is, spiritually, a null: "It's only by our lack of ghosts we're haunted." Little did he know. But then, little did any of us know. (Nature abhors a vacuum: something will fill it up, sooner or later. And so it has proven to be with the ghosts that haunt Canada.)

In 1961, the year I graduate from university, I am twenty-one, and — as part of a skimpy and motley group of Canadians you could cram into a medium-sized bus — I consider myself a writer. I am already publishing in the tiny number of literary magazines that exist, some of them printed on mimeograph machines, others — such as the much-coveted *Tamarack Review* — professionally printed and designed. I have done readings, badly, in a coffee house, with folk-singing interludes. I have worn a turtleneck sweater. I have thrown up at a party. All of these are way stations en route to the life of a female writer, which I imagine as poverty-stricken, dedicated, lonely, and potentially suicidal. But I'm up for it, because obscure masterpieces will surely result.

Nobody in my minuscule cohort of writers can picture bestsellerdom — not in Canada, and not anywhere else, either, because why would those in a real place want to publish writing from an unreal place such as Canada? We believe we will have vocations, like priests, but we will not have careers. We will have spiritual ordeals. We will have doomed affairs. We will have Camus-like depressions, and will speak of *le sale espoir*. We will have to immigrate to New York, or London, or Paris, because no one can be an artist of any worth if they remain in Canada. This is what we have been told. It is also our credo.

I straighten my itchy turtleneck sweater, draw black lines around my eyes like Juliette Gréco, wrench my curly hair into something approaching straightness, adjust my existentialist horn-rimmed glasses, and slouch off into the future.

JUMP TEN YEARS. NOW IT is 1971. So much has happened!

The assassination of Kennedy — both Kennedys. The Vietnam War protests, and the arrival in Canada of a great many draft dodgers. The end of segregation in the United States. The beginnings of the second-wave women's movement, in approximately 1968. (But note: due to the often-embattled editorial leadership of Doris Anderson at the women's magazine, *Chatelaine*, Canadian women were already familiar with many of the issues that would soon be taken up south of the border.)

The Pill and pantyhose arrived around 1966, followed swiftly by miniskirts and the "sexual revolution" in which women claimed the same sexual freedom as men, with mixed results. Widespread dope-smoking, LSD-taking, and hippies have arrived, late in the sixties. At the same moment, marriages have exploded like popcorn all over Canada, and the four-kid, open-plan suburban marriage, with the wife erasing her brain in order to be fulfilled, was effectively over. Pierre Trudeau has declared that the state has no business in the bedrooms of the nation, opening the door for the decriminalization of homosexuality. Sensible shoes have appeared. Hair has escaped from glue.

At the beginning of the decade, anthologies of Canadian poetry contained work in both French and English, as well as translations from First Nation languages — not yet called that — and Inuit, not yet called that, either. Bilingual collections were appearing. In 1967, Montreal hosted Expo '67, a pan-Canadian success story. By the end of the decade, the Quiet Revolution has come and gone, Separatism is in full swing, and writers from Quebec refuse to appear in collections that have "Canadian" in their names. This does not apply to francophone writers in other parts of Canada, such as New Brunswick, Manitoba, and Ontario, but these writers are being told by their co-linguists that they are dead ducks, doomed to extinction unless they move to Quebec.

Meanwhile, the condition of being a writer in English Canada — now being referred to as the ROC, or Rest of Canada — has undergone a sea change. Instead of heading to the cultural capitals of London, Paris, and New York, a critical mass of young writers have stayed in Canada. The poets have made contact with one another through an expanding network of public readings, and, in 1966, the League of Canadian Poets has been formed. (This took place on a lawn, as I recall.) Robert Weaver has been running his CBC radio programme, *Anthology*, throughout the decade; for many, he provides their first publication. In addition, he has published a collection of short stories that young writers have pored over, hoping some day to be included in a sequel.

Novelists and short-story writers still don't know one another, though they are increasingly aware of one another, and of several stars who have managed to get their novels published, albeit — initially — abroad: Margaret Laurence, still living in England, and Mordecai Richler, who moved back from London in time for me to meet him in Montreal in 1967/8. (Hugh MacLennan and Morley Callaghan are also in view, but seem, to the young, of a very much older generation.) Small publishers have sprung up — Coach House Press, House of

Anansi, Talon Books — while some of the earlier ones, such as Contact Press, have closed shop.

Jack McClelland, who took over the family publishing firm of McClelland & Stewart after coming back from World War II, has transformed a once-sleepy distributor that relied on school set texts into a dynamic and inventive bookery, renaming it "The Canadian Publisher." Throughout the sixties, he's been pushing "his" authors, including Irving Layton, Leonard Cohen, Mordecai Richler, Margaret Laurence, Pierre Berton, and Farley Mowat — all engaged, in one way or another, in a wrestling match with the elusive "Canadian identity." McClelland has also invented the author tour, some years before the United States would get around to it: in a country of huge distances and local media, he's found that book sales increase by a third if an author makes the rounds. In this way, prose writers have also begun to meet one another, form friendships, and consider common causes. Not many of them know what should be in a contract with a publisher, since there are, as yet, no literary agents as such in Canada, but they are on the verge of finding out.

In 1970, D.G. Jones published *Butterfly on Rock*, the first full-length study of Canadian literature to be published. It is named after a poem by Irving Layton. The butterfly in question is dead, for what that's worth, but is seen in the poem as a manifestation of the rock. Harsh bedrock, fragile life: as an identity, it's a beginning.

The Canada Council, established in 1957 to foster the arts, is upping its game, and it is through a clutch of grants to four young writers that the House of Anansi came into being, in 1966. Dennis Lee and Dave Godfrey were the founders. I was one of the writers. We kicked our meagre grant money into the company as start-up funds, got shares in return, and thus began the enterprise.

The first books Anansi published were all poetry — novels were still seen, in 1966, as a bridge too far and indeed too expensive — but the company soon saw the value and indeed the necessity of publishing books that would provide the bedrock underpinning for the butterflies of poetry that were being exuded. The 1968 *Manual for Draft-Age Immigrants to Canada* — otherwise known as "The Draft-Dodger's Manual" — was a huge hit, selling hundreds of thousands of copies. Similarly, *The Bad Trip: The Untold Story of the Spadina Expressway*, about the fight to stop the destruction of Toronto neighbourhoods that would have resulted had the Allen Expressway been extended south, was popular. Anansi also led the way with two early Idiot's Guide-style books: *Law Law Law*, which told readers how to write their own wills, conduct their own divorce proceedings, and so forth, and *V.D.*, which was the first accessible book on venereal disease. (It covered syphillus, gonorrhea, and warts, but not AIDS, which had yet to manifest itself.) Unlike some of the other small presses, Anansi had a decidedly political bent. It was shortly to champion French-into-English translations, as well as writing by such Caribbean-Canadian pioneers as Austin Clarke and Harold Sonny Ladoo — the latter unfortunately murdered after only two books. (This is another thing that bears mentioning: there were several murders and suicides in and around the emotional pressure cooker that was Canadian writing at this time.)

Now, at last: *Survival*, The Origin Story.

It's 1970/71. I am in Europe — first London, then France, then Italy, then France again — completing my second novel, *Surfacing*.

(The first one, *The Edible Woman*, was written in 1964/5, then revised in 1967/8, and was published at last in 1969. I was living in Edmonton, where I did my first official book signing in the men's sock and underwear department of the Hudson's Bay Company. I terrified a lot of men who were harmlessly shopping for their Y-fronts, and sold two copies; I was also interviewed by a stringer for *Time* magazine, who asked me whether men liked me. Those were the days! "Why don't you ask some men?" I replied, thus earning a reputation as a tough, mean bitch. So undeserved!)

It is in France where I unstick my hair: the Ethnic Look is upon us, so finally my hair is briefly fashionable. While working away at *Surfacing*, and also a commissioned screenplay of *The Edible Woman*, I receive an invitation from Dennis Lee: will I join the board of The House of Anansi? I've been doing some poetry editing for them already, in the sweat-equity way poets do, but always through the mail, at a distance. I know nothing about boards, or small publishing, or the group dynamics of small, beleaguered mini-enterprises where the piece of cheese is small, but the mice are ravenous. I am told my presence would be helpful, and having been brainwashed in youth by the Brownies, I find this ploy hard to resist. Thinking no harm, I accept. Then I return to Toronto and the gruesome reality.

I will skip over the puddles of blood on the floor that were already making for treacherous footing within the company, and cut to the chase.

It is the spring of 1972. Anansi needs another bedrock money-maker to support its ambitious new program of novel-publishing, which has kicked off in 1969 with Graeme Gibson's bestselling *Five Legs*, typeset by stoned inhabitants of Rochdale College right before motorcycle drug gangs took it over. Anansi needs, in other words, a new *V.D.* What can we collectively come up with?

I've been teaching the English-language half of a Canadian Literature course at York University, a temporary position — I'm substituting for the poet Eli Mandel, who is on sabbatical. I've based my half-course on a number of sources, literary and academic journal articles for the most part. I've just read *Butterfly on Rock*. It's groundbreaking but academic, and many of the texts referenced in it are unavailable to the general public.

"Why not a sort of *V.D.* of Canadian Literature?" I say brightly. "I keep getting asked at readings whether there is any Canadian writing, really, or whether it's just a second-rate version of American or English writing. Maybe a sort of handbook, like *The Field Guide to North American Birds*, with, you know, identifying features, and how it's different from British and American, and, and ..."

Well, why not? Worth a try, it is decided at one of our board meetings, which tend to take place in the Red Lion Tavern on Jarvis Street, not yet upmarket real estate in any way at all. At first the proposed handbook is supposed to be a hundred pages long, but Dennis Lee, in his super-editor phase at that time, holds my nose to the grindstone and twists my arm and cajoles more prose and thought out of me, and the text expands threefold and is augmented by an appendix that tells readers how to come by some of the materials covered, and add a note on films — not many of those, yet — and music — just beginning its rise.

It is decidedly a group effort. We cobble the book together in the spring of '72, and it appears in the fall of the same year. We think we might dispose of maybe five thousand copies — that would be a big number, for us — but the book receives a lot of coverage and begins galloping out of stores, and goes on to sell — over the next few years — a whopping hundred thousand. Why? Perhaps readers are now ready to hear that they are not just pallid shadows of some other country. Perhaps there are now enough well-known writers in our midst to give credibility to the argument. In retrospect, it was good timing.

With success comes negative reaction, as is so often the case. From the Left comes horror that we would talk about "cultural nationalism" — isn't nationalism supposed to be Fascist? — as well as annoyance that there are not more workers' writers in the book — it's too bourgeois. (Where, I wonder, might I have found more such workers' writers? There's Milton Acorn and Hugh Garner, and what then?) From the Right come complaints that I have written three-hundred-plus pages about something that doesn't exist.

From certain writerly quarters come peeves about this or that writer or this or that region not being represented enough; this, coupled with miscountings of what and who are actually in the book.

From the teachers of Canadian literature in universities — there aren't many of them, and they are somewhat sneered upon by those specializing in, for instance, John Donne — come various wails that seem to have to do with my amateur, heavy-footed blundering in a tiny pumpkin patch they've been cultivating as their own. Too many generalizations, too much shallow thinking: yes, there's something to that, I reflect, but luckily, having had a taste of screenwriting, I'm not looking at spending the rest of my life in academia: pot shots taken at my little tome will be largely unheard by me, and I didn't want tenure anyway.

From the Left, oddly, comes a piece in *The Canadian Forum* in which I'm depicted as climbing to victory up a pile of cut-off men's heads, heads that I myself have removed from their necks. That hurts: the *Forum* was where I first published, outside school mags, back when I was twenty. I thought it was my friend. I try to think of any men I've decapitated while clawing my way up the ladder to Canadian stardom, such as it is. (Maybe I shouldn't have unglued my hair, thus giving rise to the Medusa image that was to follow me around for years.) Who are these headless guys? Is that a metaphor? And what do my homicidal propensities have to do with Canadian Literature?

I seem to be guilty of some unspecified crime. But so it was, back in the Dark Ages, for people of my scribbling ilk and gender. With or without the bras that were either being burned or not, we were a minor public danger.

THERE. NOW I'VE BROUGHT YOU through 1972.

Skip ahead to now.

Looking back, what did I miss? A number of books and authors I didn't know about: as I've said, there was no Internet, and reprints of vanished classics were just beginning to appear. But my main aim was to make a case for the existence of Canadian Literature aimed at and accessible to the common reader, not to provide an exhaustive survey. I could have added a chapter on war writing, and one on humour, and one on the kind of big-system thinking that had been done by the likes of Harold Innes, Marshall McLuhan, and Northrop Frye: theorists of communication, all of them. But I didn't do those things. Nor was Anansi able to publish the companion anthology of writing we'd planned: it would have been too expensive.

What did *Survival* accomplish in the end, apart from helping to support Anansi's literary publishing program for years to come? Maybe it proved its case: yes, Virginia, there is a Canadian writing. Maybe it challenged future writers to prove it wrong, at least in some of its details. Maybe it pointed to vacancies, to gaps: always an invitation to fill them. A subject that is said to exist can at least be discussed, whereas one conspicuous only by its absence is harder to talk about.

In any case, now it's over to you. You're looking ahead, to the next twenty, thirty, or forty years, whereas I myself will not be here. What is writing in Canada like right at this moment? Will there be a Canadian Literature in fifty years? If so, it is you who will be making it. How different will it be from whatever it is now? Will there even be a Canada then? Will there even be people?

Let's find out.

WHY I WRITE

Lee Maracle

*F*ORTY-FIVE YEARS AGO THIS summer a group of Indigenous Youth sat around the kitchen table in my apartment, not uncommon, my apartment was always filled with Indigenous activists who were usually young. This group was ambitious, not for themselves but for our nations. I remember some of them, Larry Joseph, Joan Carter, Bill Hewitt, Ronnie Ignace, Ray Bobb, Henry Jack, and David Hanuse were regulars. There were many more. Most of the young people in this meeting were committed to something specific. Halfway through the discussion, Larry Joseph grabbed a cast-iron frying pan from inside my oven, put it on the stove and turned on the gas. He took some cedar from inside his shoe and threw some of it into the pan. He then passed it around the room. We all solemnly stated our commitments over the scent of burning cedar.

"I am going to get a PhD and set up a Native Studies program in which we don't have to learn so much about Canada and what it did to us, but instead learn about ourselves; all the stuff we should have known if we hadn't gone to residential school." This choked us. The others because they had all been to residential school, me because it had never occurred to me that they did not have the same learning opportunities from the elders that I had had.

I was next, "I am going to write books. I am going to work with story, the way we always have, you know, when the old people would start telling some ten-thousand-year-old story and by the time they got past the beginning they were telling it like it was happening now. I know writing it won't work exactly the same as telling it, but I think I can get close. I want to spiral people down into our old stories, so that these people can know who we are and who we will always want to be, as my Uncle Leonard says."

"Won't that turn out some white people who are just like us?"

"Yeah," I said with enthusiasm. Everyone got quiet. No one was sure about that.

"If they think like us then what would be the point of being different?"

"There would be no point at all." And I laughed.

"They would all be Squamish, or Stó:lō or Nu:Chahlnuth," someone said and laughed even harder. "Then they would want liberation too." The room got quiet again, still in that magic way.

Is that what Khatsahlano meant when he said to Major Mathews, "Everyone here is Squamish, just some of you aren't any good at it." Most of the youth making commitments achieved their goals many years later, but at the time one of the youth, Larry, commented, "They still would not be good at it. You offer to share something with them; they will find a way to hijack it." None of us were sure of what he meant then, but now I get it. We share our knowledge and they hijack the expertise and get themselves hired teaching us. The exploitation side of their culture is hard to defeat, but this is not about that.

Some of the people around that table died a long time ago, some are dying as I speak, and others achieved their goals. Some drifted apart from me and I don't know where they are anymore, but most held on to their convictions. There is a university on the West Coast, Malaspina College-University, that focuses on Indigenous Studies, not on what Canada did to us and they use some of my books. I succeeded in being able to tell an old story as though it were happening today. I succeeded in writing my stories in the same structure as an old longhouse tale. I learned English well enough to transform it to accommodate me. My stories are layered the way a good West Coast story is, they are poetic and they begin with the old and become modern. I became an orator and I came to understand our condition, the road to our transformation and the path to liberation in the process — all through story.

I came to understand what the elders had been trying to teach me when I was small. I came to be able to examine story for its law, politics, sociology, environmental science, literary character and its medical content. I came to realize how much of our knowledge is embedded in our stories. I also came to see that these stories were keys to our knowledge texts, our oral knowledge. I also came to understand that many of my own people did not know this — residential school interrupted our cultural continuum.

In the beginning days of my teaching career, I talked to other people about story, about the embedded knowledge in story and how that embedded knowledge was a key to a large amount of oratorical text. Even if you knew the language, we needed to be able to discuss these stories as a group and discuss the knowledge attached to them and to aggregate our own "schools of thought." I learned that writing could hasten that process.

"There are some things you can't say in English," someone interjected.

"That is because the people who speak English well generally don't speak the language and the people who speak the language don't generally speak English well. That is why the translations are so bad," I added. "We need to talk to the old ones who know the story, then talk to those a generation ahead who know both the language and the stories and whose English matches the stories. Then we need to be able to put this all in scholarly terms."

"That's three different translations. We are going to need a lot of gophers," Larry interjected. Everyone but me laughed.

"I am volunteering to be one of those gophers."

"Vi Hilbert already volunteered." She was a scholar as well as a language speaker and a story keeper. Vi was my relative. So was Janet McCloud. She did not know the language, but she knew story and her spoken language was literary. My daddy too; he knew the stories in both languages and his English, while not scholarly, was terrific for translating and transmogrifying story — he was literary in his spoken word. He was a fine poet in English. He was a fine musician in any language. He would help me, so would Vi and so would Janet. They all did. All I had to do was transform the language enough to accommodate our story and recraft it so the other people would understand.

I talked with others and we worked out the principles of our story in themselves first. We tell stories in the leanest narrative possible so that the listener will be inspired to see themselves in the story, add to the story or build a new one or shift the story's direction. The whole world has to be in the story. Someone said I tried to do too much with *Ravensong*. I felt like I wanted to do more, but if I did, others would not be able to add to it, or put themselves in it. By that he meant that I failed the narrative and did not exploit the story enough. This actually made me happy. We are not supposed to exploit anything to do with story.

Our death was always massive in the epidemics we endured. The flu still takes a number of us with it. Suicide is never singular. Divorce is massive, abuse even more massive, trauma too, comes in multiples, so the simple business of "conflict" between protagonist and antagonist makes no sense to us. Our stories are about tension between something and the people. That something could be the state and us, the medical profession and us, the education system and us, the social workers and us, or all of the foregoing and us at the same time. When these tensions converge, Canadians get confused.

OUR STORIES ARE JOURNEYS TO the centre of our world. They begin on the outside of the circle, a spoke leads the reader to the centre and back out again, to the outside of the circle, until another spoke appears and another sashay to the centre of the circle is required, then back outside. This continues until the reader has spiralled down to a moment of peace and recognition, and can then spiral out to meet the world. At the end of each spoke there is a window to the centre, where the unknown and precious thing we all love lives. It is only through this dance through story that we are able to discover the hidden and precious thing.

I would love to dance you all through *Celia's Song* and *Ravensong* and the other stories I have told, but this article is not about that. It is about the value of that to Canadians. I have a wheel of understanding. It is readily accessible. My remembering is effortless. Others must "study, study, study" to pass their exams, I just had to attend class and listen in an Indigenous way, story it up next to my already-existing wheel of understanding. No new dendrites were required for me to remember things like "economic determinism"; I know what it is and where it sits on my wheel of understanding. I know why it falls short of its goal in painting a picture of how to understand the modern world, but this article is not about that either.

It is about hearing a story from us that is written by us not as though we were you, but as though you were us. That is how I write. Any indigenous person from the West Coast can understand my writing, appreciate my story and cherish the words embedded in each paragraph. Many of the other Indigenous nations of this Island can also understand my stories, appreciate them and cherish the words embedded in each paragraph. If you are not Indigenous and you do not understand it is because you came here and thought this was Canada, this baby country made of foreigners, who killed us, usurped whatever authority we had over our lives and lands and so we could not teach you. You can learn through studying our story.

Remember when you study our story from your lens, you come to non-Indigenous conclusions about us. I am okay with that. I do not wish to naturalize anyone and transform them into us, but I have never been able to tolerate others telling me how we are and do not believe anyone but us knows who we are. I hope you are all okay with that.

Someone once asked me why I didn't just write story the way Europeans do. Sometimes I do. It depends on the story. I am working on a novel just now that I believe is a "Canadian story"; that is, it is a story about the last 150 years of this island. So I write it in typical Canadian narrative, not too many characters, no multiple themes, etc., just a simple story of "looking for our father's landscape." It is our story, both Indigenous people and non-Indigenous people's story. But if it is a Salish story, then it makes no sense to try and fit it into English Literature. I will not go to anyone's table empty-handed; that is not my tradition. I come to your table full banquet. You may not want my food, but I am okay with that, just don't pick it up, but I will not come with nothing to offer. Writing is "food," the food of the heart mind and spirit. Stories are our banquets.

I write because I cannot fall silent into a backwash of Canadiana after having produced fifteen thousand years of story. I write because I want our youth to know that we have value, we have knowledge and we have a place in this world. The place we have was carved for us by our ancestors, who loved us so much that they died that we might live.

In Coast Salish culture, ART means Way of life. Every part of our life was creative and artistic. Our life-giving creativity was meant to guide our future generations and beautify our lives. Our lives would be empty without ART. Our stories are the foundation of all our art. Prior to colonization, these stories were all oral. Some of the storytellers were keepers of story. They kept the original version alive. But some of our storytellers were artists, working with the original story. We would begin to tell an old story and then as we moved through the story we would update, modernize and create a story about today. In this way, we are constantly telling back the old story, *different but the same*, we are continuing to learn from it. We continue to glean guidance from our original stories and by telling them back different but the same we are adding to our historical continuum, creating new mythology from the old. In this way we become, different but the same as our ancestors.

We learn new things and we use these things, not to become someone else, but to augment our Coast Salish being. My learning to write was like "adding a new rafter to the longhouse." I write so that I may continue to be Salish in the colonial world I inherit. I write to influence the world I inherit. I come to the table full banquet; I am not a beggar in need of someone else's cultural capital. I have plenty of cultural capital of my own. By writing I am transmitting the cultural capital of the Salish people from which I arise to the world.

Embedded in our stories are our laws, our relationship to the earth, the sky, the waters, the animal kingdom and the bird kingdom. Even the invisible beings (bacteria, viruses, etc.) have a place in our universe. We respect all beings and do not fool ourselves into behaving as though we are the only creatures deserving of life at the cost of all others. Our stories tell us that we are no more important than a snow flea on a glacier. In fact, my son tells a story of him and an old Anishinaabe man. He told him that the white people think we are worthless. The old man says, did you thank him? "No," my son said emphatically. The old man laughed. "We are the only beings in the world that are completely worthless. We add nothing to the environment. If all the human beings died, everything else would flourish. We are the only beings that not only add nothing to other life, but we steal the very existence of other beings."

I write so that I can counter the anthropocentric belief that humans are somehow "higher beings" than anything else on earth. I write so that I can counter the sexist notion that women are unimportant. We are the transmitters of culture, the carriers of culture. Indigenous men writers write about "what happened to us," but they do not write about who we are and how we are: The women writers do that.

When I write, I transmit the Salish being, the Salish world view. I pass on who we are to my future generations.

This continent could benefit from knowing what I and other women writers know. If you want to know and understand Indigenous people, Indigenous thought and being, and then you must read the women writers. Women are still responsible for cultural transmission and they still hold up this responsibility when they write.

Indigenous women writers spend their lives learning the culture of the others and figuring out how to transmit who we are to contribute to transforming the damaging culture that the newcomers brought. We struggle to do this, gently, by nurturing a new sensibility on this continent. I struggle with them. Embedded in our story is the new story that is waiting to be born. By writing, I reach a larger audience and can continue to reach greater and greater numbers. Writing has made me an agent of transformation on a grand scale in the world I inherit. I have a voice in many countries.

LIVING HISTORY

George Elliott Clarke

I.

Outside Ottawa's Chateau Laurier, Gothic-pile hotel,
Christmas afternoon, icy, but with daylight yet staunch —
If in the shadow — the penumbra — of Parliament —
As I was exiting, with my daughter, plus her mom alongside,
A scraggly, ruddy-nosed drunkard yelled,
"What's your *Slavery Identification Number?*"
Close enough I was to my citizen comrade to spy
White foam — spittle — slather his lips,
As his kiting words took vampire bites out of the wind,
And the festive light, the shed-leaf, tree-striptease light,
Teetered suddenly, as if cliff-edged,
Though I laughed — in ashamed *Surprise* — and hurled this riposte,
"I haven't needed that for 150 years!"
My interlocutor — nay, interrogator — spat no more;
But I feared my retort was dull, an inadequate quip —
As if I were as unequipped as a eunuch —
Even as my trio hustled through steely cold to our car,
Still merry, yet wary. But I was weary,
For all my Afro-Métis Canuck life has meant constantly
Explaining, justifying, my nigger-*ex*-the-woodpile presence,

As if proclamations of *Abolition* (Brit) and *Emancipation* (Yank),
I mean, the nullifications — extinctions — of *Negro Servitude*
Were just inconvenient myths, mere "alternative facts"....

But aren't *Liberty, Justice, Equality*, just rich, white folks' words?
Ain't it a gross error for a poor or black plebe or prole to think
That doled-out dictionaries don't discriminate?
I had to muse — no *Amusement* possible — that my rejoinder
To my ruddy-schnozzled, pitted-visaged compatriot,
Overheard by the cynical greenness of pine and spruce,
Was as silly an act as spitting at a viper,
For his question, so deliberately impertinent —
And accidentally pertinent —
Had been — has been — as recurrent for me as a cold.
When have I *not* had to justify my stricken-off chains,
Not had to interpret the inquiry, "Where are you from?",
As anything but an abrupt cancellation of my citizenship?
The questioning is peremptory and intemperate,
Weaponized to gut — render — me a "spook,"
The displaced spectre of Africa, who should be readily
Terrorized, deported, exiled, jailed, lobotomized,
Castrated, deadened, executed-by-cop, anything
Lethal, fatal, so long as I just drop dead —
Get disappeared ...

II.

When I viewed that disreputable face —
The piranha mouth like barbed-wire —
And audited the *Spite* — *Animus* —
Of this spawn of probably poisonous "white-bread" parents —
Glimpsed incisors that could tear open my jugular —
Could I have assumed murky, miasmic *Pleasure*
By puffing myself up as the jerk's *Big Nigger* nemesis —
A Conradian, dark-hearted narcissist —
And shouting back, not a witticism,
But a supposedly cataclysmic expletive,
A line like, "Fuck you!"
(An Anglo-Saxonism about as satisfying as saliva),
Thus bogging myself down in his ruinous hallucination
That I'm still — a — and maybe *his* — runaway slave?

Or could I — had I been swift enough — retaliated
With fists, pitching knuckles against *Obscenity*?
How else to stifle the implicit questions,
"What's going on here? How are you free?"

III.

But how should I, must I, indulge the unethical mythology,
The archaic formula, the policed — if elusive — *Policy*,
That brown-black people remain timeless slaves?
Such was — is — the grotesque subtlety of the mischievous
Interrogative, even if its framer is one more *sumpter dolt*,
Perhaps reeking of piss and ale and slobbered tobacco,
Yet nonetheless presuming the *Authority*,
The albino *Privilege*,
To cite me as a stray from a phantasmal *Slave Quarter*,
A barracoon of anonymous dead, whose shackles
Remain as purposeful as Macbeth's spectral knives.

Admittedly, I have no *State* laurels, no gilded halo,
To align me instantly with Apollo rather than apes,
And so I'm re-enlisted as a slave on a stranger's whim —
Reversed to a primal status — chattel,
Shrouded in lice, shit, putrefaction —
Subject to whippings, brandings, rape,
So bellies go begging and hymens rip ragged,
And a poet is recast as a beast of sweat,
A skeleton of blood,
A musculature of tears…

IV.

If this poem floats a poison-gas atmosphere,
Or *Disequilibrium*,
Recognize that *Evil* is always hunting black hides,
Always stalking Africans,
To restore *Slavery* to us, as our very own cross,
As if we merit this *Oppression*,
And our desperately seized *Freedom* deserves repeal,
That we must bed down with cockroaches, rats,
Eat crap, and roof ourselves with dung.

True: Guilty people are born with every breath,
But why is my *Liberty* criminal,
And not the slavemaster's, whose whips
Hook and tear wide a mouth?
Well, *Politics* is a sinkhole of *Amorality*.

V.

My spillage
of ink
doesn't end the slippage —
the conspicuous oscillation of my identities —
"African," "Canadian," "Africadian,"
Eastern Woodland Métis —
unto the extinction of *Distinction*
once I'm branded with the blood-and-soil epithet,
"slave" —
a crashed-down, dashed-down *Identity*
(*Misnomer*).

VI.

I should be thankful for that scrawny, pale goblin's
Ferocious *Sincerity* —
His candid, Canadian, Xmas gift —
The nitty-gritty, intimidating *Conundrum*:
How can I be Afro'd, Canuck, *and* free?

There's no way to gloss over the abortion
That's my bourgeois grammar, my Royal Bank–backed *bourse*.
My interrogator's interrogative was a dagger — as were his eyes.
The guff-full primate growled as punitive as a graveyard.

VII.

My full response can only be numberless poems — *Canticles* —
And also the provision of my bank account number —
To receive way-past-due *Reparations*.

SIX SCENARIOS FOR THE END OF
CIVILIZATION AS WE KNEW IT
Nino Ricci

A TYPICAL WRITING DAY: WAKE; EAT; sit at my desk; play a game of
Spider Solitaire. Desperately run through the laurels that will come
to me — Giller Prize; Booker; film rights; Oscar for Best Adapted Screenplay —
if I ever manage to finish my new novel. Log into my author portal to find that
returns on my previous one have now exceeded sales.

Play another game of Spider Solitaire.

I used to wonder why defences of literature kept needing to be written century after century when surely the point had long ago been abundantly won.
Nowadays, I find myself composing versions of them in my head almost daily.
It is hard not to feel a creeping irrelevance in the era of The One Big Bookstore
and The One Big Publisher and The One Big Book, when everything old is just,
well, old, and when Funny Cat Videos and first-person-shooter games have
become the narratives of choice.

Don't get me wrong. I am no Luddite, and have always resisted the hell-
in-a-handbasket reflex every generation seems to give into as it goes grey, the
tendency to see itself as the last bastion against the coming deluge. History is
littered with aging gloom-and-doomers bemoaning the end of civilization as
they knew it, yet civilization has soldiered stubbornly on. While Sir Philip
Sidney, in his *Defense of Poesie*, one of the ur-texts of the defence genre, was busy
lamenting that poetry, "from almost the highest estimation of learning, is fallen

to be the laughing stock of children," William Shakespeare was sharpening his quill just up the street.

Occasionally, though, as I am starting into my third game of solitaire or disappearing into one of the myriad other rabbit holes of procrastination that modern technology has made instantaneously available, it suddenly hits me: what if this time is different? What if the digital age has brought us around to some truly quantum shift, when all the old values *really are* under siege? Apart from the occasional ice age or dark one, humanity seems to have been plodding along fairly predictably ever since *Homo sapiens* made the leap to *sapiens* 2.0 and began making music and painting caves, with not much beyond a handful of mod cons to distinguish us until now from our cave brethren telling stories around the fire to hold back the dark. But in a post-industrial, post-God, post-Darwinian, post-hard-copy world, can it any longer truly be business as usual? What might it mean to be human when our bodies can be constantly updated or our brains uploaded to the Cloud? Even more importantly, is there any point in my finishing my new novel when by the time it gets published all the old tropes could be history and the guiding metaphor of frightened brutes around the fire may have ceased to hold?

This is when the chill sets in, what the Neanderthals might have felt when they first laid eyes on *sapiens sapiens*. And as the morning drags on and my novel languishes, the scenarios spin through my head of the brave new world we might be hurtling toward, and the shrinking place it might have for the thing we once knew as literature.

1. CELEBRITY DEATHMATCH: GUTENBERG VS. JEFF BEZOS

Okay. So despite a strong recent surge, it seems e-books have not yet proved quite the game-changer tech nerds predicted they would be, their sales already languishing and publishers crowing that they were right all along to have buried their heads in the sand. Never mind that, ultimately, given their many advantages — no shipping costs, no printing costs, no waste of paper; no worries about inventory or shelf space or returns — e-books, blips aside, must surely crush the print market. The real question is whether this makes any difference. Content is content, after all, whether we get it in pixels or in print. Or — cue Marshall McLuhan — is it?

The first books that came off the Gutenberg press looked very much like the illuminated manuscripts they replaced, with the same gothic script and the same illustrations and decorative dropped caps, much as early e-books have mimicked printed ones, right down to the illusion of flippable pages. What seemed business as usual after Gutenberg, however, quickly proved otherwise. After first taking a moment to kick the Renaissance into high gear, the Gutenberg press went on to usher in the Reformation, the Enlightenment, the rise of the novel, democracy, and, arguably, the death of God, not to mention some three hundred years or so of bloody religious wars. Given this sort of precedent, e-books ought surely to have us quaking in our Blundstones.

My own e-book sales, I admit, have tended to hover in the single digits. But rather than being cause for rejoicing in the persistence of print, the poor showing suggests instead that I do not write the sort of books that are e-book-friendly; or, in other words, that my writing, in ways I don't really understand but that are somehow blatantly obvious to the average reader, is inextricably bound up with a technology that is on its way out. How is it possible, then, for me to see e-books as anything less than an existential threat? As the technology continues to establish itself, the gap between the Gutenbergians and the Bezosians can only widen, as the Bezosians begin to ask not only the obvious questions like what is a "book," after all, once you remove it from its static casing, and can it have visuals and sound, and need it move only in one direction, but much more complicated ones which my own Gutenberg brain will never be able to wrap its neurons around. This very instant, no doubt, in garrets and garages across the nation, some rough literary beast is slouching toward Bethlehem that will soon make novels, including my current in-progress one, seem as old-fashioned and quaint as rhyming poetry, the death that has so long been predicted for them having finally quietly come to pass.

2. REVENGE OF THE TELENOVELAS

Then again, in twenty years' time the debate over e-books, and indeed over the whole digital revolution of which they are merely a symptom, may have come to seem a mere footnote to some other much more momentous shift that everyone missed. Instead of the internet, it used to be TV we feared as the big-gest threat to literacy, maybe with good reason: after a hundred-year apprenticeship —

and the novel, in fact, took quite a bit longer to reach respectability — TV seems finally to have come into its own, spinning out quality serials that high-minded bohemians like me who once disdained to own televisions now spend our weekends binge-watching instead of reading novels.

When I first became aware of this phenomenon some years ago I enlisted a couple of other novelists to develop a series of our own. If TV was going to be the next big thing in narrative, I wanted in. For two years or so our little writing room chipped away at irregular intervals at our series, building a bible, sketching out story arcs, signing on with producers, even finally landing a development deal with the CBC to write a few scripts — only to have the whole enterprise go belly-up when a management change at CBC led to the axing of forty-nine of the fifty-two projects then in development, ours among them.

The good news in all this is that I discovered I probably don't have what it takes to be a TV writer. My idea of hell as a writer is having to listen to someone else's stupid idea while I'm itching to get on with my own. The bad news is that I discovered I probably don't have what it takes to be a TV writer, which means that if e-books don't make me obsolete, the telenovelas will. Think of Edmund Spenser, another of Sir Philip's contemporaries, penning his beautiful and largely forgotten *Faerie Queene* just as the Lord Chamberlain's Men, over at the Globe, were putting paid to the poetic epic and making clear that the play, instead, was the thing.

3. THE END OF TEXT

Or instead of e-books, think audiobooks.

More than half the books I "read" these days, I listen to as audiobooks. As a result, I get through a lot more books than I used to, including tomes like *The English Patient* or *The Luminaries* that I would otherwise have surely abandoned after the first hundred pages.

I can listen to books while I'm cooking, or folding laundry, or doing groceries; while I'm brushing my teeth; while I'm logging the ten thousand steps a day that my Fitbit requires of me. All those moments when, rather than doing something productive like thinking about my writing, I would otherwise just be rehashing grim doomsday scenarios that made writing seem pointless or trying to counteract these with desperate success fantasies.

I have had friends scoff at the notion that you can get the same experience of a book from listening to it as from reading it. Not the same experience, perhaps, but not necessarily an inferior one. You could even make the case that the human brain is more suited to speech than to print, given that literature arose from oral roots, and that the oral tradition — look how we flock to public readings — remains alive and well. Indeed, audio probably gives a truer, less mediated experience of a book than print, cutting out the bothersome extra step of having to make sense of a bunch of arbitrary symbols and bringing the text to us in exactly the form in which most writers have likely imagined it, as spoken word. My children will attest to this being my own case, and in company often do unflattering imitations of the constant mumbling stream that issues from behind my office door whenever I get around to any actual writing.

As formats go, then, audiobooks have even more advantages than e-books, which might explain why, as e-book sales flatline, audiobooks have become the fastest growing format in publishing. Gone are the days when they came in fifteen-cassette box sets and cost hundreds of dollars; nowadays you can fit the whole of Proust on the head of a pin and get him for $9.95 at Amazon's Audible.com, or for free at volunteer sites like Librivox. As text-to-voice technology becomes ever more sophisticated, it will soon be the case that every e-text will be instantly available in seductive-voice-of-choice audio, so that even text may end up revealing itself as merely another interim technology.

Of course, authors themselves are unlikely to dispense with text. It is hard to imagine that anything as sophisticated as *War and Peace* or *Ulysses* could be produced without the advantages that text provides for working out character or clever puns. Thus, the shift to audio might actually give writers a boost, making us, as of old, a revered class of scribes, guardians of the mystery of text. Over time, like the authors of *The Odyssey* or *Beowulf*, we will learn to incorporate into our work — cue McLuhan again — complex tonal techniques and mnemonic tricks that take full account of our new delivery system. And if the world does indeed end up going to hell in a handbasket as predicted, we may find we have truly gone full circle, back to those stories whispered around the fire at night to hold back the dark.

4. CELEBRITY DEATHMATCH: ART VS. SCIENCE

Here is the rub, though, with Scenario 3: that the same text-to-voice technology that will help do away with text is not some isolated phenomenon, but part of a much vaster technological overhaul that takes in quantum computing, reverse brain engineering, bioenhancement, and, ultimately, the war between humanity and the machine. This would be a lot to cover in the limited space I have here, so let me phrase the issue more generally in the context of the age-old battle between art and science.

Time was, in this battle, when art had the clear upper hand. We can still turn to *The Epic of Gilgamesh* for truths about being human, for instance, while science, for the bulk of its history, has been spewing mostly errant nonsense, still maintaining well into the fifteenth century that the Earth was at the centre of the universe, and into the nineteenth that God had created the universe whole cloth in or around 4004 B.C. Fast forward to the present, however, and art and science are neck and neck, with science beginning to set up shop in territory that once only the arts dared to enter. Evolutionary psychology, for instance, has revealed ophidian corners of the human brain that have left even writers aghast. But there is more: current brain projects envision delivering a fully functioning reverse-engineered silicon brain by 2030, one not only able to reproduce the subtle shifts of mind that literature has always made its stock-in-trade, but to track and explain them. Add in other advances in computing — the quantum computer, for instance, will soon make current ones seem as outmoded as digging sticks — and by then there may be few mysteries left about why we do what we do. Nor, indeed, will there be any point in writing novels, given that these computers will be able to read every last one ever penned in a matter of minutes and to deduce algorithms from them to spit out much better ones.

The only silver lining here is that advances in genetic engineering and bioenhancement might give humans — or, at least, those who can afford it — a chance for a level playing field. Indeed, this is probably the only plausible scenario in which the machines do not take over: that we learn, before it is too late, to become like them. But once we have spliced our genes and added in bioports and neural enhancements, once our body parts have become infinitely replaceable or our brains eternally preservable, what relation will we bear to that complex, messed-up piece of work that nature has spent four billion years imperfecting? And what of literature, which has always turned on the question of what it means to be human, once the human is up for grabs?

5. WALDEN II

Theoretically, perhaps, if evolution were simply allowed to run its course, it would eventually produce exactly the perfect beings we long to become: all-seeing, all-knowing, immortal; virtual gods. But who has that kind of time? The danger of technological shortcuts, however, is all the contingencies we haven't thought through, and which might end up making evolution's glacial pace seem a godsend.

Take death, for instance. So the time arrives when instead of passing on, we simply transfer our brains' OS and data from our mortal coils into more durable ones, and thus live, conceivably, forever. This would be big, certainly qualifying as one of humanity's game-changers, since death has always been at the top of the list of the things we hate about being human. But isn't it also, sort of, our favourite topic? In literature, it has always provided not only the age-old structuring principle of beginning, middle, and end, but the big questions. Death gives dignity to characters' actions, and irony; it ennobles and humbles; it begs the question of meaning, and seems to refute it. It is also what gives stakes, and without stakes, as every creative writing student knows, there is no story.

If the optimists get their way, then, and we end up in a kind of *Walden II* world where death is banished and everything is hunky-dory, it seems likely that even Shakespeare will begin to seem a little beside the point. In such a world, the forces that drive most of us to write at all — fear; obsession; more fear — will have ceased to operate. Instead, we will sit by the pond in our machine bodies, feeling nostalgic about the days when apocalypse stalked the earth and wondering why eternal life feels so oddly like death.

Of course, the optimists never do get their way in the end, any more than the pessimists do. Utopia, it seems, is just the other side of apocalypse, the two joined in one of those black-and-white binaries that often make human brains seem little better than those of computers. The truth always ends up being a lot messier — more prosaic, in a way, but also more mysterious and unforeseen. Some peculiarity of electrical currents or quantum shifts ends up making the transfer of brains a non-starter. Or global warming happens, and Florida and Indonesia disappear beneath rising seas, yet somehow life goes on, with none of the Armageddon-like closure of real apocalypse. And meanwhile the writers will still be at it, setting out into the grey zone that the utopians and catastrophists missed, the only ones who can chart our way through it.

6. COMPLEXITY

Some years ago, at a trial pitting Canada Customs against Vancouver's Little Sisters bookstore, I was called in as an expert witness to discuss the literary merit of some of the books Customs had seized on their way to the store. I was thrown into a panic at the time by how little hard thought I had given before then to what criteria might determine such a murky thing as "literary merit," and by the seeming impossibility of ever communicating such criteria, should I happen upon them, with sufficient concision and rigour to have them hold up in court. What I ended up with, I suppose, was my own defence of literature, reverse-engineering what I thought good literature did from what it seemed I myself was trying to do in my own stumbling attempts at it.

Of the various criteria I came up with, the one that seemed most to go to the heart of the matter was one that I labelled "complexity." By this I meant the extent to which a work tries to build in a level of interconnectedness and detail and nuance that gives an intimation, at least, of the impossible complexity of the world. This notion has a lot to do with why I bother to write at all, out of a hope, at bottom, of somehow fitting in the whole of creation, so that every bit of light is shaded with the million wavelengths of it we can't quite see, every bit of truth with the million qualifications of it we can't know. It also has to do with why as a writer I have always resisted the sorts of pigeonholes — whether of genre or content or style or of ethnicity or nation — that seem to want to reduce this ethos of inclusiveness to something like the specialization to which all the other, less ambitious, branches of knowledge inevitably tend. "Overambitious projects may be objectionable in many fields," Italo Calvino writes in his own contribution to the defence genre, *Six Memos for the Next Millennium*, "but not in literature. Literature remains alive only if we set ourselves immeasurable goals, far beyond all hope of achievement."

In a world of specialists, then, writers remain the last great generalists, madly plugging away at the hopeless task of making sense of everything. "And no list could hold what I wanted," Alice Munro writes at the end of *Lives of Girls and Women*, in a passage that has long served as me as a kind of manifesto, "for what I wanted was every last thing, every layer of speech and thought, stroke of light on bark or walls, every smell, pothole, pain, crack, delusion, held still and held together — radiant, everlasting." It would be hard to design a machine so dysfunctional that it kept tilting away at the impossible, an algorithm so buggy that it kept trying to name what couldn't be named. Fortunately, for these jobs we have writers.

Not so fortunately, my morning is shot by now. On my browser, some thirty tabs are open, everything from cave art and transhumanism to an OED check on the etymology of "solitaire" and a YouTube cat video. As for my novel, there is always the afternoon: eat, nap, sit at my desk; then begin again.

MIND THE GAP
Pascale Quiviger

*W*HEN REFLECTING ON BOTH BEING a writer and being Canadian, I find that my work lacks the backdrop of a specific cultural landscape. I have been based outside Canada for half my life, and the very idea of a base has always been shaky. My foreignness isn't just the product of emigration: emigration itself is the product of my relationship to language.

I grew up in a linguistic gap, which finally manifested in moving abroad. In the long run, I have developed a chronic sense of "not quite fitting," which seems to befit the times we live in. You could say I had the perfect linguistic start to experience today's global confusion.

Many think of Canada as bilingual. But that doesn't cover it: French Canadians use not one, but two languages. Strictly speaking, *joual* (the dialect) does not merit the status of a language: it doesn't tick the necessary boxes. All the same, it exists as an unmistakable counterpart to "proper" French, and an awkward one at that. The counterpart of something proper will always be improper.

Linguistic masquerading has long been familiar to French Canadians. I remember how my grandmother, Marguerite, a highly successful fashion designer and businesswoman, had to speak English at work. In those days, power jobs didn't happen in French. Ironically, this has also been true of France's linguistic minorities. My father is from the last generation to have spoken exclusively Breton at home and endured a traumatic assimilation. *It is forbidden to spit on the grass and to speak Breton*, said the (French) sign on the lawn of his boarding school.

I WAS BORN IN MONTREAL. When my turn came to start school, I spoke with the foreign accent imported by my mum from her studies in Paris, and by my dad from his life minus Breton. I soon lost it to blend in with my classmates. When I was nine, English became a compulsory part of our school curriculum. It was ever so difficult, but worth the effort. First, *Sesame Street* wasn't encrypted anymore. Second, the secret code used by our parents for adult topics was finally unveiled. English was power. At around the same time, the teacher started to alert us to anglicisms camouflaged in our daily *joual*. Like so many hand grenades, they threatened the survival of French in North America. As she patiently disarmed them, and tightened the grammatical screw, a very disturbing fact dawned on me: our dialect *was not really French*.

Worse: it was a *threat to French*.

Fortunately, I didn't realize what became obvious later; namely that *joual* sounds to others like a nasal potato mash and isn't much valued. A shame, really, since it is a vigourous, colourful, quick, precise and witty dialect; a rich blend of English and indigenous vocabulary, kneaded in French (old and modern), and peppered with quirky bits created from scratch. "Use with caution" was the subtext of our school training. It was okay to speak *joual* among ourselves, but we wouldn't hear it on any serious TV or radio program. In writing, willingly or not, it always bore the mark of a political statement. Besides, we couldn't agree on the spelling.

Thus it was that I inherited a linguistic minority gene from both my parents. Today, Breton only survives on life support in specifically designed schools, taught in a way old folks find too formal to be real. Québécois *joual* is alive and kicking, but trapped in its own contradiction — embodying the fight for the French it constantly undermines. For me, language was never going to be something to relax into and find certainty within. It would always carry a hint of shame, grief, hope and dissatisfaction.

In my twenties, I took sanctuary in a third language: Italian. Made to be spoken out loud and generously gestured, it allowed me to reinvent myself outside of that native paradox. I stayed in Tuscany for ten years of bountiful nature, fabulous pasta and impossible beauty, far, far from the harsh facts of winter and the humbling scale of Canadian wilderness. *Tutto bene*. But it must have become too familiar, for I eventually pushed the eject button. I resettled abroad from abroad — in the UK, of all countries. The motherland of the invader. The root of all evils. It took me seven years to see beyond toxic atavism.

And now, here I am, sitting between three of four chairs, and attempting to write in English. I work, live and love in the UK, but I won't call it home. It is too late to call anywhere home. But in truth, there is a strange perfection in the mismatch. For one thing, it opens a sort of cultural duty-free, very conducive to creative freedom. It carries a dull bereavement with it, but also the privilege of seeing things in a refracted light.

What does this mean in terms of writing? If language determines the structure of our thoughts, what happens when language occupies such shifting ground? How do you write when your most congenial expression is best avoided, when exiled from it for twenty years?

I knew I would write as soon as I started to read. I needed words to write with, and French was closest at hand. I tried hard. Sadly, no matter how many pages I've filled, French has yet to become the perfect glove. Too precious, too formal, too contorted; I long for something lighter, more direct and more casual. This has a lot to do with the gap between the spoken and the written form. It varies from one language to the next. In English, it is narrow. In Italian, it is deep. In French, it is manageable to start with; but as a Québécois who shaped her mind to *joual*, I find it difficult to cross. Somehow, everything I write is half a translation.

Part of my unease goes beyond French and *joual*; it concerns the nature of language itself. What are words for? They act as a bridge between people and, as such, they fundamentally address separation and the need for connection. Moreover, they never contain the solid objects they stand for, nor fully carry the thoughts they spring from. Language is on an impossible mission — and always fails. As much as it generates communication, it also secretly speaks of an unbridgeable distance. It tells of a very human ache, an existential solitude.

Such solitude feels especially acute at this point in our history. We have lost traditional structures that used to define our individual place in the world. This is the price to pay for self-determination; freedom of choice is a hugely positive step forward. But parameters are also lost to wars, globalization and environmental negligence. Around us, millions of people are displaced. The internet provides a goldmine of information but no discrimination. Governments reduce the meaning of life to economic charts. Rulers blatantly lie and stay in power. Corporations hold the reins of democracies, and democracies try to hold the reins of tyrannies. Nature, now unpredictable, makes apocalypse a strong possibility. Earth has become a confusing place.

We want to access knowledge but feel we know too much. We are showered in the suffering of others; a wonderful occasion to develop compassion, which often turns into indifference. More solitude. The closer we seem, the further we feel. The smaller the planet, the more difficult it is to hold.

UNCERTAIN IDENTITIES IN A FRAGMENTED world: how irresistible to turn inwards, to find solace in a selfie … How satisfying to define ourselves in the controlled habitat of a screen. But does that make us feel whole? No. The parts don't add up, the sum is never enough. Who are we, really?

You can hang on for dear life to a sense of purpose, trying hard to believe in a coherent narrative. But lucidity forbids it. It throws you out of the mainstream and sticks you into the margin. If there is a road, it is filled with potholes. You have to walk within the gaps.

> Gaps are not comfortable, but they are fruitful in their way.
> Not being a nation or a creed, they offer an alternate dwelling place.
> Living in a margin doesn't make you less. It might be the right
> place to be when the mainstream isn't.
> So, I try to get on with it.
> I write from within the gaps.
> I write about the gaps.
> And as I write, more gaps appear.

My job exists in a no man's land: no salary to speak of, no boss, no team, no workdays nor holidays, no structure other than self-imposed duty. I have developed a wandering office style, settling anywhere with enough of a surface: the kitchen counter, the nearby café, and, above all, the allotment shed. My only enduring landmark is to be found in ether: some subtle scent I've been tracking all along while — from outside — I seem to meander.

My tales are filled with in-betweeners: comatose or schizophrenic patients, dreamers, ghosts, angels, lovers, mutants. These are marginal people trying to find themselves and meet others within the margin. Explicitly or not, they question what it means to be human right now. They live in unnamed cities, cursed forests and imaginary islands, houses that may or may not exist; fictions within fiction that have readers candidly ask if they are true or not.

Well, no (they are invented).

Well, yes (once invented, they exist).

I happily hold both answers; an overactive imagination has long contaminated basic common sense.

It was inevitable. The tales are so vivid that the physical world pales accordingly.

Fiction constantly reveals the fragile status of what we call reality.

I never break my back to shovel stuff on the page; I never scratch my brain for ideas. Scenarios float into place; characters present themselves fully clothed and with clear intentions.

All they ask for is a mind available enough to catch them into the net of language.

In short: they already exist.

I don't try to find them, they find me.

There is a condition for this to happen.

I have to reach my outer limits to connect with

— what? —

something.

Something between a Higher Self and an undefined Other.

Call it Inspiration, call it The Force.

My job is not about pitching something I have to say,

but to give a shape to something that wants to be said.

It requires such self-effacement

that there is barely enough self left to witness the encounter.

The skin feels loose and time is distorted.

Sometimes what wants to be said is so far off shore that words struggle to haul it in.

If this sounds like writing from a ouija board, that is often how it feels.
To catch the drift of tales, I have to sit in undefined spaces where some unworldly thing consents to spread its wings and cast its shadow.
I wish to live under that wing, in that shadow.
I see no better use for my foreignness.

No better use for *our* foreignness: my work tries to connect with something much bigger than all of us.
It tries to free the meaning we often leave in the closet; an invisible body screaming to be let out.
Writing becomes a meditation with keypad.

I start by focussing on the breath and looking at my thoughts.
Eventually, thoughts vanish and emptiness is everything.
  Gaps open unto
  gaps
  like unending fractals.
  Reality cracks again.
  Any fundamental difference between fiction, night dreams and material reality is flattened.
  There are made of the same fluid substance.
  All are illusions, or none of them are.

My relationship with language takes me to a place where language is redundant.

A place where words are still budding
no sound yet, no spelling,
only a potentiality.

A no-place-yet
where universes are just about to bang
forms to arise
consciousness to choose a mind
and mind a body.

There,
past and future collapse
into Now
and without time
goodbye to space.

No chairs
no gap.

I meditate.

Everything else goes overboard
the hook for my coat
the name of my dog
but silence allows the words to come
emptiness makes me kinder
and exile allows me to come back.

Back to the margin.

I will always live in a margin.
Because my grandmother spoke English downtown and my dad learned
     to spit in French.
Because human beings were granted a mind that could embrace galaxies
think the unthinkable
and turn unto itself
to bite its tail.

Who has never felt exiled?
Who hasn't sensed, even just once, that they are so much more than their
    physical body?
Who hasn't felt an existential kinship with stranded refugees?
Who still believes that selfies hold a self?

We are a mystery
landed on a threshold
at the narrow end of infinity.

Hence, fiction.
True fiction.
It springs from the gap, feeds on it, makes it inhabitable, deeper, wider and wilder:
it blazes a track in the faraway land
it joins the dots on the white page
it salutes the sun and bends in the wind
it greets emptiness like the only star.

My solitude is bound to be extreme.

But here
in my carefully irrigated desert
I invite
the reader.

The reader
steps into the book
contributes to the gap
and makes it unique, again.

Somehow
we are together.

For that companionship in unbridgeable space,
I write.

WHO WILL WAVE BACK? NOTES TOWARD WHY I WRITE
Rita Wong

*A*S SOMEONE WHO HAS LOVED reading from an early age, I started writing to intuit and test who I am. My ancestors come from the Pearl River Delta in southern China, where they depended, generation after generation, on the land's fertility for life. When my parents moved to Treaty 7 territory, Calgary, where I was born, I inherited both their Chinese histories, as well as the responsibilities that come with living as an uninvited guest in someone else's home. Whether or not those histories and responsibilities were taught to me, they still apply. I cannot know who I am without knowing where I am.

Living and writing on the unceded Coast Salish territories, also known as Vancouver, for the past twenty-three years, I have a responsibility to the land and its peoples. My lifelong homework is to learn how respect is enacted and renewed with the Tsleil-Waututh, the Musqueam, the Squamish, the Stó:lō, for starters.

Writing can be a humble exercise of deep freedom. In the context of a colonized society that reduces freedom into superficial consumer choices or bluntly eliminates that freedom through systemic violence, writing can question unjust hierarchies and unthinking habits that need to be reconsidered. It can make space for the imagination to move swiftly as dragonflies at dusk, or as easily as otters floating affectionately together. It makes room for a world where every creature has a place, every life form matters. So why do people become so desensitized to the world's simple wonders? Why does injustice and violence persist and get massively misdirected at vulnerable people and places? In asking necessary questions, writers nourish the conditions that support others to exercise their deep freedom. This individual agency cannot be divorced from collective well-being. As Rosemary Brown reminds us, "until all of us have made it, none of us have made it."[1]

Recognizing whose homelands I am on, then, offers guidance on how to conduct myself as a Chinese woman whose way, *dao*, must be reinvented. For now I begin by acknowledging how much I have learned from Tsleil-Waututh poets who, from Chief Dan George[2] to Lee Maracle, have done their utmost to speak and write what needs to be said so as to create the conditions for a good relationship with the land and waters, and with each other. Lee reminds us that when we are on Salish territory, we are Salish citizens, even if we aren't very good at it, even if we don't realize it. Once we realize this, we can learn to become better relations. Another way to phrase it, as Secwepemc leader Arthur Manuel did so succinctly, is to understand that Crown title is a burden on Aboriginal title, not the other way around.[3]

TODAY, CHIEF DAN GEORGE'S DESCENDANTS have formed the Tsleil-Waututh Sacred Trust to actively protect their home from colonial destruction through the proposed Kinder Morgan pipeline expansion.[4] I consider the pipeline to be a lawless intrusion, and this expansion further violates Salish law. What skills or aptitudes do I have to offer in fulfilling my joyful responsibility to uphold Salish law? While there are many other ways, thankfully, writing is one way.

Writing saved my life, giving me a place to raise my voice, to not be wiped out or conscripted into someone else's ideas or stereotypes of what I was supposed to be. In a society that implicitly or explicitly demeaned and belittled non-white people, writing offered a way to turn anger and anguish into something I could see on a page, outside me, a process of refusing to internalize what was projected onto me. Instead of merely absorbing or inflicting pain upon myself, I could feel that pain, but not be reduced to it, because there was more to the story, to my story, to others' stories. Over time, combined with reading, writing nourished my capacity to respect others' perspectives, whether of this time and place, or past, or future ones. One life opens a window into others' lives, if you listen carefully.

'I work for the ancestors. — sx̌ɬemtəna:t, St'agid Jaad, Audrey Siegl, independent activist from the traditional territory of the Musqueam.*[5]

*Kwi Awt Stelmexw is a Skwxwú7mesh phrase that can be interpreted
as "the last people" or "the coming after people". These in turn have been
translated to mean "ancestors" or "future generations." We took this name
as a reminder that we are the ancestors to those unborn children to come.*[6]

Kwi Awt Stelmexw is a Squamish language revitalization program whose
name reminds me to think and write intergenerationally. When Audrey Siegl
invokes her ancestors, she reminds us that we are beholden to laws of this land
that predate and surpass temporarily imposed colonial frames. Larissa Lai men-
tions that she's been told, because time is cyclical, not linear, our children are our
ancestors, so when we are responsible to the future, we are also responsible to
the past.

This long view is what draws me, what reading and writing provide, if we
follow them with care, entering the ongoing conversation through each individual
story that gives us a glimpse into the larger realm.[7]

Reading was a lifeline as I grew up in Calgary in the seventies and eighties.
A studious girl, I would sit behind the cash register of the family grocery store,
reading for hours in between customers, stretching my imagination through
words that took me out of the often tedious confines of a small business that was
open 9:00 a.m. to 9:00 p.m., seven days a week.

I KEPT A JOURNAL AND wrote because it helped me to make sense of the world
around me — a world that did not reflect me or my family in its normatively
white discourses — and to assert my place in that world by making space for
my feelings, thoughts, and questions to breathe. In a very white city at a very
white time, feeling connected to Cantonese heritage — however fragmented
and fraught — was crucial to me, in the precise and idiosyncratic forms that it
took in my sometimes cranky and historically traumatized, but mostly loving
family. So much was unsaid and unsayable, but writing poems helped me to
reach toward what needed to be said, despite the intimidating forces of ideology that smoothed over or denied the contradictions of our daily lives. Even
if I spoke English well and watched too much American television, I regarded

myself and my family as steadily *tang yen* (southern Chinese people), not chinks, as one customer (the mother of a classmate) called us. Fragments of family stories, and larger silences, gestured toward historical traumas I sensed but could not narrate. In experiencing this, I could at times sense it in others. For instance, though we were living in their territory, back then I did not yet have the words to say I was on the traditional homelands of the Niitsitapi (Black-foot), Nakoda (Stoney) and Tsuut'ina First Nation. Having these words now changes my perception, my responsibilities on Treaty 7 land, what I am attuned toward if I want to end the systemic violence that has wasted too many lives.

Fast forward into the early nineties, after graduating from the University of Calgary with a major in English and a minor in East Asian Studies, I lived overseas, teaching English for a year in Japan and then in China. I wrote as a process of place-making, a way to orient myself through rapid changes, and as a form of witnessing the world, though I would not have called it that back then. One poem I wrote, during a journey along the Yangtze River before the Three Gorges Dam was built, says:

> i look for the big sky
> but clouds suffocate me
> rain defeat for the dispossessed.
> families pushed out of homes,
> mouths gaping hunger.
> stone soup, stone face,
> cracking as earth reveals herself through us
>
> without memory, we die fast & brutal
> flooded by greed
> our drowned, bloated arms wave
> and who will wave back?[8]

Having written this, I felt a responsibility to act on the feelings that had generated these words, to honour the words and be guided by them to oppose the dam. I wasn't sure how or what I could do, but I kept paying attention.

I followed Probe International's work, and when I was back in Canada, living in Vancouver, spoke to the Chinese media about my opposition to this destructive dam. As John Berger phrased it, "Far from my dragging politics into art, art has dragged me into politics."[9]

In its striving for insight and compassion, writing is also a form of giving back, waving back — to our ancestors, to the communities that make our lives possible (as well as the ones that are an obstacle to our lives), to the generations to come, and to the land and water if we stretch ourselves to take the long view. Renewing these relationships — through writing and other means, too — is a commitment to life's interdependence, a recognition that one's well-being depends on others' well-being, both human and nonhuman.

I have been incredibly fortunate in my journey as a writer to be guided by some very strong voices[10] and generous spirits. Having experienced racism growing up in Calgary, I knew I needed to develop anti-racist strategies out of self-defence. But it was at a life-changing workshop that Lee Maracle conducted with the Women of Colour Collective in Calgary in the mid nineties where I realized, as Lee lucidly told us, that racism is a product of colonization. If I wanted to address racism, sexism, and classism, I would need to address their root, the colonial violence that normalizes these and other unacceptable injustices. Lee clarified for us that, in a society that is effectively at war against racialized people, it can be an act of courage just to get up in the morning and keep going.

LEE'S INFLUENCE, ALONG WITH THE efforts of the Lubicon Cree to educate the public about the horrific effects of oil extraction on their traditional territories, which came to prominence during the Calgary Winter Olympics in 1988, helped me to approach the interrelatedness of oppression, and the urgency of decolonization. Lee writes in *Talking to the Diaspora*, "my body has always understood justice."[11] I love this reminder. The body also knows what injustice feels like, from hot rage to an icy calculation, and words help me to convey the shapes of those injustices, how they need to be called out and stopped, so that our minds, bodies, hearts, and spirits may live, and even flourish. I can't say that I've experienced that much justice in my life, but when I have felt its glimmering, I would describe it as a reciprocal sense of feeling connected and related to the world: a process where it has your back and you have its in return.[12]

My first book of poems, *monkeypuzzle*, accumulated images and tools to articulate one possibility of what Chinese ancestry means in contemporary Canada. What does it mean to own your own life (and to devote it in a service to yourself that is simultaneously a service to others), when dominant colonial and capitalist systems work in so many ways to reinforce power imbalances that effectively steal our very lives and subtle truths from us? Underneath those alienating and objectifying systems, I would argue, is a quiet humanity, at risk but surviving like weeds, unevenly growing back despite attacks on them. One poem in *monkeypuzzle* responds to the history of a woman, "China Annie," who ran away from her "owner" to marry her lover;[13] she was "charged with grand larceny for stealing herself." The work of stealing back our lives recurs in so many ways and forms; from indentured labour to the patenting of genetic material to the prison industrial complex, systems that unjustly turn life into mere property need to be challenged, dismantled, and reconfigured so that life can be autonomous, can just be.

I'm curious about what is embedded in our everyday lives, the queerness that comes into view when we look and feel a little more closely, whether that's the exploited labour in the stories of the clothes we wear and the trash we discard, the insidious pollution we are immersed in, or the grounded history underneath our feet being obscured by colonial narratives, what SKY Lee calls imperial delirium.[14] As Dionne Brand writes in *Bread Out of Stone*, "Poetry is here, just *here*. Something wrestling with how we live, something dangerous, something honest."[15]

The stories of this land's peoples are necessary to guide us through the delirium. For instance, the Anishinaabe prophecy of the eighth fire[16] — a time when people from all four directions may respectfully come together for the sake of the earth and each other — inspires me, for I feel that we each have a humble role to play in nourishing this fire of peace through paying attention, through learning, and sharing that learning, as writers, readers, speakers, listeners.

OVER THE PAST DECADE, MY writing journey has been sparked and nourished by Secwepemc-Syilx visual storyteller/filmmaker Dorothy Christian's call to protect sacred waters, to realize that water is the embodiment of spirit. This journey has taken me up north to gatherings held by the Keepers of the Water, committed to protecting the Arctic Ocean watershed. To learn from the land is to love the smell of spruce trees and campfire smoke, the cool feel of submerging your feet in clear lake water, to hear the vastness of the wind. In Wollaston Lake, Saskatchewan (2010), and Lac Brochet, Manitoba (2011), we could feel how inseparable people are from the land, as I heard Dene elder after elder attest to the power of water.[17] The generous hospitality I experienced up north taught me how powerful and loving communities can be, even as they are under siege from colonial intrusion. As a city creature, I know I could not survive in the bush on my own. While it's an honour to visit the bush, my work is situated in the city, in examining our relations with the waters buried under the concrete in sewers and pipes, for instance, and in following how water's cyclical path connects us to unseen places far away. Some might come to voice this relation through bodily intelligence, sensory awareness, song, dance, art, medicine, conversation — I come to it through words, through an entwined process of reading and writing.

Those of us living in cities rely too heavily on the sacrifices of land and water up north, due to resource extraction that has severely damaged and polluted people's homes, and reduced their ability to live with and from the land as they have for millennia. This sets up a relationship where we owe a debt to those whose homes have been destroyed or damaged for our urban lifestyles. Reciprocity is called for — it sings in our bones if we take the time to listen. We stop the pattern of colonial destruction by living more simply, more mindfully, by taking the power of the land's words and Indigenous stories seriously. Writing, then, is what paradoxically returns me to land, to community. As the Unist'ot'en say, heal the land, heal the people.[18]

Some days I write with the feeling that I am a reluctant worker who some-how finds herself on the *Titanic*, trying to find and make life boats out of the Leap Manifesto while the ship's captain is rearranging chairs on the deck. I didn't choose this industrial behemoth, but here I am anyway, trying to organize with my coworkers while not believing in capitalist bosses. If there's a boss, it's the ocean, the earth, the sky. The workers and passengers have different skills and gifts that could contribute to our collective survival, if we figure out how to work together in a respectful relationship with the ocean, the earth, the sky.

I keep breathing and writing because panicking on the *Titanic* doesn't help. Learning from folks who care about building canoes, simply and lovingly, might. Thankfully, the canoe is an Indigenous technology that is culturally strong along the west coast and elsewhere.[19] I am not a strong paddler, but I have had the honour of paddling for the Peace River on Treaty 8 territory as well as paddling with the Tsleil-Waututh Sacred Trust to protect the Burrard Inlet.

Canoes are vessels that teach the importance of observation, timing, and respect for water and place.[20] When the West Moberly and Prophet River First Nations host the annual Paddle for the Peace in northeastern B.C. on Treaty 8 territories, inviting everyone who loves the land to paddle together in the Peace River and to protect it from the Site C dam, what is enacted is a relationship that honours the treaties. Ecological literacy is crucial — one party to the treaty has not kept up its responsibilities, and the other party is still waiting for the delinquents to catch up with them, to learn the laws of this land that have been so blatantly violated and trespassed by colonial governments.

One might ask: can a poem stop a dam and reassert Indigenous laws? Probably not by itself, but in solidarity with people organizing on many levels, language, poetry, and story have a crucial role to play in providing an alternative to violent force. When poets gather, we may sometimes accomplish more together than we could alone. At the 2016 Paddle for the Peace, Nuu-chah-nulth-Kwawkwaka'wakw poet Valeen Jules and I asked Helen Knott[21] from the Prophet River First Nation, what could we do? She responded simply, "You can organize a poetry slam in Vancouver." And so Poets for the Peace was born, and events have taken place across Canada, raising thousands of dollars to support the Treaty 8 First Nations in their legal battle against the voracious colonial state.[22]

After opposing the Three Gorges Dam more than twenty years ago, I enter another battle with so many others — paddlers, farmers, First Nations, citizens groups in B.C., Canada and the world — to stand with the Peace River, which is named after a historical peace agreement between the Cree and Dane-Zaa peoples. When I turn on the light switch at home, I imagine following the electricity lines all the way from Vancouver up the grid, a fourteen-hour drive north to the W.A.C. Bennett Dam on the Peace, built in the sixties, when it massively and traumatically flooded and displaced people and animals from their homes, poisoning the waters with methyl mercury releases. Being implicated in this brutal history every time I use electricity, I have a responsibility to prevent further violence. Poetry teaches, decade after decade, that actions follow words.

Talk of "reconciliation" is merely hollow rhetoric or cynical manipulation of traumatized peoples, unless actions back up the words: to not reinflict the violences of the past again today. The purpose of Canada's residential schools, the Sixties Scoop, and today's child apprehension agencies was/is to force Indigenous people off the land and keep them disconnected, disempowered, so that wealth could be extracted from their homelands. This is a colonial pattern that people around the world are all too familiar with, unfortunately. And it is a writer's task to refuse to accept this unjust violent tearing away of people from their homes. It is a writer's task to keep looking, speaking, singing, writing, remembering so as to change the field of what is possible, here and around the world we call home.

> *"My freedom is not to be as they want me to be, but to enlarge my prison*
> *cell, and carry on my song of the door."*
>
> — *MAHMOUD DARWISH*[23]

This is why I write: because this process of coming to language, to words, keeps alive a commitment to be better relations with one another, to not merely absorb and repeat colonial violence unthinkingly, but to enact the kinship we are capable of, if we try, and to live better stories with each breath, each action, we offer the earth.

NOTES

1. Rosemary Brown, words etched into the concrete outside Allard Law School, University of British Columbia.
2. Janet Rogers, "Has Anything Changed? Revisiting Chief Dan George's Iconic 'Lament for Confederation,'" CBC, May 5, 2017, *http://www.cbc.ca/2017/has-anything-changed-revisiting-chief-dan-george-s-iconic-lament-for-confederation-1.4079657* [Accessed June 20, 2017].
3. Arthur Manuel, *Unsettling Canada* (Toronto: Between the Lines, 2015).

4. Tsleil-Waututh Nation, Sacred Trust Initiative, *https://twnsacredtrust.ca.*

5. Audrey Siegl, talk given at The Human Right to Housing and the Vancouver Situation, SFU Woodward, June 5, 2017.

6. Kwi Awt Stelmexw, *https://www.kwiawtstelmexw.com/about/.*

7. I wonder at how words like *care* and *beholden* resonate differently after recently hearing Christina Sharpe's work, *In the Wake: On Blackness and Being.* Refusing to accept pervasive anti-blackness, she precisely delineates black survival, word by word, image by image, till the weather changes. She crafts lifelines in the wake of slavery, from a history that is also our present. This deserves its own essay or book, but for now, I would simply like to bow my head in respect to her necessary, brilliant work, *In the Wake: A Salon in Honor of Christina Sharpe. Barnard College.* Feb. 2, 2017, *https://vimeo.com/203012536.*

8. Rita Wong, "lips shape yangtze, *chang jiang*, river longing," in *monkeypuzzle* (Vancouver: Press Gang, 1998), 73–4.

9. John Berger, quoted in Parul Sehgal, "Arundhati Roy's Fascinating Mess," *The Atlantic*, July/August 2017, *https://www.theatlantic.com/magazine/archive/2017/07/arundhati-roys-fascinating-mess/528684/.*

10. In addition to Lee Maracle, I would like to acknowledge some early teachers and mentors who encouraged me while I lived in Calgary: Della Zeegers, Donna Kelly, Fred Wah, Claire Harris (who advised me to join the Writers Union and the League of Canadian Poets upon the publication of my first book), SKY Lee, and more.

11. Lee Maracle, "Blind Justice," in *Talking to the Diaspora* (Winnipeg: ARP Books, 2015).

12. Lillian Allen, "The Poetry of Things," in *Psychic Unrest* (Toronto: Insomniac, 1999), 13–15.

13. Judy Yung, *Chinese Women of America: A Pictorial History* (Seattle: University of Washington Press, 1986).

14. SKY Lee, Keynote speech: "Imagining Asian and Native Women: Deconstructing from Contact to Modern Times Conference," Western Washington University, March 2, 2002.

15. Dionne Brand, *Bread Out of Stone* (Toronto: Coach House Press, 1994).

16. Eighth Fire, CBC, *http://www.cbc.ca/8thfire/.*

17. "Water Is All of Us: Report from the Fifth Annual Keepers of the Water Gathering," *The Dominion: News from the Grassroots, August 24, 2011, http://www.dominion paper.ca/articles/4154.*

18. Unist'ot'en Camp, *http://unistoten.camp/.*

19. See, for instance, Peter Cole, *Coyote and Raven Go Canoeing: Coming Home to the Village* (Montereal and Kingston: McGill-Queen's University Press, 2006), and

tribal canoe journeys, *http://www.cbc.ca/news/indigenous/tribal-canoe-journey-campbell-river-1.4213295*.

20. See Tarah Hogue, "learning to canoe and learning to listen are the same," *http://www.vozavoz.ca/aresponse/julie-nagam*.

21. Helen Knott's blog: *https://reclaimthewarrior.com/*.

22. Poets for the Peace, *http://www.poetsforthepeace.ca/*.

23. Mahmoud Darwish, "Four Personal Addresses," in *Unfortunately, It Was Paradise: Selected Poems* (Berkeley: University of California Press, 2003), 179–82.

WANDERING HOME: ON THE DOORSTEP
OF A CANADIAN ATHEIST IN MID-WINTER

Camilla Gibb

*O*NE DAY, AT THE HEIGHT of my loneliness, I opened the door to two West African women holding a copy of *The Watchtower*. I knew what was coming — in fact, I generally avoid opening my door to well-dressed people in pairs for just this reason. They smiled, spoke about the Bible and held out their magazine. I don't remember exactly what they said, because I was immediately taken away by them, taken out of my house and the isolation of my postpartum anguish, taken back to the sweltering lushness of a botanical garden in Limbe, on the coast of Cameroon.

I had been a graduate student at the time, preparing to do fieldwork on the other side of Africa, but in the interim I had gone to visit a British friend from Oxford, a forester who had taken on the job of managing the garden, one of the most biodiverse sites in the world. His American girlfriend didn't want me there; this was clear from the start. I was offered a bunk in the visiting researchers' dorm with its cockroaches and communal shower, down the hill from the colonial mansion where they lived. I was invited up the hill once for drinks.

I turned for company, instead, to the people around me: my friend's team of researchers, five Cameroonians who were collecting samples of traditional medicinal plants from around the country for an educational garden. I accompanied them on one expedition that took us several thousand feet up the side of Mount Cameroon, trudging through mud and perspiring jungle, one of the crew leading the way with a machete to cut a path through vegetation when necessary. I was the slowest of the group, unaccustomed to the heat and the elevation. Not much far ahead of me was Julia, a soft-spoken woman in her early thirties, my eyes following her ample khaki-covered behind, who turned around to check on my progress and offered a hand periodically to pull me up through mud.

We were tentative and shy with each other at first, but we laughed a great deal as the trek wore on, laughed and talked more as our breath returned, descending a trail toward a lake. We ate lunch by the water, then stripped down and waded in to pull up reeds from the muddy bottom, collecting specimens for the garden on the coast.

A friendship quickly developed; a friendship with an urgency more common to lovers. My time in Cameroon was brief, not enough to satisfy our mutual curiosity and affection for one another. We kept in touch, but in the letters that followed my departure, God was such a constant and insistent presence that I rather feel He came between us. Several years later, when Limbe turned dark and violent, my friend the forester moved to Indonesia and Julia and I lost contact. I have worried about her, but perhaps the God who got in the way of our friendship is also the God who has kept her safe.

I wanted to ask the Jehovah's Witnesses on my doorstep if they come from Cameroon. I wanted to ask them all sorts of questions that are none of my business. I wonder what has brought them here, to the doorstep of a Canadian atheist in mid-winter, what and how the journey has been. My baby was sick, though; it wasn't the right moment, so they left me with a copy of their magazine and said they would come back another time. Four months later the very same thing occurred — a new copy of the *The Watchtower*, their cautious warmth, a sick baby, another time, the unfulfilled desire for the company of a story, the kind of story I used to seek, the kind of story I used to tell, before I lost language to grief, before I had a baby, back when I was a wanderer and witness in the world.

I wanted to invite them in, even though I knew God would soon get in the way, because my world had become so small.

When I was in public school I knew and liked a girl who did not celebrate Christmas. I worried for her, not for spiritual reasons, but in material terms. When the Lord's Prayer (the only nod to religion at our public school) was broadcast over the PA system after the national anthem each morning, Rhonda left our grade five classroom to stand out in the hall. If Rhonda was allowed to leave the classroom, I should be, too, I reasoned. I was an atheist — I'd been told this when I was about six by my father — I didn't believe in the Lord. But why do others believe in God? I remember asking him. He told me humans were too weak to live with questions they could not answer, such as what happens after we die, and why we are born at all. He spoke of humans as if they were other creatures, creatures we were clearly not because we didn't seek recourse in such fantasy.

So, at eleven, I stood outside with Rhonda in the hallway, separating myself out in the spirit of my father's arrogance, an act meant to comment less upon my religious views than on the absence of rationality amongst my peers. I was raised not to belong. I assumed this was the case for Rhonda, too. I could not have been more wrong, of course: Rhonda's declaration was all about belonging very strongly somewhere, amongst the Jehovah's Witnesses, somewhere just as separate from me as it was separate from every other kid at school. Our silence in the hallway every morning was mutual, but not shared.

Given my father's explanation, humans seemed to me a very mysterious lot, a species I might aspire to belong to if only I could understand how they worked. It is perhaps not surprising that I became first a social anthropologist, making religion — Islam — the subject of my research. It is not at all surprising that I became a writer.

I HAVE A FRIEND, A great writer I will call Pilar, who was also once a wanderer. Upon first meeting I recognized in her a familiar compulsion for escape, an attachment to the fantasy and vain hope that to be somewhere else is to be someone else, the preparedness to do the work of learning the language of that somewhere else, the propensity to becoming impassioned about its politics, the inevitability of engaging in some defiant, forbidden love affair, and the constant companionship of writing throughout, writing as a means of making sense and finding meaning in oneself and the world.

I recognized all these things so viscerally that I disliked her quite intensely at the start, as perhaps, she did me. It took me years to understand my reaction, years during which I grew to respect and love this woman to the extent that my world would now be so much less without her. Neither of us, now in our late forties, can call ourselves wanderers anymore. We have become domesticated, living in houses and raising children in the same country in which we grew up.

"Don't you envy her life?" I asked Pilar a few months ago, referring to a mutual friend and contemporary who continues to wander, a woman whose writing is garnering considerable praise and reward.

"No," said Pilar. "It was lonely. I wanted a home."

"But isn't that exactly why we write?" I might have said to Pilar. "Because it is always lonely? Because we are always in want of a home?"

I had, in fact, expected her to say yes; I had expected one of us, at least, to say *yes*. But *yes* is too simple an answer, particularly for a question that isn't really a question at all.

In part, I was referring to a problem we share with many other female writers, one that our mutual friend, whom I'll call Deirdre (*wanderer* in Gaelic), has managed to avoid. To mother is to be participant in the destruction of the very conditions that enabled you to write, particularly in the case of fiction. Often, in the early years, sustained thought or immersion elsewhere can only be achieved through some form of dissociation (and the consequent burden of guilt). Time and space are fundamentally altered, becoming as ordered and finely attenuated as the keys of piano. But you do not play the piano. And you cannot learn because the child is asleep. And when he is awake it is his piano lessons that take precedence.

That last fact is enduring. Your presence in the world has been permanently altered. You will never again be an autonomous entity; your consciousness is now permanently tied to an external referent. Your ego no longer entirely resides in you. But while the books and career might prove to matter less as consequence, the need to write remains a rabid gnawing animal. What and how do you feed it?

Leonard Cohen's biographer wrote that "romantic relationships tended to get in the way of the isolation and space, the distance and longing his writing required." I used to worry that certain things — love, material stability, anti-depressants — would relieve me of a discomfort I address through writing — I worried in this way before I had experienced the kind of pain that renders language meaningless. As lonely as it is, there is a certain privilege in being able to cultivate and maintain the distance necessary in order to write. "How do you reconcile the need for distance with being the critical engine of a family?" I might have asked Pilar. Perhaps that is the question I meant to ask in the first place. It may be impossible to be a mother and answer this question in a way that does not imply the neglect of children.

I am trying to raise a child who has no place in my fiction. I am trying to give her the conditions for cultivating a very different prevailing narrative of her own. I am trying, in fact, not to write her story, and let her live in the world, rather than in my head.

When I was my daughter's age, I wrote my first short story — told from the perspective of an icicle. I attempted a "novel" soon after that, the story of a child who lived with the squirrels on the roof of her parents' house. In some ways, this is the story I have been writing ever since, one of alienation, exile and estrangement. And hope. It is my hope that my characters find some meaningful connection to others, some sense of belonging, before book's end. That place might even be with God, as it is for the characters in one novel. God does not get in the way of my writing.

How could I explain to the Jehovah's Witnesses that distance and longing allow me to write about God? That this is the very best I can ever do, that distance enables me to get closer than I otherwise ever could? How can I explain this to them when they have not returned to my door? My baby is no longer a baby and while she will dispossess herself of me in time, in pieces, this will not return me to the life of a wanderer, one who might have sought them out, made an honest effort to learn the way of Jehovah, accompanied them on a trip back to Cameroon to see their parents, hoping, all the while, that I might be able to locate a woman named Julia, and might one day be able to write a story of forbidden love between two women, one of them a Jehovah's Witness, the other, a botanist cultivating a garden in Cameroon.

That is a novel I will not write. Motherhood and grief and middle age and years of psychoanalysis have conspired to give me a certain unexpected permanence. This might be what people call home. If there are really are only two stories in the world as Tolstoy said, perhaps there comes a time in a writer's life where one's protagonist is less likely to go on a journey than she is to encounter a stranger who comes to town. This might explain my hunger to invite the West

African Jehovah's Witnesses in for tea. I have never written fiction set in the city in which I live, rarely even in this country — I've not found the necessary distance, but then, I haven't even sought it, tending instead, to write about people and places far away.

The Jehovah's Witnesses and I inhabit this city, but move so very differently within it that we do not share it. We follow different maps, but while theirs quite deliberately intersects with mine, mine does not intersect with theirs. Perhaps they can alter my perceptions of this place, make it strange, make me the stranger. I once asked another Jehovah's Witness who came to my door some years ago if she knew my old classmate Rhonda. She praised Rhonda, saying she was doing good missionary work. If we tend to think of missionizing as something that happens in Africa, the West African Jehovah's Witnesses on my doorstep represent a total inversion of that idea. Without a sense of home, I wrote in search of one. Now that I have a home I can afford to welcome ideas that disrupt it.

OF DISLOCATION AND CREATION
Lawrence Hill

$\mathcal{I}$N HIS ADAPTATION OF THE traditional song "Wandering," James Taylor sings about a man who spends his life uprooted and observing. "Wandering" came out on Taylor's album *Gorilla* in 1975. I was a teenager, and the song seemed to define my very molecules, which identified with the man who belongs nowhere. He looks in on life as if it is a framed painting. From time to time he tries to crawl into it, but he will be perpetually expelled. If I hadn't become a wanderer myself, I may never have become a writer.

A stroke of luck in high school set in motion my own life of wandering and writing. At the age of seventeen, I won a scholarship and used the money to travel in Europe. Four decades have passed since that first trip overseas, but I still remember — as clearly as an old melody — the feeling of standing on the outside of life and looking in on it and using writing as a means to unite the divergent sensations.

My hair was a long, curly, messy mop, and my summer skin was brown, and thoughts of the Black side of my family and my own emerging Blackness were never far from my own consciousness as I discovered how openly and unabashedly racist Europeans could be. I saw gendarmes stop Blacks for no apparent reason in the streets of Paris, and I stood outside a Brussels nightclub until spotting a handwritten sign that said *Défense aux noirs* ("No Blacks allowed"). I was experiencing an emerging racial consciousness, but along with it grew the awareness that my imagination soared when I found myself in places of unbelonging: on trains hurtling across the French countryside; in the

Louvre trying to make sense of Monet's *Water Lilies*; in a Dutch village befuddled by the sight of men stumbling around in mourning because their soccer team had lost the World Cup final to West Germany; spending all day climbing in the Alps near Chambéry, France and walking down into a village as night descended and finally finding shelter in barn of a farmer who offered wine when I showed up with a friend up at the door (*"vous préférez du rouge ou du blanc?"*) and on our way out in the morning, crusty bread and black coffee with the kick of defibrillators.

I spent $175 to live for eleven weeks in Europe that summer of 1974, stretching out my travel budget by staying in barns, train stations and youth hostels, and by carrying a jar of apricot jam and buying bread and cheese in lieu of restaurant meals. While watching Europeans go about their lives, daily writing made me feel that I, too, was doing something worthwhile. Writing what I saw, creating descriptions and short scenes, made me feel that I was making sense of life and advancing my own ambitions.

Two years later, I returned to Spain. I had finished my first year at the University of British Columbia (studying creative writing, French, and economics) and decided to take a year off to travel and write. I flew to Spain with Jack Veugelers, the same childhood friend with whom I had travelled in Europe at the age of seventeen. This time, we were both anxious to settle into a pattern of creative work: Jack as a painter, and I as a writer. We rented an apartment in the village of Águilas on the Mediterranean coast of Spain. About halfway between Murcia and Almería, it was off the main north-south highway and in 1976 it attracted little tourist traffic.

In my apartment building, in the flat adjacent to mine, a woman ran an afternoon typing school. We came to a prompt arrangement. Each morning, in exchange for the rental fee of a few hundred pesetas a day, she reached over the balcony and handed me a manual Spanish typewriter. It worked beautifully. I would hammer away at an unending short story for several hours, desperate to crank out every possible word before having to surrender the typewriter in time for the afternoon typing class.

It was a spacious flat. To house the rental typewriter, I set up a writing desk and chair in my room. Being away from home, with only rare contact by letters or pay phone with my family, made it easier to write. There wasn't much to do in Águilas. I would go for a run along the Mediterranean every day. Although I had not a shred of religious belief, I sang in a church choir — to improve my Spanish. Also to practise, I chatted as much as I could with neighbours, storekeepers, and with all the market vendors. I wasn't much of a drinker, but occasionally would have a beer or a ginger ale in the local bar and listen to 45s featuring Jim Croce, Paul Simon, Diana Ross, and Janis Ian. If they could sing passionately, I felt, surely I could write the same way.

Each day, I crossed town to chat with the baker and to buy cocos — a dough-textured ball of butter, flour, sugar, vanilla, and shredded coconut. Indeed, I ate them so faithfully that on January 6, Epiphany, the baker surprised me with a gift of a dozen cocos.

Hauled over from Canada in my knapsack or purchased second-hand in Paris and Barcelona, I had books by Faulkner and Hemingway and devoured them — especially Hemingway's *A Moveable Feast, Death in the Afternoon, For Whom the Bell Tolls* and all of his short stories — and counterbalanced them with James Baldwin's essays and novels, Richard Wright's *Native Son* and *Black Boy*, and Ralph Ellison's *The Invisible Man*. I left the books behind as I finished them. Living in Spanish each day also injected a sense of excitement into my work on the page in English.

Apart from running and reading and making meals with Jack and learning how to make coffee — the first efforts involved boiling entire coffee beans in water, which produced such a tepid, half brown, watery mixture that I marched back to the market to ask the woman who had sold me the beans why they weren't producing a decent coffee — I had nothing to do but write. I was living off the funds I had earned during a summer job, and didn't want to waste a cent or a second. I felt that writing was necessary to justify my year away from university and to make good use of my time in Spain.

What did I write about that year in Spain? At the time, I had two obsessions. One of my best friends had committed suicide and I was struggling to come to terms with it. In my dreams, he accused me of being hypocritical for continuing to live in a corrupt world. I tried to make sense of his death and my life in a short story called "Where Are the People?" I wrote several drafts of it, and continued to work on it after returning to Canada and taking a job as a CP Rail train operator in Gull Lake, Saskatchewan, in the summer of 1977. I didn't ever feel that I nailed that story, and didn't publish it, but more than thirty years later I returned to the themes of that story, set it in Gull Lake, and published it as "Meet You at the Door" in *The Walrus* in 2011.

During the months of writing in Águilas, my other obsession was my own heartbreak. A year earlier, in my first year at university, I had fallen in love with a woman who, about half a year into our relationship, took up with a friend of mine. Part of the reason I went off to Spain was to get away from that scene and rediscover a sense of joy in life — joy that can be so easily quashed when love turns bad. I wrote a very bad story about a young man recovering from his emotional suffering. Perhaps it was good for me to write a bad story, because it helped me distinguish between bad and not-so-bad writing coming off my own pen, and also helped me understand the limits of autobiographical fiction: follow your own story too closely, and the prose becomes leaden.

I made a stupid mistake near the end of my months of writing in Spain. I had hitchhiked to Granada to visit the Alhambra and to buy a classical guitar from the craftsman who made it, and upon my return to Águilas, discovered that the woman I had fallen in love with the year earlier had come to visit me in Águilas. I parted ways with my travelling buddy Jack and took up with her again. We ended up staying together in a flat in village in the French Alps called Villard de Lans. We only cohabited for a few weeks — long enough to discover that the relationship was going nowhere. I look back and cringe at my own stupidity, but I suppose it was good for me to suffer subsequently in solitude, because as I kept travelling to Italy and Greece, I kept writing.

Putting down words — even ones that I knew did not deserve to be published — helped me feel that I was doing something important, and made me believe that I was inching toward a worthy goal. I set stories in the places I found myself, as a way of growing closer to them, of taming them, of declaring to myself and perhaps timidly to anyone who would listen: I will write my way into a sense of belonging. Nestled up in the hills above Grenoble, and a fabulous location for cross-country skiing (which I loved), Villard-de-Lans was one of the most beautiful villages I had ever seen. But I was shaking off lovesickness, again. To pass the time, distract myself, and become more fluent in French, I took a job for a few weeks as a dishwasher in a restaurant and small inn in the village. Working for dismal under-the-table wages and meals, I stayed only long enough to discover that the waiters and dishwashers were expected to eat the guests' leftovers. I quit the job, thinking that perhaps one day a bio on a published story of mine might read, "Lawrence Hill has worked as a dishwasher in France." I thought that might sound cool. A story of mine came out some years later and did carry that line in the section of contributors' bios, but thanks to a typo, the bio mentioned that I had once been a "fishwasher in France." Not quite so cool. Nobody ever challenged me on that claim, perhaps because the story likely found no more than a dozen readers.

After I left France with the clear understanding that the romantic relationship was over and must never be resuscitated, I travelled — with my knapsack, notebook, and guitar — to Italy and Greece. I kept writing, and playing from a music book I had purchased in Granada, and revelling in the sounds of languages that were not my own. After French and Spanish, Italian sounded easy to understand. It felt like a friendship waiting to be made. I discovered that for a young writer, one of the most stimulating acts is to travel and write in a place where one's native language is not spoken. It was exciting verbally, but I also found that living alone, abroad and heartbroken, forced me to think more clearly about who I was, where I came from, what my own mixed-race ancestry meant to me, and what I wanted to do with my life.

In the spring of 1977, I decided to return to Canada, aware that I would need to find a summer job to pay for my second year of university.

Something happened in Athens, en route to the airport from which I would fly home to Toronto, which would affect my writing life years later. I had been a runner for many years, and always walked quickly too, so it came as something as a surprise to me to be overtaken on the walk to the bus stop by an older man — by which I mean, far older than my twenty years — decked out in blue jeans and a jean jacket. He stopped at the same city bus stop that I had earmarked, and we got to talking while we waited.

His name was Ernie Gremm, and he was from Abbey, Saskatchewan, and on his way back to the wheat farm that he owned and ran. He was a fast-talking, opinionated bachelor who said he spent every winter travelling abroad. He claimed to have been an air force pilot, and to be wealthy enough to buy many of the establishments at which he had been eating and drinking. We had a drink at the airport, and ended up choosing seats together on the flight home.

He enjoyed telling me that although he was "hornier than a fourteen-peckered owl," he had always escaped what he described as the prison of marriage.

Not long after our flight took off from Athens, Ernie tapped me on the arm and predicted that we would soon make an emergency landing. Why, I asked. Because, he said, we were flying in circles, with the sun coming in one window, then on the other side of the plane, and then back to the first side. That meant the airplane was dumping fuel, he said, because you couldn't land with a full tank of fuel. Minutes later, the pilot came on the air to announce that we had a problem with the aircraft and would make an emergency landing in Amsterdam. We landed safely, and were put up for a night in a hotel. The airline company required us to double up in hotel rooms, so I ended up sharing a room with Ernie. The next day, we flew on to Canada, without any further hiccups. We exchanged addresses at Pearson, and went our separate ways: me to visit my parents in Don Mills, Ontario, and Ernie to work on his farm.

Although I would have been welcome to stay with my parents in the Toronto suburb where I had grown up, and to find a job there, and although I could feel that they were perplexed and hurt to see me take off within a week of returning home, I felt the need to live and work in a new place, alone, and to write. I flew to Calgary, carrying on my lap the full-sized L.C. Smith typewriter that my mother had given me, and on which I had learned to type. I couch surfed in the home of some friends.

Day after day, I pestered the folks at CP Rail for a job until they taught me how to be a train operator and sent me to Gull Lake, Saskatchewan — population about four hundred, with no lake in sight and no seagulls, either — to work for four months. I worked alone in a one-man train station, from 7:00 p.m. to 3:00 a.m. each day, and often staying on till 6:00 a.m.

It was a tiny station — a two-room shack with an indoor toilet — and nobody came to the station because Gull Lake was too small to qualify as a stop for passenger trains. Each night, I watched the prairie sun go down. Often, I saw it come up. I was alone. I took my typewriter and classical guitar in the station, because I had only one or two intense hours of work to do each night. The work involved typing out rushed, coded messages called in by radio from the dispatcher in Calgary, and then standing on the very edge of the station platform while mile-long freight trains highballed by. I would clip the dispatcher's messages onto a long wooden hoop shaped like a number 9, and hold it way overhead for the engineer — leaning out his window — to snatch as he passed at seventy kilometres an hour and for the conductor to grab as he leaned out of the caboose. Between trains, there was nothing to do. Sleeping on the job could get you fired, so I spent the nights staring out the windows, scratching my chin, thinking about my life and what I wanted to do with it, writing, reading, and playing the guitar.

That summer, I rented — for the princely fee of $25 a week — a bachelor's suite in the basement belonging to an old, sympathetic white woman named Elizabeth Bucheler. She was about eighty years old — the age of my grand-mothers — and was still an avid gardener, cook and baker. After she got used to the sight of me — dark skin, wild afro, always typing or playing the guitar or going for long runs under the endless prairie skies — she began to ply me with potatoes she had just pulled from the garden, and with apple pie, and with meatloaf. We ate together several times a week. Elizabeth was my only regular companion that summer, and we became comfortable with each other.

While I was in Gull Lake, I spent my spare time writing for the *Gull Lake Advance* — a local weekly newspaper that paid me twenty-five cents per column inch. I wrote the longest pieces I could manage in order to squeeze out more payment from the newspaper. I covered a high school track-and-field race, a chuckwagon race, a visit to a local Hutterite colony, a court case in Swift Current. I detailed the nuts and bolts of my job as a CP Rail train operator, and whatever else they would let me write about. At night, on the job, I reworked the short story from Spain about the young man haunted by the suicide of his best friend, as well as a fictionalized account about one of my cousins — a troubled black youth in Washington, D.C. — called "Goddamn." That summer was one of the best seasons of my life for writing, perhaps because I had the stimulation of living in a place that seemed and felt foreign, but also because I had the calming influences of a salary, a clean bed and a shared domestic life with Elizabeth Bucheler. It didn't hurt to have unlimited hours to stare out the windows and to write during the prairie sunsets, nights and dawns. It also helped to have my old, faithful L.C. Smith typewriter with which to bash out my short stories.

During that summer, I made a call to Ernie Gremm and discovered that his wheat farm in Abbey was only 125 kilometres away. On a weekend off, I hitchhiked to Abbey to pay him a visit. Ernie picked me up at the local food store. He bought some food, wouldn't let me pay, and I remember him tossing the cans and bread down on the checkout counter as if they were hockey pucks or sacks of nails. He drove me in a pickup truck to his place, and had classical music playing on the radio. Ernie was one of the male species who seemed to have driven — and owned — a different car every year since he was sixteen. All along the grassy, square perimeter of land by his farmhouse, old cars and pickup trucks sat rusting between the trees. He had rigged up a shower on his front lawn, under a massive barrel of water loaded onto an overhead platform. When he wanted to piss, he stood on the front porch and let it rip. He listened to a transistor radio in his simple farmhouse kitchen, but even though he travelled the world each winter, refused to shell out for batteries. On his kitchen counter, he had his radio wired to an old battery from one of his abandoned cars. The battery, it seemed, was not quite as dead as the car from which it had been removed.

Ernie told me that I should open the fridge and help myself, but that I was not to touch his Heineken beer. If I wanted a drink, I was to stick to the Canadian labels. Fine with me: I've never enjoyed beer, and mostly drank water, tea, and coffee. I remember what he fed me, the night that I stayed at his place: roasted chicken, kept moist with water and a bit of lemon juice. And in porcelain salad bowls, he served the side dish — diced tomatoes spooned from the can. I had never eaten canned tomatoes straight up. But in Ernie's farmhouse, they tasted delicious.

Ernie relished a good political debate. He asked me for whom I voted, and I told him that I had liked David Barrett when he had been the NDP premier of British Columbia. He surprised me by saying that he was a Conservative, and hated the NDP. We did a bit of battle, and he seemed to enjoy the disagreement.

Then he asked me if I liked the taste of wheat. I asked what he meant. The taste of wheat, he said. I said I had never tasted wheat. He was shocked. How could I not know the taste of wheat? Did city boys from Toronto have no respect for the Saskatchewan wheat farmer? He took me outside and dropped some kernels into my palm. I tossed them into my mouth, and discovered a rich, nutty taste. Ernie seemed satisfied to see that my real education had finally begun.

I saw Ernie one more time after that. He came to Gull Lake a few weeks after our meeting in Abbey, to consider buying a piece of farm equipment at auction. I watched as he examined and then declined to buy the equipment in question. We had a coffee in town and said goodbye, and although I never saw him again, I received a few letters and my parents would sometimes report that he had called and left messages for me, while passing through Toronto.

My summer came to an end. I had written a fair amount in the preceding twelve months and in the fall of 1977 I began my second year at UBC. I took more undergraduate creative-writing courses, but at the end of the year decided to major in economics and to switch to the Université Laval in Quebec City, where my courses would be in French. I decided that year that I would do my best to become a writer, but that I would learn the craft on my own and study something else to expand my knowledge and skills.

In 1978, I moved to Quebec City to commence courses at Laval, and took up residence near the Plains of Abraham, on Avenue Cartier, in a tiny "1 1/2" — an apartment with a bedroom barely big enough to fit a bed, a minuscule kitchen for eating, studying, and writing, and a bathroom. Again, I found it stimulating to work on short stories in English while living in another language. I did write several stories that year, but spent most of it overwhelmed by the need to become fluent in French and to pursue my degree in economics.

The next summer, I travelled as a volunteer with the nonprofit group Crossroads International to Niger, on a cultural exchange and tree-planting mission. The trip altered forever my inclinations, passions, and commitment as a writer, and changed my life forever.

Crossroads — or *Carrefour* as it is known in French — sent small groups of Québécois (and willing Anglos who could speak French) to French West African countries — such as Senegal, Mali, Niger, and Cameroon — to take part in African-run grassroots community development projects (such as tree-planting and house-building). The idea was to participate with and support African peoples in their own community development projects, as a means of understanding them better and developing better ties between our country and theirs. Upon landing in Niger, I became aware of a raw and powerful desire in my own heart to be seen and recognized as a person of African descent, and to be welcomed as a long-lost brother. I wondered each day if people might see or intuit or just know that my own father was black — an African American, who immigrated with my white mother to Canada the day after they married in Washington, D.C. — and I became consumed with this need that seemed to shoot out of nowhere. I was travelling and working alongside six white Québécois who were my friends and fellow Crossroaders, but in the initial stages I wanted nothing other than to drop them and to disappear into the bosoms of my new acquaintances from Niger. This tension, anxiety, and striving for a new sense of belonging continued for a week or two until I became suddenly ill with gastroenteritis. I became stricken with ceaseless vomiting and diarrhea. I could not get out of bed unassisted or stand on my own.

My friends from Quebec saved my life when they took me to the hospital in Niamey, the nation's capital, which had to be one of the poorest hospitals in the world. In that hospital, a friend had to stay with you to provide food, drink and support. My friends took turns sleeping on a mattress on the floor by my bed and checking in with me as I received blood transfusions and IV drips. In the fog and discomfort of my illness, I recognized that my white friends were keeping me alive, and that it was possible to love them and to explore a new interest in Africa and Africans, and I ceased in those awful, uncomfortable days to be the least bit preoccupied by notions of my own racial identity. I was black, and white. I had both ancestral strains. It didn't matter what anybody else saw in me. I knew what I was, and from that point forward in life I felt no further anxiety about how others might see me racially. But I also felt excited by exploring themes of blackness and identity in my writing. That summer marked the beginning of a lifelong preoccupation, in my own fiction and nonfiction, with migration, home, identity, and belonging, and with drawing connections between Blacks in Canada and those throughout the African Diaspora.

Within months of returning to Canada, I wrote an autobiographical short story, "My Side of the Fence," recounting the experience of falling ill in Niger while striving for a sense of racial belonging. It appeared in 1980 in the now-defunct Toronto literary quarterly *Descant*, and became my first published short story.

I returned three more times as a Crossroads volunteer to Africa — to Cameroon, Mali, and much later to Swaziland — and have spent the last thirty-five years as a volunteer (and for some years now as an honorary patron) with

Crossroads in Canada. Each trip seemed to confirm and cement my need and desire to explore Black themes, create Black characters, and imagine stories — short fiction, novels and a television adaptation of my novel *The Book of Negroes* — that involved Black folks on both sides of the Atlantic. It became the material I wanted to work with, as I wrote fiction and essays that I hoped would be of universal interest.

I kept writing short stories through university, and by the time I graduated with a degree in economics in 1980, knew that I did not want to spend my lifetime pursuing any career other than that of a writer. The economics degree might seem odd, given my artistic interests, but it helped. I worked as a newspaper reporter from 1982 to 1985, initially for *The Globe and Mail*, and then for the bulk of that time for the *Winnipeg Free Press*, and was called upon to cover a federal budget and write about other economic issues, especially after becoming the Parliamentary and Supreme Court correspondent in Ottawa for the *Winnipeg Free Press*.

In those years of reporting, my fiction did not progress much. I kept writing short stories in my spare time, but I was working too hard to have the time or energy to write fiction with gusto. All the fiction writers I knew who had also been journalists had eventually quit their work as journalists to write novels. While holding that job as Ottawa bureau chief for the *Winnipeg Free Press* at the age of twenty-seven, I remember worrying that I was getting old. The notion of aging seemed especially troubling, because working as a journalist was not how I truly wanted to live. I quit the job — anxious to do so before reaching the old age of forty and becoming bitter over not pursuing my one dream in life — and moved once more back to Spain.

Before leaving Canada, the arrival of an unexpected letter made it much easier for me to quit my job and begin writing again. A registered letter arrived from a law firm in Saskatchewan. I wondered if it was a scam. Opening the enveloped, I found a letter from an estate lawyer who informed me that Ernie Gremm had died and left me $5,000 in his will. The envelope contained a list of all of the recipients of his largesse. He had indeed been a wealthy man, and had left sums of $5,000 and more to many people. I have always looked back at that moment imagining that Ernie was looking at me from a distance, whispering: "Don't drink my Heineken beer, but here's a little boost.

Go do what you need and want to do. Make your life count, young lad."

It was the third time I had gone to Spain to write, but the first time that I went as an adult, with high school and university degrees in hand, some savings in the bank and the ability to make decisions about how to manage my life as a writer. I had no car, no mortgage, no pets, and no debt. I was married to my first wife, Joanne Savoie, who quit her job to move with me to Spain. We travelled for a few weeks to Paris, Barcelona, Valencia, and Ibiza, but quickly settled into three towns or cities — Salamanca, Sanlúcar de Barrameda and Santiago de Compostela, each one for three to six months — where I fell into a routine of writing, reading, and running. I bought a portable Olivetti Spanish typewriter and worked on short stories daily. Again, I think the most valuable gift was that of time and space to write, and to muddle, and to read, and to let my mind bathe with the greatest of leisure in all of my ideas, characters, and plots. Looking back, I feel that I was fortunate to develop my skills in an era devoid of electronic distractions. I sent letters to my family and friends, and occasionally called home from a dysfunctional pay phone in Sanlúcar de Barrameda that let me make long-distance calls for free, but I had no emails, text messages, or cellphone calls to pull me from the task of writing. To this date, I do my best, and most sustained work when I manage to divorce myself from those distractions.

In Spain, I gave myself silly motivational promises, usually along the lines of food or travel rewards, such as "I get to take Joanne and me out to dinner in a fine restaurant once I have finished drafts and revisions of three new stories" or "We get to take a train from Santiago de Compostela down into northern Portugal and stay in a pleasant inn for the weekend, once I finish two more stories." It was a great year. I spent most of my waking hours writing, reading and running. Joanne took Spanish-language and dance courses and made friends easily. We lived cheaply — our rent was less than $200 Canadian per month, and with the exception of coffee, which I have always loved taking in Spanish bars and cafés, we almost always ate at home. I came back to Canada with more than a dozen finished stories. Only two or so of them went on to be published, but that was fine with me. I knew they weren't great. But writing them had given me the opportunity to learn quickly. One of the benefits of writing short stories is that your flaws announce themselves quickly and overtly. Fixing them on second or third draft puts you on the steepest part of the learning curve. Looking back, I was fortunate not to have put undue pressure on myself by expecting that I would return home from Europe with a publishable manuscript. I didn't have any such manuscript, but I did have the confidence to tackle my first novel, *Some Great Thing*. My decision was firm: I would organize my life to make writing my priority, and would set up paying work to fall into a supporting role.

It has been thirty-two years since I returned home from that last year-long writing binge in Spain. In the interim, I divorced, remarried a few years later and raised a blended family of five children with my wife, Miranda Hill. A year ago, Miranda and the children (all grown now) and I went to Spain to celebrate my sixtieth birthday. Travelling to the country was, for me, much more than a chance to see the people and the sights and to revel in the language that had intrigued me so profoundly when I was young. It was also an opportunity to celebrate the act of living and writing away from home as one of the most important factors in opening up my creative life.

KNOWN STRANGER
Michael Helm

I. in tongues

> How can one pray when another oneself would be
> listening to the prayer? That is why one should only pray in
> unknown words. Render enigma to enigma, enigma for
> enigma. Lift what is mystery in yourself to what is mystery
> in itself. There is something in you that is equal to what
> surpasses you.

I WROTE MY FIRST NOVEL WITH two notecards pinned to a corkboard above my desk. On one were these translated lines from Paul Valery. However pretentious it sounds now, the thought that as I wrote I might access an uncharted language close to true prayer appealed to me. As a boy of twelve I'd been to revival meetings and seen my mother speaking in tongues, and though glossolalia isn't exactly prayer, I at first had no other way of thinking about it but as prayer in unknown words. One afternoon in a big tent in the true backwoods of Alberta, the service, led by an American preacher of some apparent fame who performed apparent miracles there before us, I myself received the apparent gift. A language rose up in me like — what? — fire on a resined stave. Whatever came over me was physical, a lightness, a bearing upwards and, to express now in more than one sense a senseless thing, utterly strange. Speaking that way involved a brief lack of self-consciousness, but I was a shy kid and self-consciousness took its place again before long. Afterwards I kept this language, and the event of the language, to myself, wandering away from the fellowship and into the woods, staring at seeming patterns in the birchbark, closing my eyes and wondering how the invisible world could be so much larger than the visible one. And, alone, speaking again, trunk-lined to God. How did my holy tongue sound? The others I'd heard sounded pretty distinct from one another. I think mine tended toward two- and three-syllable bursts with much repetition and a sort of continuous patter, as if God was trying to sell me something, or vice versa.

When I recall it now, the language seems a little like that of my oldest brother John. He was born brain-damaged and has always been out of time, unlocatable amid measures of age and language and development markers that don't add up. He still gets most excited about Santa Claus, his word for Santa being one of the few he can say well enough that his family understands him. He has about twenty or thirty such words. I won't attempt to reproduce them phonetically. The reproductions would be rudely approximate — the words as he says them exist somehow outside of alphabets — and anyway John can't give his consent to be quoted. Because of his excitement over dogs, Christmas gifts, the prospect of seeing family, at times he can seem a kind of ecstatic innocent. One summer afternoon when we were boys — I must have been six or seven, he sixteen or seventeen — alone in the living room of our house, he stood up out of his chair and began making sounds that weren't from his singular language. He moved in my direction, stiffly, in stabbing steps, seemingly entranced, in what I didn't know was an epileptic seizure, and fell to the floor. I called for our mother, who came running and told me to get a spoon, which I brought, apprehending all, comprehending nothing. I watched as she kneeled over him and pressed the spoon against his tongue. As if, I thought, this affliction was in his mouth, as if his half sense had turned on him.

By my teens, then, I knew that a voice made strange had a great force of presence, and inside that presence could be almighty powers, loving or chaotic, able to save a life or take it. And I came to learn there was also power in the unsaid. Though I like reading the best fiction in the autobiographical first person, it has no draw for me as a writer. Even here as I write I'm uneasy, having entered into family story, stuff I've always chosen to leave off the record.

The tree where I come from is dark and gnarled and belongs to the prairie gothic. The stories, true ones, are of derangements, murders, heroisms, outsize tragedies, salvations, and seers. Most of these stories were never spoken of at home, not by the time I came along, a late last child. In what was spoken, the subtext was huge and the text sometimes cryptic. And beyond the family, in the little town of a thousand people, hours from anywhere unlike it, silence always had the last say. The mostly Anglo-Protestant stoics were dominated by, maybe subjugated to an empty landscape and killing climate. There was gossip but not much confession, wry humour but not much complaint. A lot of talk was expended to keep steady the understanding that almost everything went without saying. Early in boyhood I knew that language in its usual form could not fully describe or explain the nature of important things. Joys, fears, beliefs, high dramas, the mysteries of speech itself, in some ways these were allied with silence, and if I were to say anything about them, I'd better respect the power of the unformed and unsaid inside expression.

THE POET ROBERT HASS, ON the distinction between shamanism and spirit possession:

> Shamanism ... [is] usually a fully developed, male-dominated, politically central evolution of spirit possession; ... in the harshly repressed lives of women in most primitive societies, new songs, chants, visions, and psychic experiences keep welling up into cults which have their force because they are outside the entrenched means to vision. Because rhythm has direct access to the unconscious, because it can hypnotize us, enter our bodies and make us move, it is a power. And power is political.[1]

Why do I feel some belonging in the idea of being "outside the entrenched means to vision"? Hass connects such ecstatic rhythms to American vernacular speech and poetry. I connect them to the vernacular of the place I'm from, my particular non-American middle of nowhere; to images from boyhood; and to the secular prayers and performances of literary art.

I'm not saying that all novels need to be visionary or should have the intensity of spirit possession. Very few writers have the talent to bring and sustain that sheer linguistic power, though I admit that when reading these few writers, I sometimes wonder why I read anyone else. Not every line can be a cry from the heart, as someone once said. What most writers seem to want is a voice that feels urgent and real, whether baroque, clipped, ludic, or smartly flattened into absence of style in the high art of artlessness.

The idea has many levels, but at the simplest one, writing in an uncharted language means writing quarter-turned away from the words and phrases worn thin from use in the general surround. The idea that words are simply functional, tools employed to convey ideas or describe things, cannot account for their mystery and power. Functional language takes skill to use well, but I've always gone to the language arts to escape or complicate that function. The first measure of any literary fiction is whether or not the writer knows the difference between transparent language, that of instructional manuals and textbooks, and literary/poetic language. Open any novel. Read the first paragraph, flip to any middle page and read a few lines. Are they alive? Are they new? Is the writing free of auto-language, clichés, adjective-noun combinations we've seen before?[2] Does it hold intelligent mystery? Count the dimensions. Do the lines cast shadows and do the shadows move?

It's an old saw, but however strong the draw of life, of people and our follies and failings, of reading, however much training and work it takes for a writer to transform her sheer need to say into an organic style, language begins in the body. The body, both uniquely itself and like the bodies of others, registers the forces of nature and history. Everything reverberates, even at levels we aren't aware of. Why do dogs behave strangely prior to an earthquake? One theory is that they hear something that humans cannot, and some among us notice or half-notice the dogs and feel a foreboding. But, of course, there are fainter intimations, the kind we take in below conscious awareness. We simply do not know all that we bodily know. Some of it is outside our range of understanding. People have an outer known, and even if we could see what's there, it might not have a name.

II. in pictures

Nothing so discredits a theory of art as the suggestion that creative expression is mystical. What I'm talking about isn't so much mystical or metaphysical as unsayably physical. Nature and history register in the body whose modified energies are somehow converted into art. In this way writing can be deeply personal whether or not it's outwardly autobiographical or playing with first person positions. It's personal, too, when it displays distinct markers. These show up in diction, syntax, sound, and images. Images are necessarily apart from language even as they're simultaneously a part of it for being made of words. To the degree they're apart, they're supra- or subtextual, and the ones that seem to recur organically in the work of certain writers can be among the most personal elements in the writing.

It's interesting to think of images from one writer resituated in the work of another. Why do certain impressions strike one person more strongly than the next? Sometimes it's because ideas attach to them, or gradations of emotion very like ones that she feels. In trying to understand the organization and natural laws of her own psyche, a writer can pay attention to what gets repeated in the work or her thoughts about it. Some of the strongest images that come back to me include a figure speaking from within or possessed by fire; an enigma rising up at the point where all rational thought has been expended; and a movement, usually westward, sailing, riding, searching, into the unknown. In canto 26 of the *Inferno,* on his last voyage, Ulysses turns his back on the light of the world, God, and sails west in a vain quest for knowledge of "the world beyond the sun." Having sighted Mount Purgatory, he plots his course, but a storm blows in and wrecks the ship. It goes under, we are told, "as pleased Another." We learn his story because, in the eighth circle of Hell, Ulysses is doomed to tell it perpetually from within a flame.

The image of the punished sailor speaking in the flame is the inverse of verse, specifically the lines in Acts about the "cloven tongues like as of fire" that on Pentecost "sat upon" the Apostles. My mother read me, showed me the verse. In one take she could open her Bible to any passage she wished to find. I see her sitting at the kitchen table in the evening, reading scripture, the cigarette tip quickened and vivified with each breath as she drew it down. As in the tent, at the table I learned that the Apostles were "filled with the Holy Ghost" and "began to speak with other tongues, as the Spirit gave them utterance." The unknown tongues are of course outside reason and sense, and make me think now of another image, sighted on a different ocean. "The palm at the end of the mind,/Beyond the last thought, rises/In the bronze decor." In the palm is a bird that sings "a foreign song." Wallace Stevens's vision is of death and a realm where, one imagines, they talk strangely, if they talk at all. Seeing the bird, hearing it, we know that "it is not the reason/That makes us happy or unhappy." Beyond the last thought, beyond reason, is enigma and song, and a little weather. Which is to say, poetry. Stevens and his palms (there are others) share their small colony in my imagination with the King James version of Acts and Dante's version of Ulysses. But also with Miles Davis: "Play above what you know and finish before you're done."

AND WHAT ABOUT VISUAL ART, pictures free of language? These, too, can seem to connect figuratively certain moments and events in our lives to our ideas about them and to the world outside them. The connection has something to do with the way history inspires forms. Through stop-time images, some painters allow us to glimpse an unnamed constant, something we sense but can't see precisely, an energy whirling along all the way from creation to kingdom come. That it can't be fully captured leads us to doubt its existence, but we can hold tight to doubt. We believe in doubt.

Like certain writers, painters can render doubt through the very thing others use in attempting to abolish it: exactness. In the seventeenth century, Vermeer used the camera obscura to help him secure exactness in paintings. But the works leave unanswered questions. In the painting usually called *Girl Reading a Letter by an Open Window* the doubt is narrative. Who has written the letter? A lover? A soldier off at war? Is the open fruit on the table a symbol of marital infidelity, an allusion to the transgression of Eve, as some art historians suggest? In *Woman in Blue Reading a Letter* we have more ambiguity. Not simply, who has written the letter, but is the woman pregnant? Besides the material wealth commonly recorded in Dutch domestic paintings of the time, what's suggested by the box of pearls barely visible on the table? John Berger writes:

> The fundamental difference between Vermeer and the other Dutch interior painters is that everything in the interior he paints refers to events outside the room. Their spirit is the opposite of the domestic. The function of the closed-in corner of the room is to remind us of the infinite.

I like that Berger connects the narrative and political-historical with the infinite, and that he identifies a peculiar quality in Vermeer, the interior and exterior worlds presented together, which is also, in related senses, a quality of fiction. It's as if certain artists, in different centuries, in different arts, are all glimpsing the same thing.

We see more correspondences if we follow later allusions to the women Vermeer painted. Especially (but not exclusively) in his figurative paintings, Gerhard Richter offers something like a painterly equivalent to novelistic prose. Richter's well-known photorealist allusion to Vermeer is *Lesende*. As in the Vermeer, we see a woman reading, in profile, her left side visible, her hair tied up, in this case with a scrunchie, here immortalized. The pearls in the box in Vermeer are now a pearl or fake-pearl necklace. But the light is from the opposite direction, from behind. And we can see what she's looking at — a newspaper or review supplement — but is she in fact reading at all, or looking at the image mid-page? And where exactly is she? These observations and questions aren't original to me. Richter's figurative paintings have always generated responses, on technique, on their possible political dimensions, some at odds with others. The artist's own statements can be elusive or slyly contradictory, and just produce more questions. This kind of uncertainty feels modern. *Lesende* ("Reading") is painting as snapshot, with the background out of focus. It has the casualness of a film photograph, but the casualness is constructed and so we see not just surfaces but depths, only some of which are art-historical.

Richter sometimes draws, too, from the lived-historical, the autobiographical. The woman in *Lesende* is his wife, Sabine. He's painted from photographs members of his family who were in the Nazi party (*Uncle Rudi*) or killed by it. Richter's aunt (see *Aunt Marianne*) was one of thousands of mentally ill people sterilized and "euthanized" by starvation, likely by the very man who became Richter's father-in-law. These autobiographical paintings (Richter himself, as a child, is in *Aunt Marianne*) are only slightly more readable than those at some remove from the first person. Most complex and elusive is his fifteen-painting sequence, *Baader-Meinhof* (October 18, 1977), from 1988, remarkable, blurred photorealist paintings of the Red Army Faction members, alive and dead. Richter described this series of paintings as "dull grey, mostly very blurred, diffuse. Their presence is the hard to bear refusal to answer." Later he said the paintings were about "compassion and grief." The critic Kaja Silverman writes that "painting is more for Richter than an aesthetic practice. It is also a way of inhabiting the world, a mode of thinking ..." Richter: "I might also call it redemption. Or hope — the hope that I can after all effect something through painting." It's worth noting that Richter, a virtuosic artist, has little respect for "mere virtuosity." He has found his own language, quarter-turned away from simple, functional representation.

NOW LET'S REVERSE THE ANGLE and return to images in writing, putting the prose before the picture. In the story "Baader-Meinhof" we find one of Don DeLillo's characters in an art gallery, looking at Richter's paintings. It isn't just the uncertain image in the painting that's described, but the uncertain perception of the artwork:

> In the painting of the coffins being carried through a large crowd, she didn't know they were coffins at first. It took her a long moment to see the crowd itself. There was the crowd, mostly an ashy blur with a few figures in the center-right foreground discernible as individuals stand-ing with their backs to the viewer, and then there was a break near the top of the canvas, a pale strip of earth or roadway, and then another mass of people or trees, and it took some time to understand that the three whitish objects near the center of the picture were coffins being carried through the crowds or simply propped on biers.

The word "crowd" appears four times (hiding the word "word"), an assertion of an indistinct thing. DeLillo describes the struggle to understand, a subject that's enormous in our lived experience and therefore true-feeling and belief-making in our readerly experience. On some level this struggle is political; on another it occurs in that most contested of spaces, the enclosed self.

DeLillo has added a third layer of mediation to the captured event (fiction rendering painting rendering the photo on which the painting is based). Blur exists within or on the margins of a form rendered with rare exactness. Like words, material forms vibrate at the edges. The image is there in Tomas Tranströmer's poem "Out in the Open": "I have seen the cross hanging in the cool church vaults./At times it resembles a split-second snapshot of something/ moving at tremendous speed." Like reality, certain artworks hum with disturbance and are ever unresolved. Maybe that's why they seem to know us. Maybe the peculiarities of their features fit into our own features of reception or intuition, and the art becomes for us a kind of perfect, known stranger. In fiction, it isn't simply ourselves that we recognize in the predicaments of a given story. It's the particular mix of us and not, sense and not, there and not, all the base pairs of a distinct telling, its determining codes, all the secrets awaiting their expression that we sometimes find in those places where the sure and unsure meet.

III. in story

The other quotation pinned above my desk when I started out, from Emerson: "A true method ... tells its own story, makes its own feet, creates its own form. Is its own apology."

MY AUNT ALICE FIRST APPEARED to me in my mid-teens as a pair of pink slippers being wrapped in red-and-gold paper. I'd walked into the kitchen. Mom was at the table. "Who are those for?" I'd never heard of Aunt Alice. From that Christmas forward, cards from her were put out for display with the others. The jitterscript handwriting, legible to Mom but not me. In the private collection of books and papers discovered after Mom died was a yearbook. During the war Alice had trained as a nurse in Toronto and graduated at the top of her class. Her classmates wished her well. All else we know is that she and my mother were very close, that she was a talented musician, and that after graduating she came west and soon thereafter something happened. Depression? Schizophrenic episode? We, Alice's nieces and nephews, don't know, but health professionals were engaged and a treatment proposed. Abdicating his position, her father made his oldest daughter, my mother, sign the forms, and Alice was medically lobotomized.

She lived the rest of her life in North Battleford, about two hours from our town. Her youngest sister Joan had a family there and visited her often. She lived part of that time in a large brick psychiatric hospital and part of it in the community. I came to learn that my mom and dad saw Alice there. I've seen pictures of them together from the sixties or seventies. And I came to understand that Mom confided these few details in my oldest sister, and must have decided at some point that all her children should know of Alice, or at least of her existence. After both my parents had died, my siblings and I talked about arranging to meet Alice, but decided against it. She died in 2013.

The story of Alice, for me, is part of the story of my mother, the one I'm telling in this essay, in a few images, a few hard facts. I won't tell the fuller story about Mom, of poverty, heroism (hers), the death of a soldier off at war, a Job's worth of burdens, conversion, and faith. Of these, I heard her speak only once of the heroism, not because she was proud (she hid away the commendation from the Queen) but because it was one of the few times in her life that she had had an adventure. And once she spoke of the soldier. The image is of her reading a love letter from him that arrived the day after his parents received the news that he'd been killed in action.

Of the burdens she said nothing. She did say a lot about faith.

IF THE FIRST KNOWN SIGNIFICANCE of formative experiences is emotional, the last is political. A rural kid witnesses his mother in a spiritual trance, speaking strangely, and soon thereafter believes he himself has been possessed by the spirit of the Holy Ghost. He's told he has spoken a lost or divine language. Years later, when he sees the phenomenon as an induced emoting, both an eruption of spiritual sensation and part of a designed exploitation of people in need, he can still access the feeling (not just the memory of the feeling) of possession. It's either akin to what some artists feel as they're making art or it's the same thing. The feeling is personal, private, and yet places him on the margins of a marginal community, back in a remote place like the one he came from. Not to suggest that his eyes roll back in his head and he begins channelling when he sits at his desk, but this remote place twice on the margins is where he goes to write.

It's also a place that can't really be known, even to himself. When some writers are most moved by the spirit, they're least conscious of what's happening to them. This escaping of self-consciousness seems to make them more receptive. They seem to be speaking (writing) *in* one place but *from* another, *in* one moment but *of* another and *from* the moment to come. The state is alive and in flux, and to the degree that it's open and has been prepared for, it responds to the immediate world and history, and maybe to harbingers of the future. Walter Benjamin wrote: "Without exception the great writers make their deductions in a world that comes after them, as the streets of Paris in Baudelaire's poems were there only after 1900 and Dostoevsky's characters, too, did not pre-date him." If we see the real world through the imagined one, the real one is changed. But there's more to this idea. These unselfconscious, semi-possessed writers present reality as it is, but not as it is self-evidently; they write of the world as it's becoming, both brightly through new evidences, and dimly, so dimly that they can perceive it intuitively, construing the whispers inside a white noise. Afterward some will find meanings and structures they weren't conscious of in their making. Some of these meanings can only be read sideways, and their refusal to resolve into neat order feels necessary or even emancipatory. The poet Wendell Berry wrote: "As soon as the generals and the politicos can predict the motions of your mind, lose it."

Here I'm talking about artistic concerns that only gesture at the political. Artists can be engaged with the world or they can try to remove themselves to a place far outside the common exchange, out there with prophets and other seers. But of course it's not possible to be entirely outside of things. Agnes Martin left the New York art world, traveled the continent, and ended up living on a mesa in New Mexico. Of her shift from figurative to grid paintings, Martin claimed that she'd found a form with "no hint of any cause in this world." But it was the world that led her to the shift. The act of turning a back means nothing without someone or something to turn the back to.[3]

If a writer is awake to things, her instincts necessarily have moral and political dimensions. If these dimensions are foremost, the demands on the form are extreme, and writers who fail to meet them write thinly, issue fiction or meretricious sentimental stuff that tends to sell a lot. But when writers do meet the demands, something new enters the world. It's out ahead and turns to look back at us now and then. What is that look? Is it reassuring? Is it sly? Is it two or more things at once? What if, page to page, there's more than one thing going on *all* the time?

What if the writing offers recognition *and* strangeness? As a reader, as a writer, this radical push-pull is what I look for.

A few weeks ago my brother's heart stopped. Because a doctor just happened to be nearby, John was resuscitated. In hospital he acquired an infection that specialists worried could be necrotizing fasciitis. One or another of his siblings was with him every day for two weeks, partly to translate for the doctors and nurses. He's very good-natured, and, as I learned, physically brave. For a few days it seemed he was losing touch with the world and what he loves in it, but one afternoon he woke briefly and saw a flock of pigeons wheeling outside the window, said his word for "birdies," and fell back asleep, dreaming of what I can't imagine, and I knew, in the wake of what I'd understood, in that moment of strange recognition, that he was returning to himself.

NOTES

1. "Listening and Making." Hass is describing the findings of English anthropologist Ian Lewis.

2. Do you find a "national treasure" or an "honest effort," a "current climate" or "mass exodus" or "animated discussion" or even a "sunny day" — cheap prefab words brought home in the back of a third-hand junker?

3. My mother and Martin were born into the same world, the same Saskatchewan, ten years and one hundred miles apart, but lived universes from one another. In her last years, my mother, who always wanted to be a writer, took up painting.

A PORT ACCENT
Michael Ondaatje

*S*OMEONE ONCE MENTIONED THE PHRASE "a port accent" to me. A ship will dock at Aden or Port Said, and the overheard talk in those harbours will be not so much the language of that country, but a language based on commerce — speedy, efficient, an informal *esperanto* among the ship chandlers, a lingo crushing nouns and phrases from various languages together rather like the commentaries during hockey games in Quebec that include French and English colloquialisms. This non-existent but useful language is understood by any water-sider along the Suez Canal or along any Asian or African coast. Calvino comically exaggerates this method of communication when speaking of Marco Polo on his travels:

> Newly arrived and totally ignorant of the Levantine languages, Marco Polo could express himself only with gestures, leaps, cries of wonder and of horror, animal barkings or hootings, or with objects he took from his knapsacks — ostrich plumes, pea-shooters, quartzes — which he arranged in front of him.[1]

The word *pidgin* derives from the Chinese pronunciation of the English word *business*. It is often the language we hear in multilingual kitchens where cooks and waiters speak in mime or shorthand. It is the language that is hinted at and leapt into in G.V. Desani's *All About H. Hatterr* and in Sam Selvon's great book, *The Lonely Londoners*. It is that informal and active language Rushdie often embraces in *Midnight Children*, in response to the portrait of English India in E.M. Forster. Rushdie some years later will speak generously and perceptively on how in a way *Passage to India* inspired him to draw on his own Indian English voice.

I was very lucky when I was at Cambridge that I overlapped briefly with E.M. Forster. We were at the same college, King's, and I met him a few times, and he was interested in my Indian background and I was interested in his Indian background, and I was a great admirer of *A Passage to India*. But actually, when I started to write *Midnight's Children*, in some ways I wrote it against that very cool, controlled, Forsterian English.... I began to wonder what a language might sound like that was not cool but hot, that was noisy and crowded and vulgar and sensual in a way that the Indian reality is. And that, in a way, is not represented by that Forsterian language.

And so, certainly, the language project of *Midnight's Children* was, in some degree, a conscious piece of writing against the language in which English people have written about India, most notably in *A Passage to India*, which I think is a masterpiece, so it's not that I want to criticize the book. Sometimes you find out your voice ... by trying to write like other people. Sometimes you find it by trying to write unlike other people, and, for me, trying to write unlike Forster was a way in which I found out how to write.[2]

In contrast one sees a writer like V.S. Naipaul having to choose the official dialect so he can exist in the canon. Whereas for me, during a festival in Jamaica, one of the great moments was hearing Cindy Breakspeare stand up and read from an early Naipaul novel in a West Indian dialect. It was a wonder, and one longed to have Naipaul witness the power of the voice and the response to the dialect he had walked away from, that included port accents and dialects as well as literary wit and pacing.

At one end of the scale, writers such as James and Conrad and Naipaul, and many other unlikely outsiders, came up the Thames and slipped into the established voice of English literature. But many arrived and hung on to a home-born voice, as can be heard, for instance, captured in those Trinidadian songs by new immigrant musicians in the 1950s such as Lord Kitchener; and especially Lord Beginner in his classic song on cricket, "Victory Test Match." One can find such examples on a remarkable album called *London Is the Place for Me.*

2.

A GENERATION OR TWO EARLIER, Gandhi, after a sea journey to England, published a few of his journal entries in a magazine called *The Vegetarian.* It's a tender recollection, remembering how he lived on the sweetmeats and fruit he had brought on board with him, and how he played the ship's piano. Up at eight in the morning, he found the arrangements of the water closets astonishing: "We do not get water there, and are obliged to use pieces of paper." Gandhi is quite sentimental about his attachment to London, "with its teaching institutions, public galleries, public parks and vegetarian restaurants." According to various reports he was apparently always in the best of spirits during his sea journeys, spending most of the night "under the canopy of the starlit sky."

But, in 1909, on a journey from London to Cape Town, a fifteen-day journey by ship, Gandhi decided to write *Hind Swaraj*, a book that formulated a plan for Indian Independence. It was to be his first book, and this is one of the great stories of a book being written at sea. "The obsession was so great that he began writing on the ship stationary with a pencil. The thoughts were coming so furiously that he could not stop writing. When his right hand began to ache, he switched to writing with his left."[3] This would become a habit all Gandhi's life. Whenever his right hand got tired, he wrote with the left. His left hand's writing was apparently more legible.

Tagore had also made a crucial journey, from India to England by ship in 1912, that would completely change his life. He spent the whole journey translating and reworking his Bengali poems from Gitanjali. And it was this manuscript, lionized by Yeats and other English poets shortly afterwards, that led to him being awarded the Nobel Prize.

3.

"TO HAVE A GREAT LANGUAGE," it is said, "you first of all must have a great Navy." For it's essential to have a map of your territories. A map clarifies at a glance the political perspective of the mapmaker, as to where power lies. We look at "North America" and automatically are used to seeing Canada far away to the north, in its less significant distance. Marlow in *Heart of Darkness* looks at a map of Africa and sees a still untranslated white space in the distance, where whatever is there is still unrevealed. We look at maps of Sri Lanka, and find Colombo will always be at the centre, at the horizon line of our gaze, while far into the north is Jaffna.

But in a remarkable recent work by T. Shanaathanan, called *The Incomplete Thombu*, the book startlingly begins with an almost unrecognizable map of Sri Lanka — until you realize it is upside down (with place names and towns printed the right way up). So Point Pedro and Keerimalai and Kodikamam are surprisingly at our natural eye level, while the southern part of the island, where the power and the narrative voice usually exist, are now somewhere to the distant north, in fact not even on the map — it is offstage. The farthest north, or "south," we get is Vavuniya.

Winslow's Tamil dictionary defines a *Thombu* as a public register of lands — it is a word not used in any country outside Sri Lanka. And what we have in Shanaathanan's book, like any *Thombu*, is not only a glance and interpretation of a place, but an in-depth study of a region's local history, with careful documenting of properties and lands belonging to Tamil-speaking people prior to "single or multiple displacements" from their homes in the north of Sri Lanka between 1983 and 2009. The way the data is presented is multiple: first there's an informal drawing by the displaced occupant of what he remembers of the property and where things had existed — a well, a fence, a palmyrah tree, an office, a vegetable garden. This is followed by an architectural drawing of the same site based on that informal drawing, then a quiet, devastating statement by the owners of how the property was lost. And then a drawing by Shanaathanan based on an image from that statement.

But it is Shanaathanan's reinvented and realigned map at the start of his book that prepares the reader for this more accurate perspective in order to discover what really took place on the Jaffna Peninsula in a time of war. It is no longer just an abstract land of salt-water lagoons and a surrounding sea, supposedly unmapped and unrecorded and distant.

4.

IN THE EARLY TWENTIETH CENTURY the most popular bestsellers had to do with adventurous travel abroad, mostly about English travellers going abroad. Marlow's river journey was just one of that genre. *King Solomon's Mines*, the Tarzan novels, etc., etc. The list is endless. On a smaller scale you even had Toad's yearning for such adventurous travel in *The Wind in the Willows* — which may have been the best book of the lot. Kenneth Rexroth summarizing an essential habit of plot in Sherlock Holmes stories summarized it as, "India, China, the South Seas, the Far West, his characters come home from the ends of the earth to blackmail and murder each other."

But world literature is full of reverse journeys by other cultures. And the air currents of literary influences that result in the merging of art forms, subject matter, alternate perspectives, and above all, translations, alter our world subliminally and more profoundly than we know. We move, drift, climb into, and tunnel from one country to another. It is the central story of our time. Compare all this porousness to that line by William Carlos Williams: "The Pure products of America go crazy."

Yes, they do. Whereas this crashing together of places and genres, somewhat like the invention of those fluid port accents, is joyous, quick-witted, at times almost unbelievable. As in the meeting and friendship between the Cambridge mathematician G.H. Hardy with the completely unknown Indian mathematical genius, Ramanujan, in 1913, or the way Ford Madox Ford, the heir of pre-Raphaelites, sat down to discuss "literary impressionism" with a Polish sea captain named Józef Korzeniowski. There are meetings and influences everywhere. James M. Cain, author of dark noir novels such as *The Postman Always Rings Twice*, said his favourite book of all time was *Alice in Wonderland*. (In a reversal, Wittgenstein supposedly loved thrillers.) And C.L.R. James, a lifelong Marxist who wrote *The Black Jacobins* on the Haitian Revolution and *Beyond a Boundary*, one of the great books on cricket and politics, grew up in Trinidad loving Thackeray's *Vanity Fair*. "Thackeray, not Marx, bears the heaviest responsibility for me," he said, claiming to almost know it by heart.

WE LEARN FROM THE OLD as well as the new, just as today we can translate ourselves with the abundance of available foreign work, this great gift of the twentieth century where we learn what is beyond a boundary. Gandhi's politics, V.S. Naipaul points out, were greatly influenced by Ruskin. He even translated Ruskin into Gujarati. The Polish artist Czapski gave weekly lectures on Proust while in a prisoner of war camp three hundred miles from Moscow. Milosz in 1943 Warsaw was translating *The Waste Land*. Janusz would stage Tagore's *The Post Office* with a group of orphans in the Warsaw Ghetto. Adam Zagajewski writes that Ernst Jünger was reading the sixteenth-century poet, Ariosto, while in the trenches in 1917, and at the same time collecting more than a hundred species of beetle. And there's Ananda Coomaraswamy, from Sri Lanka, one of the great gatherers of Asian art, showing this influential collection to Jacob Epstein and Eric Gill while in London.

Writers are not just altered by the influence of language. Robert Creeley admitted his line breaks were learned by carefully listening to Miles Davis's version of "But Not for Me." We are told Krishnamurti loved Westerns. And in the strangest connection that I have come across between art forms — the jazz musician Charlie Parker (so a recent biographer believes) was possibly drawn to heroin because of his lifelong love of Sherlock Holmes stories and the great fictional detective's similar addiction.

Violette Leduc, the author of *La Batarde*, once remarked, "Recently I pressed Beckett's *Molloy* against one cheek, then against the other. A great writer is a great brother, he just falls into your life, it is stronger than any bond of blood." Those bonds of blood and inheritance in literature exist not just between countries, but between the Then and the Now. Writers might leap back in time to retell a story by an overlooked voice or character, as Jean Rhys, born and growing up in the Caribbean, did with the first Mrs. Rochester in *Wide Sargasso Sea*, "her right hand married to Jane Eyre," as Derek Walcott has written. Coetzee also does that in *The Master of St. Petersberg*, unravelling a version of Dostoyevsky by focusing on and investigating a suppressed chapter in the Russian's novel, *Demons*, that was never reinstated. This too is our inheritance. We are, let's face it, this mix of time and place. And not the pure products of America going crazy. So that somewhere, in such a world swirled by so many political and literary trade winds, one almost imagines the possibility of a meeting between Capability Brown and Calamity Jane.

It is where and when the left hand meets to right. It's a much better alternative than characters returning from the ends of the earth to blackmail and murder each other.

NOTES

1. Italo Calvino, *Invisible Cities.*
2. See: *https://www.theguardian.com/books/2017/may/27/thirty-years-of-hay-festival-christopher-hitchens-margaret-atwood-hilary-mantel-in-conversation.*
3. See: *http://www.liveindia.com/freedomfighters/MohandasKaramchandGandhi.html.*

FALSE CONSCIOUSNESS

Leanne Betasamosake Simpson

1.

ziibi is writing her story
one drop at a time
one breath after another
carving it into the clay and bedrock
embellishing it with snow melt and rain drops
moving it from headwaters to ocean
owah. ziibi is writing her story

the part at the beginning is dead slow
expansive
hard to paddle, because there is no current
more like a lake than the river
more like a river than a story
more like a song made of terns and eagles,
bears and whitefish,
beaver, moose.
owah. ziibi is singing her song

story picks up a little in the middle

but it's too big and too long and you're lost
seemingly no beginning
seemingly no ending
point to point
one bend after another
aching stroke after aching stroke
always sun, always mosquitoes
owah. ziibi is writing her story

story gets really moving near the end
current is fast
there are ramparts and rapids and smoke
we're all sure we're going somewhere
and no one feels lost
story after story after story
merged into black spruce, birch
mint, bush tea
the sky

ziibi is writing her story
one drop at a time
one breath after another
carving it into clay and bedrock
embellishing it with snow melt and rain drops
moving it from headwaters to ocean
owah. ziibi is writing her story

2.

they told me: stories are seeds

they told me: seeds are hot-wired with the potential and the kinetic of
    the everything

they told me: birds carry the seeds and with the right conditions, some
    grow

they told me: weweni, because sometimes the stories are not stories,

they are the intended

i) sheer egoism (read: we stand on guard for thee)
ii) aesthetic enthusiasm (read: white luxury)
iii) historic impulse (read: white whimsical)
iv) political purpose (read: bowling, knitting, retweets)

she told me: stories are our birthright

she told me: stories are beings in their own right

she told me: just whisper

she told me: tellers are conduits, nothing else

perseverance. love. luck. endurance.

he told me: stories die trapped in the deadness of bleached trees

he told me: stories are smothered in the smugness of english

he told me: stories stand next to meaningless in the uni-dimensionality
    of capitalism

he told me: stories are only freedom in the ethos of sound and relation

live what it means to be human, because you are a cancelled human.

we (exclusive) told me: your body is a node in our assemblage

we (exclusive) told me: you as story

we (exclusive) told me: write, but don't pretend it means something

we (exclusive) told me: write, while we ignite into revolutions

write, but only as labour in bringing opaque to purpose

3.

there was broken weather
never-ending rain
and then the flood.
basements were ruined
internets caught on fire
burned from nothing to nothing
green toxic blue fumes
we sat on the log. again. together.

in the absence of light
we picked 10-dollar bills
out of each other's bone marrow

in the absence of rupture
we took turns
falling into dream

diving deeper and deeper
in the deficit of oxygen
through
insult and call out
ego and ego
swimming
drowning
sinking

i reach out for
my paw full of earth
and instead
you hold my hand.

NOTES
In Nishnaabemowin *ziibi* means river, *weweni* means carefully.

ABOUT THE AUTHORS

MARGARET ATWOOD was born in 1939 in Ottawa and spent the earlier part of her youth in the woods for two-thirds of every year. Her novels include *The Handmaid's Tale* and *Alias Grace* — both of which have recently been serialized for streaming — *The Blind Assassin* (which won the Booker Prize in 2000), The MaddAddam Trilogy, *The Heart Goes Last*, and *Hag-Seed*, a novel revisiting of *The Tempest*. Her most recent collection of poetry is *The Door*. Her nonfiction works include *Survival*, her 1972 attempt to demonstrate that Canadian literature did — at that time — exist, *Payback: Debt and the Shadow Side of Wealth*, and *A Writer on Writing*. Her most recent graphic series is *Angel Catbird*. She has served in various capacities with several organizations, including PEN International and BirdLife International. She continues to be surprised by human behaviour, both noble and not.

NICOLE BROSSARD. Born in Montreal in 1943. Poet, novelist, and essayist, twice Governor General's Literary Award winner for her poetry, Nicole Brossard has published more than forty books since 1965. Many among those books have been translated into English: *Mauve Desert*, *The Aerial Letter*, *Lovhers*, *The Blue Books*, *Installations*, *Museum of Bone and Water*, *Yesterday at the Hotel Clarendon*, and *Notebook of Roses and Civilization* (translated by Erín Moure and Robert Majzels, shortlisted for the 2008 Griffin International Poetry Prize).

She has cofounded and codirected the avant-garde literary magazine *La Barre du Jour* (1965–1975), has codirected the film *Some American Feminists* (1976) and coedited the acclaimed *Anthologie de la poésie des femmes au Québec*, first published in 1991 then in 2003. She has also won le Grand Prix de Poésie du Festival International de Trois-Rivières in 1989 and in 1999. In 1991, she was awarded le Prix Athanase-David (the highest literary recognition in Quebec). She is a member of l'Académie des lettres du Québec. She won the W.O. Mitchell 2003 Prize and the Canadian Council of Arts Molson Prize in 2006.

Her work has influenced a whole generation of poets and feminists and has been translated widely into English and Spanish and is also available in German, Italian, Japanese, Slovenian, Romanian, Catalan, Portuguese, and other languages. In 2010 she was made an officer of the Order of Canada and in 2013 a chevalière de l'Ordre national du Québec.

Her most recent books in English are *White Piano* (translated by Erín Moure and Robert Majzels, 2013) and *Ardour* (translated by Angela Carr, 2015). In 2013 she received le Prix international de littérature francophone Benjamin Fondane.

Nicole Brossard writes and lives in Montréal.

DAVID CHARIANDY was born in Toronto and now lives in Vancouver. His first novel, entitled *Soucouyant* was nominated for several literary prizes and published internationally. His second novel, *Brother*, won the 2017 Rogers Writers' Trust Fiction Award.

GEORGE ELLIOTT CLARKE: The fourth Poet Laureate of Toronto (2012–15) and seventh Parliamentary Poet Laureate (2016–17), George Elliott Clarke is a revered artist in song, drama, fiction, screenplay, essays, and poetry. Now teaching African-Canadian literature at the University of Toronto, Clarke has taught at Duke, McGill, the University of British Columbia, and Harvard. He holds eight honorary doctorates, plus appointments to the Order of Nova Scotia and the Order of Canada. His recognitions include the Pierre Elliott Trudeau Fellows Prize, the Governor General's Literary Award for Poetry, the National Magazine Gold Award for Poetry, the Premiul Poesis (Romania), the Dartmouth Book Award for Fiction, the Eric Hoffer Book Award for Poetry (U.S.), and the Dr. Martin Luther King Jr. Achievement Award. Clarke's work is the subject of *Africadian Atlantic: Essays on George Elliott Clarke* (2012), edited by Joseph Pivato.

SHEILA FISCHMAN undertook her first translation, Roch Carrier's first novel *La Guerre, Yes Sir!*, as a way to immerse herself in the French language as spoken here and now. Despite years of French courses at school and university, she was far from bilingual.

The book was a success, she enjoyed the exercise, even discovered that she might have a certain knack for it. Nearly two hundred translations later she believes that she made the right decision when she moved to Montreal to try making her living as a literary translator.

She has been awarded prizes, honorary doctorates, and the Molson Prize in the Arts — the first translator to be so honoured. A member of the Order of Canada and a *chevalière* of l'Ordre national du Québec, she has become by choice a proud Montrealer and Quebecer. She says that translation is not what she does but who she is.

CAMILLA GIBB is the author of four novels, including *Mouthing the Words* and *Sweetness in the Belly*, as well as a memoir, *This Is Happy*.

HIROMI GOTO is an emigrant from Japan who gratefully resides on the Unceded Musqueam, Skwxwú7mesh, and Tsleil-Waututh Territories. Her first novel, *Chorus of Mushrooms*, a tale of three generations of Japanese-Canadian women living in the Alberta prairies, explores immigration, cultural dissonance, systemic racism, the nature of storytelling, and post-coloniality. Her novel was the 1995 Commonwealth Writers' Prize Best First Book, Canada and Caribbean Region, and co-winner of the Canada-Japan Book Award. Her second adult novel, *The Kappa Child*, was awarded the 2001 James Tiptree Jr. Memorial Award. She's published three novels for children and youth, a book of poetry, and a collection of short stories (adult). Her other honours include The Sunburst Award and the Carl Brandon Parallax Award. Hiromi is a mentor in The Writer's Studio Program at Simon Fraser University, a mentor for The Pierre Elliott Trudeau Foundation, and is a board member of *Plenitude* magazine. She is currently at work trying to decolonize her relationship to writing, and to be a responsible guest on Turtle Island.

RAWI HAGE, born in 1964 in Beirut, is a child of the war. At the age of eighteen, Hage immigrated to the United States. In New York, after Arabic and French, he adopted his third language, which became the one he would write in: English. He's the recipient of many national and international awards. His work has been translated into thirty languages. He resides in Montreal.

MICHAEL HELM was born in Saskatchewan. He attended the universities of Saskatchewan and Toronto. His novels *After James*, *Cities of Refuge*, *In the Place of Last Things*, and *The Projectionist* are all national or international prize finalists. His nonfiction includes writings on social justice workers, bioscientists, and reading in translation; and critical essays on fiction, poetry, photography, and painting. He's an editor at *Brick* magazine and teaches in the Creative Writing program at York University. He lives in rural Ontario.

STEPHEN HENIGHAN is the author of five novels, most recently *The Path of the Jaguar* (2016) and *Mr. Singh Among the Fugitives* (2017), four short-story collections, including *Blue River and Red Earth* (2018), and six books of non-fiction, notably *Sandino's Nation: Ernesto Cardenal and Sergio Ramírez Writing Nicaragua, 1940–2012* (2014). Henighan's short stories have been published in more than thirty-five magazines and anthologies, including *Lettre Internationale*, *International Quarterly*, *Ploughshares*, *The Malahat Review*, *Best Canadian Stories*, *The Fiddlehead*, *The New Quarterly*, and *Queen's Quarterly*. He has published essays and feature articles in *The Times Literary Supplement*, the *Montreal Gazette*, *The Walrus*, *Toronto Life*, *The Globe and Mail*, *Guernica* (New York), and *The Quarterly Conversation*, and scholarly articles in *The Modern Language Review*, *Comparative Literature Studies*, *The Journal of Transatlantic Studies*, *Bulletin of Hispanic Studies*, *Hispanic Review*, and numerous other journals. Henighan is a columnist for *Geist* magazine and has translated novels into English from Portuguese and Romanian. He won first prize in the 2016 McNally Robinson/*Prairie Fire* Short Fiction Contest and has been a finalist for the Governor General's Literary Award, the Canada Prize in the Humanities, a National Magazine Award, a Western Magazine Award, and the *Malahat Review* Novella Contest. He lives in Guelph, Ontario.

LAWRENCE HILL, a professor of creative writing at the University of Guelph, is the author of ten books, including *The Illegal*, *The Book of Negroes*, *Any Known Blood*, and *Black Berry, Sweet Juice: On Being Black and White in Canada*. He is the winner of various awards, including The Commonwealth Writers' Prize, the Rogers Writers' Trust Fiction Prize, and two-time winner of CBC Radio's Canada Reads. Hill delivered the 2013 Massey Lectures, based on his nonfiction book *Blood: The Stuff of Life*. He co-wrote the adaptation for the six-part television miniseries *The Book of Negroes*, which attracted millions of viewers in the United States and Canada and won eleven Canadian Screen Awards in 2016. The recipient of seven honorary doctorates from Canadian universities, as well as the 2017 Canada Council for the Arts Molson Prize, Hill served as chair of the jury of the 2016 Scotiabank Giller Prize. He is the grandson and son of African-American soldiers who served with the American Army during the First and Second World Wars, respectively, and is working on a new novel about the African-American soldiers who helped build the Alaska Highway in 1942–43. He is a Member of the Order of Canada, and lives with his family in Hamilton, Ontario, and in Woody Point, Newfoundland.

GREG HOLLINGSHEAD has published seven books of fiction, including *The Roaring Girl*, *The Healer*, *Bedlam*, and, most recently, *Act Normal*. He has won the Governor General's Literary Award for Fiction and the Rogers Writers' Trust Fiction Prize and been shortlisted for the Giller Prize. Currently professor emeritus at the University of Alberta and Member of the Order of Canada, in 2011–12 Greg served as chair of the Writers' Union of Canada and from 1999 to 2017 as director of the Writing Studio at the Banff Centre. He lives in Toronto with his wife Rosa Spricer, a psychologist in private practice.

LEE MARACLE is the author of a number of critically acclaimed literary works and is the co-editor of a number of anthologies, including the award-winning publication, *My Home As I Remember*. Ms. Maracle is a member of the Stó:lō nation. In 2009, Maracle received an Honorary Doctor of Letters from St. Thomas University. Maracle recently received the Queen's Diamond Jubilee Medal and the premier's award for excellence in the arts. Her latest works are the novel *Celia's*

Song, Memory Serves and other Words (creative non-fiction), and *Talking to the Diaspora*.

LISA MOORE has written two collections of short stories, *Degrees of Nakedness* and *Open*, and four novels, *Alligator*, *February*, *Caught*, and, for young adults, *Flannery*. She has adapted her novel *February* for the stage. Her most recent work was a radio-play collaboration that included several writers and was produced for the Woody Point Short Waves, Short Stories series. Lisa has written for the magazines *Canadian Art*, *Walrus*, *Azure*, *Elle*, and *Brick*, as well as *The Globe and Mail*, the *National Post*, and the *Guardian*. She is working on a collection of short stories and painting a series of waterfalls. Lisa teaches creative writing at Memorial University in Newfoundland.

MICHAEL ONDAATJE was born in Sri Lanka in 1943, and in 1962 he moved to Canada. He is the author of several novels, books of poetry, a memoir, and a nonfiction book on film editing. His books of poetry include *The Cinnamon Peeler* and *Handwriting*. His novels include *The English Patient*, *In the Skin of a Lion*, *Anil's Ghost*, *Divisadero*, and *The Cat's Table*. He lives in Toronto.

HEATHER O'NEILL is a novelist, short-story writer, screenwriter, and essayist. Her work, which includes *Lullabies for Little Criminals*, *The Girl Who Was Saturday Night*, and *Daydreams of Angels*, has been shortlisted for the Governor General's Literary Award for Fiction, The Orange Prize for Fiction, and the Scotiabank Giller Prize for two consecutive years. She has won CBC Canada Reads, the Paragraphe MacLennan Prize for Fiction, and the Danuta Gleed Literary Award. Her latest novel, *The Lonely Hearts Hotel*, was published in February 2017. Born and raised in Montreal, O'Neill lives there today.

MARIE HÉLÈNE POITRAS is a Montreal writer who was born in 1975 in Ottawa. In 2016, together with Léah Clermont-Dion, she published the nonfiction book *Les superbes*. She won the prix littéraire France-Québec for her novel *Griffintown*, which was subsequently published in France, Italy, and in an English translation by Sheila Fischman by Cormorant Books. Her first novel, *Soudain le Minotaure*, won the Prix Anne-Hébert. She is also the author of the collection of short stories, *La mort de Mignonne et autres histoires*, and a series for young adults, *Rock & Rose*. She works for Radio-Canada.

PASCALE QUIVIGER was born in Montreal in 1969. She obtained a master's degree in philosophy from Université de Montréal and a studio arts degree from Concordia University. She has published five novels, one short-story collection, an essay, and two art books. Her first novel, *Le cercle parfait*, was awarded a Governal General's Literary Award for French Fiction, and its English translation was shortlisted for the Scotiabank Giller Prize. After spending ten years in Italy, Pascale moved to Nottingham (U.K.) in 2008. She currently works as a writer, a painter, and a hypnotherapist. She lives with her daughter, her husband, and their little dog.

NINO RICCI's first novel was the internationally acclaimed *Lives of the Saints*, published in seventeen countries and the winner a host of awards, including the Governor General's Literary Award for Fiction and England's Betty Trask Award and Winifred Holtby Memorial Prize. It formed the first volume of a trilogy that continued with *In a Glass House* and *Where She Has Gone*, shortlisted for the Giller Prize. The *Lives of the Saints* trilogy was adapted as a television miniseries starring Sophia Loren, Jessica Paré, and Kris Kristofferson.

Ricci is also the author of the novels *Testament*, winner of the Trillium Award, and *The Origin of Species*, which earned him a second Governor General's Literary Award. His short biography *Pierre Elliott Trudeau* formed part of Penguin's Extraordinary Canadians series. His most recent novel is *Sleep*, a national bestseller and winner of the Canadian Authors Award for Fiction. Ricci was appointed to the Order of Canada in 2011, and is a past president of PEN Canada. He lives in Toronto with his wife, writer Erika de Vasconcelos, and their children.

EDEN ROBINSON is a Haisla/Heiltsuk author who grew up in Haisla, British Columbia. Her first book, *Traplines*, a collection of short stories, won the Winifred Holtby Memorial Prize and was a *New York Times* Notable Book of the Year in 1998. *Monkey Beach*, her first novel, was shortlisted for both The Giller Prize and the Governor General's Literary Award for Fiction in 2000 and won the B.C. Book Prize's Ethel Wilson Fiction Prize. Her latest novel, *Son of a Trickster*, was shortlisted for the 2017 Scotiabank Giller Prize.

LEANNE BETASAMOSAKE SIMPSON is a Michi Saagiig Nishnaabeg scholar, writer, and artist. She is on the faculty at the Dechinta Centre for Research and Learning in Denendeh and is a distinguished visiting professor at Ryerson University in Toronto. She is author of *As We Have Always Done*, *Dancing on Our Turtle's Back*, *The Gift Is in the Making*, *Islands of Decolonial Love*, and *This Accident of Being Lost*, which was shortlisted for the Rogers Writers' Trust Fiction Prize. Leanne is a member of Alderville First Nation, in Ontario, Canada.

MADELEINE THIEN was born in Vancouver. Her novels and stories have been translated into twenty-five languages and her essays have appeared in the *Guardian*, *The Globe and Mail*, *Granta*, *Brick*, the *New York Times*, and elsewhere. Her most recent book, *Do Not Say We Have Nothing*, about art, music, and revolution in twentieth-century China, won the 2016 Scotiabank Giller Prize and the 2016 Governor General's Literary Award for Fiction, and was shortlisted for the Man Booker Prize, the Baileys Women's Prize for Fiction, and the Folio Prize. The youngest daughter of Malaysian-Chinese immigrants to Canada, she lives in Montreal.

JUDITH THOMPSON is the artistic director of RARE Theatre, a theatre dedicated to providing a professional opportunity for those who are rarely represented to be seen and heard on our stages. She is the author of over twenty plays. She is most proud of winning the Amnesty International Award for her play *Palace of the End*, and being named an Officer of the Order of Canada. She is a director, an actor, and a professor of theatre studies at the University of Guelph.

RICHARD VAN CAMP is an Eisner Award–nominated bestselling author and storyteller from Fort Smith, Northwest Territories. He's also a proud member of the Tlicho Dene. With over twenty books to his name, his novel, *The Lesser Blessed*, is a feature film with First Generation Films.

M G VASSANJI was born in Nairobi, Kenya, raised in Dar es Salaam, Tanzania, and attended university in the United States. He came to Canada as a post-doctoral fellow in theoretical nuclear physics in September 1978 and stayed. He is the author of seven novels, two collections of short stories, a travel memoir about India, a travel memoir about East Africa, and a biography of Mordecai Richler in the Extraordinary Canadians series. His first novel received the Commonwealth First Book Prize (Africa region); since then he has twice won the Giller Prize for fiction and once the Governor General's Literary Award for Nonfiction. In 1981 he co-founded the literary journal *The Toronto South Asian Review*, which he edited for twenty years. In 1985 the journal branched into the book publisher TSAR, which in turn transformed in 2015 into Mawenzi House Publishers and continues to promote new Canadian literature. He is a member of the Order of Canada.

RITA WONG learns from and with water as an (un)settler living on unceded Coast Salish territories, who has responsibilities to build better relationships than colonization could imagine. With Dorothy Christian, she co-edited the anthology *downstream: reimagining water* (Wilfrid Laurier University Press, 2017). Wong has written four books of poetry: *monkeypuzzle* (Press Gang, 1998), *forage* (Nightwood, 2007, awarded the Dorothy Livesay Poetry Prize and Canada Reads Poetry 2011), *sybil unrest* (co-written with Larissa Lai, LINEBooks, 2008 and New Star, 2013), and *undercurrent* (Nightwood, 2015), as well as one graphic collection with Cindy Mochizuki, *perpetual* (Nightwood, 2015). She works as an associate professor at Emily Carr University of Art and Design, where she also serves as president of its unionized Faculty Association. When life allows, she enjoys spending time with rivers.

ABOUT THE EDITORS

TESSA MCWATT is the author of six novels and two books for young people. Her fiction has been nominated for the Governor General's Literary Award, the Toronto Book Award, and the OCM Bocas Prize for Caribbean Literature. She is the winner of the 2018 Eccles British Library Writer's Award, is a librettist, and also is a professor of creative writing at the University of East London.

RABINDRANATH MAHARAJ is the author of five novels and three short-story collections. His last novel, *The Amazing Absorbing Boy*, won both the Toronto Book Award and the Trillium Book Award (English). Previous books were nominated for various awards, including the Commonwealth Writers' Prize, the Chapters/Books in Canada First Novel Award, and the Rogers Writers' Trust Fiction Prize. In January 2013, he was awarded the Queen Elizabeth II Diamond Jubilee Medal. Maharaj resides in Ajax, Ontario.

DIONNE BRAND is a poet, novelist, and essayist. She was Poet Laureate of the City of Toronto from 2009 to 2012. An award-winning poet, Dionne Brand won both the Governor General's Literary Award and the Trillium Book Award for her volume *Land to Light On*. She's won the Pat Lowther Award for Poetry for her volume *thirsty*. And her volume *Ossuaries* won the 2011 Griffin Poetry Prize. Brand's critically acclaimed novel, *What We All Long For*, won the Toronto Book Award and her 2014 novel, *Love Enough*, was short listed for the Trillium Book Award. Her fiction includes the novels *In Another Place, Not Here*, and *At the Full and Change of the Moon*. Brand's nonfiction work,

A Map to the Door of No Return, has been widely taken up in scholarly work on the Black Diaspora.

ACKNOWLEDGEMENTS

THE EDITORS ARE DEEPLY GRATEFUL to the writers in this collection for the elegance, generosity, and eloquence with which they tackled our questions.

Thank you to Marc Côté for enthusiasm from the outset. This project would not have come to fruition without his input, support, and prescience.

Thanks to the Canada Council's New Chapter Grant, which made this book possible.

Thanks to Leslie Sanders and Christina Sharpe for their clear eyes and keen readings.

Thanks also to everyone associated with Cormorant Books who helped to bring this anthology into the world.

THE PUBLISHER GRATEFULLY ACKNOWLEDGES THAT the editing, writing of the introduction, and the writing of all authors' contributions to *Luminous Ink: Writers on Writing in Canada* was made possible by a grant from the New Chapters Program of The Canada Council for the Arts. This program was designed to contribute to the celebration of Canada's sesquicentenary. We acknowledge the support of the Canada Council for the Arts, which last year invested $153 million to bring the arts to Canadians throughout the country.